Mural Painting in Ancient Peru

DUCCIO BONAVIA

Mural Painting in Ancient Peru

TRANSLATED BY PATRICIA J. LYON

Indiana University Press —————————————————————— *Bloomington*

The preparation and publication of this volume were supported by grants from the Translations Program and Publications Program of the National Endowment for the Humanities, an independent federal agency.

Manufactured in the United States of America

Library of Congress Cataloging in Publication Data

Bonavia, Duccio, 1935–
Mural painting in ancient Peru.

Translation of: Ricchata quellccani.
Bibliography: p.
Includes index.
1. Indians of South America—Peru—Painting.
2. Mural painting and decoration—Peru.   3. Indians of
South America—Peru—Antiquities.   4. Peru—Antiquities.
I. Title.
F3429.3.A7B6413   1985   751.7′3′0985   84-47883
ISBN 0-253-33940-5

1 2 3 4 5   89 88 87 86 85

Contents

FOREWORD BY JOHN HOWLAND ROWE   vii
PREFACE   ix
TRANSLATOR'S NOTE   xi

1. The Background   1
2. The Early Andean Images   9
3. Further Developments   35
4. The Moche Tradition   47
5. Late Expressions on the North Coast   111
6. Late Manifestations on the Central Coast   135
7. Murals in the Inca Empire   151
8. Materials and Techniques   177
9. Final Considerations   187

APPENDIX: PIGMENT ANALYSIS AND COMMENTS BY CARLOS NÚÑEZ
          VILLAVICENCIO   197
NOTES   205
REFERENCES   207
CREDITS FOR ILLUSTRATIONS   217
INDEX OF PERSONS AND AUTHORS CITED   219
INDEX OF MONUMENTS   223

Color plates follow p. 34

FOREWORD

Duccio Bonavia has discovered a whole field of ancient Peruvian art that the rest of us had hardly noted. Many individual mural paintings have been described and illustrated, but Bonavia is the first to survey the entire field and point out its importance.

All known ancient Peruvian mural paintings were executed on clay plaster. Mexican and Mayan mural paintings were done on lime plaster, which is both more durable and more respectable by European standards. Clay is a building material for which most art historians and archaeologists have no respect, and it is easily overlooked in consequence. Clearly, ancient Peruvians had a different system of values, in which clay might be as noble a material as stone. At the Temple of Viracocha, the Incas decorated panels of fine stonework with a design in fine clay plaster. To appreciate what the ancient Peruvians accomplished, we need to recover their values and see what they were trying to do in their own terms.

Bonavia has tried to make such generalizations as he could about ancient Peruvian mural painting, and his book stimulated me to think more generally about problems of color in architecture. Color in architecture involves more than painting. That fine clay plaster on the stonework at the Temple of Viracocha is not painted; it is a thin layer of reddish clay. I examined it carefully, because it was red enough so that my first thought was that it was painted. At Machu Picchu, the Incas applied a yellow clay to the stonework of the buildings. This clay plaster is likewise not painted; the yellow is the color of the clay. In these cases, at any rate, it appears that the Incas achieved colored walls by selecting clays of attractive colors for their plaster. At Pikillaqta, which is a Huari site near Cuzco, a white lime or gypsum plaster was used to finish walls. This plaster was not painted,

and it was probably used because the builders liked its gleaming white color, rather than because they were interested in the physical properties of the material. Here, then, is a bit of context for thinking about the use of paint.

A recurrent theme of the book is the fragility of Peruvian mural painting and the speed with which it is destroyed in consequence. It is virtually impossible to protect mural paintings once they are exposed, and the ones spared by vandals are destroyed in a few years by the elements. Pachacamac is a major tourist attraction, and the Peruvian authorities made several attempts to preserve the mural paintings exposed there in 1938, including mounting sheets of glass in front of them, but those paintings have gone like the rest. Bonavia has led the way in recording mural paintings himself and recovering surviving information on murals which have been destroyed.

An earlier version of this book was published in Spanish in 1974 by the Banco Industrial in Lima. The edition was small, and the book was out of print before many of the people interested in ancient Peruvian art and archaeology knew of its existence. Bonavia's message has not yet been communicated to the audience for which it was meant, and it needs to go forth again. Besides revising the text of 1974, Bonavia has provided much new material, so that about a third of the present text is new, and new illustrations have been added in proportion. As a result, the book incorporates many important discoveries made since the earlier version was written.

I join the author and the translator in inviting readers to discover a new world of ancient art.

JOHN HOWLAND ROWE

PREFACE

This English edition is a completely restructured, enlarged, and updated version of my work on prehispanic mural paintings of the Andean area that was published in Spanish in 1974 under the title *Ricchata quellccani; pinturas murales prehispánicas*.

This study began in 1958 when I first saw a Moche mural. My old and unforgettable friend, the late Hans Horkheimer, took me to see it, and with him I began to love aboriginal Peruvian art as well as to understand its tragedy. Since then I have been seeking and accumulating evidence. I have never seen with my own eyes many of the paintings dealt with in this book, while others that I did know and study, no longer exist. And those that remain are destined to disappear unless things change. Yet many remain hidden in ruined structures, covered with rubble, concealed by old walls, or buried in sand, and the task of the archaeologist continues. In the prologue to the first edition of this book I said: "As these pages go to press I receive word of new paintings . . ." and the phrase is still applicable in spite of the decade that has passed.

On this long trail of discovery I have had many companions and friends without whose help these lines would not have been written. To those named below and to those involuntarily omitted, to all, my sincere thanks.

The research began as a professional exercise. In 1974, however, I received help from the Ford Foundation, which allowed me to complete the preparation of the first edition, and in 1982 I had support from the Consejo Nacional de Ciencia y Tecnología of Peru for preparation of the map that appears on p. 2.

In the preparation of the original manuscript and the preceding research I was helped by many people. Worthy of special mention are Jorge Rondón and Oscar Lostaunau, who not only gave me invaluable firsthand information but also went with me into the field and offered advice based on their years of experience. John Harrison placed at my disposal his photographic files, which are of exceptional value as the first record of a later renowned discovery: the ruins of Puncurí and Cerro Blanco.

Unhesitating collaboration was provided by Toribio Mejía Xesspe, Georg Petersen, Donald Collier, Donald Thompson, Junius Bird, and Michael Moseley. Some sent me unpublished information on collections in North American museums; others opened their private libraries to me. Important technical and theoretical aspects were discussed with Richard Schaedel, Gordon Willey, Armando Hartmann, and George Kubler, from all of whom I received valued guidance.

In the compilation of the graphic record, so fundamental to this work, I have been generously aided by Juan Ossio, Abraham Guillén, Antonio Rodríguez Suy Suy, Gustavo Alvarez Sánchez, and the authorities of the Colegio León Pinelo, who allowed me to use material from the Archivo Hans Horkheimer. All the graphics of the first edition were in the hands of Antonio Hartmann, who, with singular expertise, revived old images faded by time.

Spectrographic analyses of the pigments were provided through the disinterested collaboration of the Cerro de Pasco Corporation, in whose laboratories at La Oroya the samples were examined at the request of George Kirkner and H. B. Wadia.

Ramiro Castro de la Mata not only accompanied me on some trips but also read the first version of the manuscript, upon which he provided useful suggestions. The great erudition of Eduardo Jahnsen has also left its traces on many aspects of the book.

But my deepest gratitude goes to Rogger Ravines, my closest friend of many years, with whom I have shared so many interests and hopes, some joys, and many unpleasantnesses. He urged me to write this work, which, without his constant advice and help, would never have been completed.

I certainly cannot fail to mention the support of the Banco Industrial del Perú, which made the first edition of this work possible. It is important to understand that the bank saw the publication as a contribution to scientific research, and to that end even the beauty of the edition was sacrificed to document examples of little aesthetic, but great scientific, value. Such an attitude is almost impossible to conceive in a country such as Peru. Thus they permitted the dissemination of much valuable material that had for years been overlooked in archives. In that regard, the contribution of Fernando Palao Alvarez, who directed and designed the original edition, was invaluable.

In preparing this second edition I have also received help from many people. Many points of the text were discussed with John H. Rowe, and his advice has permitted certain improvements.

Several aspects of the discussion of paintings of the north coast have been markedly enlarged thanks to the unpublished materials provided to me by Christopher Donnan, Ricardo Morales Gamarra, Izumi Shimada, and Martha Anders. Both Donald Proulx and Richard Schaedel contributed their field experience, clarifying specific points upon which there was some doubt.

Wolfgang Haberland of the Hamburgisches Museum für Völkerkunde was kind enough to allow me the opportunity to examine the materials left there by Heinrich Brüning, and also allowed me to reproduce some of the original illustrations of the Huaca Pintada, which are of incalculable value. It was long thought that this important mural had vanished, leaving no record whatsoever.

Once more I must thank the graciousness of the directors of the Banco Industrial del Perú, who allowed me to use the graphic materials prepared for the first edition. Their generosity has contributed considerably to the preparation of this edition.

I owe special thanks to Patricia Lyon, who undertook to translate the text from Spanish to English. Not only has she achieved this goal without distorting the meaning of the original, but throughout the work she has made valuable suggestions for bettering the edition. Her expertise made this task, normally wearying and difficult, agreeable and easy, resulting in a worthwhile human and professional experience.

I cannot end without mentioning the publishers of this English version of my book, who have given me the opportunity to acquaint a wider public with the cultural riches of ancient Peru.

For me there remains the inner satisfaction of having preserved from oblivion this cultural heritage that belongs to humanity. It would be naïve to hope that this work might serve to awaken interest and emotion to protect and preserve what remains of the mural art that is our legacy from the ancient Peruvians. That is irretrievably condemned to be destroyed.

DUCCIO BONAVIA
Lima, 1982

TRANSLATOR'S NOTE

Any translation demands a series of decisions on the part of the translator. Not simply the word-by-word choice between shades of meaning, but also such details as what not to translate and whether or not to accent place names. In the present work I decided not to translate the names of sites or of institutions (museums, universities). Site names frequently have no translation, as when a site is named in an unknown language for a long-abandoned settlement. In other cases the name may tell us more of modern oral tradition than of the site itself (i.e., Huaca del Sol, Huaca de la Luna, and Fortaleza de Paramonga). One term, however, occurs so often in the names of coastal archaeological sites that the reader deserves an explanation. That word is *huaca*, also written *guaca* and *wak'a*, which comes from the language of the Incas, Quechua, and originally meant a holy or sacred place (hill, rock, cave) or object, whether natural or manufactured (i.e., building, figurine, statue, stone, plant). Today, *huaca* is frequently applied on the coast to any mound, especially to the many stepped adobe platforms and large buildings built on platforms so common in that part of Peru. The possibly derivative term *huaquero*, which is applied to those people whose income comes, entirely or in part, from the looting and sale of ancient remains, I have generally translated as "looter," but sometimes as "treasure hunter." I have accented all names as in Spanish, although some (i.e., Chavín, Chimú, and Pachacámac) are so common in English that the accent is often omitted, for the convenience of those unacquainted with that area. I have, however, maintained the original spelling and accentuation in quotes.

All quotations from sources in English have been taken directly from the original. I translated all other quotes from the original language, except for a few cases in which a reasonably accurate English translation had already been made (e.g., Ubbelohde-Doering, 1967). The source of the quote is always the one cited. In a few cases I was unable to use the original Spanish source, relying on the material provided to me by Dr. Bonavia. These cases include all letters written in Spanish, newspaper articles, and Peruvian theses except Bonavia, 1965a, as well as Haase, 1958; León Barandiarán, 1938; Mueller and Mae, 1969; Samaniego Román, 1973; and Tello, 1939b.

I am grateful to the National Endowment for the Humanities for funding this translation, to Duccio Bonavia for being extraordinarily prompt and thorough in his comments on the translation, to Elizabeth F. Wolfe for checking my German translations, and to John Rowe for locating and transporting dozens and dozens of books.

PATRICIA J. LYON
Berkeley, 1983

Mural Painting in Ancient Peru

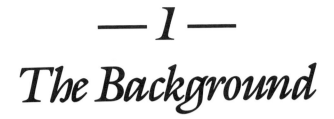

— 1 —

The Background

One of the greatest civilizations of the world flourished in the Central Andean region. Here geography and history combine uniquely and incomparably. In this land of violent contrasts, with infinite microclimates and landscapes, unsuspected riches and staggering hardships, natural forces are expressed in all their strength, each facet of the mighty whole demanding individual understanding. This then is the land where, after battling the cosmos for millennia, the native American created an amazing civilization, a culture not yet fully compre-

hended but one that is unparalleled as a magnificent example of the human will.

Between the equator and the Tropic of Capricorn, the land rises from the shores of an ocean not quite as pacific as its name would indicate to heights that form the highest mountains in the world after the Himalayas. Here the classical rules of geography and historical causation have been broken in a violent and still unresolved confrontation.

The coastal desert, although smaller, calls to mind the

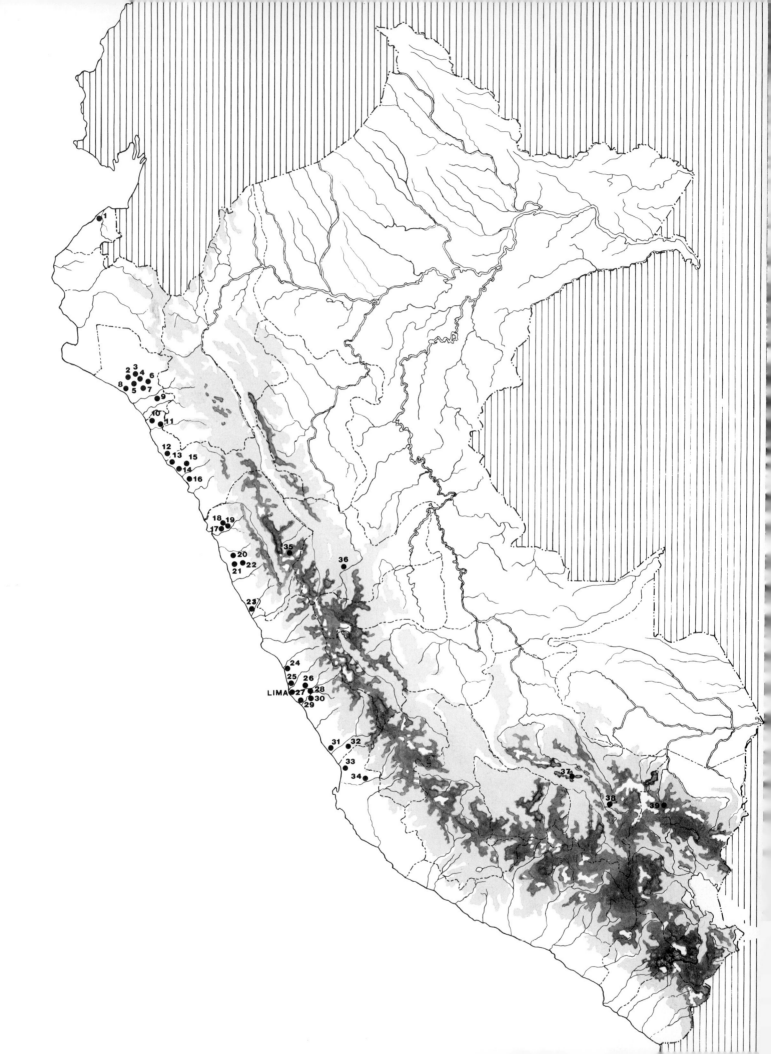

Gobi or Sahara because of its dryness. Its monotony is broken by small oases, but in some places no rain has ever fallen. Mere kilometers from the sea begin the spurs of the Andes, which eventually rise from sea level to more than six thousand meters, from tropical valleys to barren wastes of eternal snow. Through geologic time torrential rivers have cut deep narrow canyons between the mountain chains. On the eastern slopes of the massif lie the hot tropical lands of the green Amazonian rain forest, which covers an immense area—exuberant, unexplored, unconquered by man.

MAIN LOCATIONS MENTIONED IN TEXT

1. Tumbes
2. Huaca Pintada
3. Huaca del Oro
4. La Mayanga
5. Túcume
6. Huaca Lucía
7. Huaca Corte
8. Chornancap
9. Pampa Grande
10. Huaca Cotón
11. Gallito Ciego
12. Huaca Licapa
13. Casa Grande
14. Chanchan
15. Huaca del Dragón
16. Huaca del Sol and
    Huaca de la Luna
17. Pañamarca
18. Cerro Blanco
19. Puncurí
20. Cerro Sechín
21. Chanquillo
22. Moxeque
23. Paramonga
24. Cerro Trinidad
25. Cerro Culebra
26. Ñaña
27. Lima (Armatambo, Huadca, Huaca
    Concha, Mateo Salado, Garagay)
28. San Juan
29. Pachacámac
30. Campo de las Flores
31. Guarco
32. Incahuasi
33. Huaca de la Centinela
34. Tambo Colorado
35. Chavín de Huántar
36. Kotosh
37. Cuzco and Sacsahuaman
38. Temple of Viracocha at Raqchi,
    San Pedro de Cacha
39. Macusani

While other great cultures developed where the climate and other geographical conditions are more or less uniform, the Andean peoples created one of the most original and important civilizations of the ancient world in response to the challenge of a hostile environment. In the deserts of South America people lived as in the Middle East, seeking water underground or bringing it from the heights by means of impressive engineering works. On the high Andean plains they raised cities, as in Nepal, where those from other places can hardly breathe. They fought the tangle of the rain forest, as in India. And when the precipitousness of the mountainsides seemed to preclude agriculture, the basis of the economy, they cut into the slopes and created agricultural terraces. Only in cooperation could the force be found to overcome such natural obstacles, cooperation that culminated in the Inca empire. Before arriving at this synthesis, however, many thousands of years passed, years filled with trials and errors that yielded knowledge, though the cost of the learning was high.

The terms used in describing this cultural development require explanation. Archaeologists have created a system of arbitrary time divisions to simplify the task of reconstructing, understanding, and explaining the past. The development was actually uninterrupted, a continuum cut by the artificial periods into which we have divided it. Although there are indeed elements that mark these divisions, they are not rigid, and the changes are much more subtle than they appear.

In the course of the development of Andean culture, three great moments of cultural unification have been identified. These periods, in which similar traditions are found throughout the region, are called *Horizons*. They alternate with two intervals called *Intermediate Periods*, in which cultural expressions were specific to each locale, resulting in regional diversification (Table 1). While there are various interpretations of the horizons, they are of interest only to the specialist. For our purposes the reader need simply be aware that each horizon is identified by the appearance of a complex of elements characteristic of a single region, so that they are sometimes mistakenly called the Chavín, Huari, and Inca horizons.

The period preceding the use or invention of pottery is, by definition, preceramic, but in Peru it has been divided into two stages called Lithic and Preceramic. The Lithic encompasses the time from human arrival on this continent until the first appearance of textiles. The economy was apparently that of nomadic hunters. The Preceramic witnesses a change toward sedentary life and the first steps toward agriculture and plant domestica-

TABLE 1

TEMPORAL AND SPATIAL PLACEMENT OF PRINCIPAL PAINTED MONUMENTS

PERIOD	YEARS (approx.)	SOUTH COAST		CENTRAL COAST		NORTH
		Styles	Sites	Styles	Sites	Styles
COLONIAL ↑	1534	Ica 10				
LATE HORIZON		Ica 9 Ica Inca	Incahuasi Guarco Tambo Colorado Huaca de la Centinela	Inca	Ñaña, San Juan, Huadca Armatambo Campo de las Flores	Chimú Inca
LATE INTERMEDIATE PERIOD	1440	Ica 8 ↑ 1		Chancay	Pachacámac Mateo Salado	Chimú
MIDDLE HORIZON	800	Ica Epigonal Pinilla Ica Pachacámac Atarco Nasca 9		Pachacámac Nievería	Huaca Concha	Lambayeque Huari Norteño Moche ↑ V
EARLY INTERMEDIATE PERIOD	500 — A.D. —— B.C.	8 ↑ Nasca		Lima 8 ↑ 1 Baños de Boza/ Villa el Salvador ↓ Miramar	Cerro Trinidad Cerro Culebra	IV Moche I
		1		Negative Decorated		Gallinazo Salinar
EARLY HORIZON	500	10 ↑ Ocucaje (Paracas) 1		Colinas Ancón	Garagay ↑ ↓	Cupisnique ↑
INITIAL PERIOD	1400	Erizo		Rímac Incised Chira/Villa		Guañape
PRECERAMIC ↓	1800					

Designed by Duccio Bonavia, 1983.
[1] Presumed painting published by Carrión Cachot (1942).
[2] Painting reported by Orrego (1927) and Schaedel (1978).

COAST	ALTIPLANO		CENTRAL HIGHLANDS HUALLAGA		CALLEJON DE HUAYLAS	
Sites	*Styles*	*Sites*	*Styles*	*Sites*	*Styles*	*Sites*
Tumbes Paramonga	Chucuito	Chullpas de Macusani	Chupacho Inca		Local Inca	
Túcume	Collao					
↑ Chanchan | Huaca Pintada?¹	Sillustani		?		Aquilpa	
Huaca del Dragón Huaca Corte Huaca del Oro Chornancap Huaca Pintada² La Mayanga Huaca de la Luna Pampa Grande Pañamarca	Expansive Tiahuanaco		?		Honco	
			Higueras			
	?				Recuay	
			Kotosh White-on-Red			
Huaca Cotón Huaca Licapa						
Sechín, Puncurí Cerro Blanco Moxeque Casa Grande	↑ Pucara Incatunuhuiri ↓		Kotosh San Blas		Chavín	Chavín de Huántar
Chanquillo?			Kotosh Sajarapataj			
Huaca Lucía	Qaluyu		Kotosh Chavín			
↑ Caballo Muerto			Kotosh Huairajirca Mito		Huaricoto	
	?			Kotosh?		

tion. Between the lengthy preceramic era and the first horizon, the Early Horizon, the control of agriculture brought about a change in economic systems, from the exploitation of nature, that is, a parasitic form of life (fishing, hunting, gathering), to a system of production.

The Early Horizon is already a time of intensive agriculture, calendric knowledge, cultist practices, and some complexity in social organization. It is followed by the Early Intermediate Period of regional diversification, in which various groups achieved considerable progress; some, who already had well-developed social organization, progressed in technical or artistic fields, others, in specific organizational areas. These local developments were cut short by the spread from Huari of the first imperial state in the Andes, which, in the Middle Horizon, imposed drastic changes on many aspects of life.

In the Late Intermediate Period, when the southern yoke had disappeared, a series of confederations formed, and throughout the entire region there spread the concept of urbanism and related organization. The Incas, being better organized, overcame the other groups until they had formed an empire whose course was halted by the Europeans.

In spite of regionalism and apparent differences, however, there are certain basic elements with which the Central Andeans achieved their cultural creation, including subsistence based on intensive agriculture using plants domesticated in the region; native animals held in common; identical agricultural tools and techniques; use of the same materials and techniques in architecture and in various crafts; a social and political superstructure that controlled society, as well as a series of common elements in social, political, and religious organization. All these factors resulted in a cultural unity that specialists have called the Andean Co-tradition, encompassing an area comprising the Peruvian coast and highlands and the basin of Lake Titicaca extending into Bolivia, together with some marginal zones.

Art represents not only one of the most interesting aspects of the culture of the aboriginal Americans, but also one of its outstanding manifestations, a true approximation to their beliefs. The tradition is very ancient, lost in the dawn of humanity. Various approaches to its study have enriched volumes on the history of art. Nevertheless, there is one facet of this art mentioned by no one: murals. The very knowledge of their existence has remained exclusive property of archaeologists. Consequently, little is known of them, documentation is almost nil, and direct evidence virtually nonexistent. Time and neglect have erased all.

Even as it opens a new chapter of Peruvian art, this study leads to woeful conclusions. Our entire legacy amounts to but a handful of serious studies together with a mountain of useless material, error piled on error, speculation on speculation, fantasy on fantasy. Of the splendid reality of an era there remains far too little. Because of the innumerable examples that have been irretrievably lost, a complete history of prehispanic Peruvian art can now never be written. Since only a few examples remain, and those in imminent danger of destruction, the aim of this work is to gather the greatest possible amount of evidence on the painted murals of ancient Peru, leaving aside literary pretensions.

Before considering the evidence, however, I wish to define some concepts that are frequently confused and might lead to erroneous interpretations (see Macera, 1975, p. 60). The concepts in question are rock art, murals, and wall painting.

Rock art is executed on natural rock faces and uses special techniques. Although it is not confined to any particular time period, and indeed is still being executed, the most outstanding examples of rock painting belong to lithic times, the age of the early nomadic hunters of the American continent. They brought with them the ancient tradition of the Old World Upper Palaeolithic and doubtless continued it in America. I do not believe that this art is an exclusively Western phenomenon, as some authors have asserted (see Leroi-Gourhan, 1965).

Murals, in turn, are the decoration applied to building walls using several specific and specialized techniques. They are the expression of a symbolic language, only minor aspects of which we have been able to interpret and understand.

Despite the differences between murals and rock art, the former is undeniably a continuation of the latter within a single tradition. An interesting example of the transition between the two is found in the Udima paintings in the department of Cajamarca (Mejía Xesspe, 1968), which constitute prolegomena to the pictorial expression of the centuries preceding the expansion of Chavín art.

We have no way of knowing when mural painting reached its peak, since there is no record of it. We can appreciate the phenomenon in only a very fragmented fashion. Indeed, the reoccupation of houses and palaces and especially the remodeling of ceremonial sites were common occurrences in antiquity and have played an important role in the loss of many architectural details of the earliest epochs. Such loss, however, is as nothing in comparison to the destruction wrought by modern vandals, as will be seen.

The sheer quantity of decoration in the last prehispanic period would suggest that wall paintings were a typically Inca phenomenon. Such an impression is surely false, however, a function of the fact that we have only the most recent evidence, which, for that very reason, has reached us most easily. We have much more and better data regarding paintings of the Early Intermediate Period than we have for other periods, providing a guide for the interpretation of all such remains. Amidst all the problems, one positive factor stands out: all the murals can be more or less securely dated, with the single exception of the temple of the oracle of the Lima Valley, which I attribute to the Late Horizon, and which will be dealt with in chapter 7.

The simple painting of the walls of buildings has great antiquity throughout the world. In Peru it goes back to the Preceramic, when either exterior or interior walls, although predominantly the latter, were smeared with some color. It has been widely thought that painted buildings had some special significance or served some specific function (e.g., Kroeber, 1949, p. 415). I have observed, however, that, especially in late periods, groups of dwellings with painted walls do not always have other than domestic functions. On the other hand, in some cases, especially in temples, floors were also painted.

One further aspect of architectural adornment consists of walls, painted or not, that bear decoration in high, low, or flat relief. Such treatment, along with sculpture, stelae, columns, pilasters, and other architectonic elements, constitutes artistic expression with meaning similar to that of the painted murals. In the present study such decoration will be dealt with only very briefly, as needed to serve as examples or to provide context for the painted murals. My personal research was devoted to the painted adornments, and detailed analysis of these other modes of ornamentation has yet to be carried out.

Mural painting had a special value in the native world that has not been adequately discussed. It must have embodied important magico-religious aspects, and I think that its persistence through time demonstrates its importance; we are dealing with a tradition that goes back to the origins of Andean culture and continues through the Colonial Period to the present. Even without considering rock art we find that there are pictorial representations in native Peruvian architecture all the way from the Initial Period to the Late Horizon. In the following chapters the theme will be dealt with in chronological order, from the earliest to latest. Within each period, I shall first discuss the coastal sites and then the highland ones, each group arranged from south to north.

—2—
The Early Andean Images

The Preceramic peoples lived in houses of clay and stone as well as ones of poles and thatch. Only in the final Preceramic periods did architecture begin to display sophistication. There appeared more elaborate and complex structures, especially on the central and north central coast, probably somehow related to religion. In many cases the walls of these buildings were painted. According to Engel (1967, p. 251), up to four colors were used at El Paraíso. At the site of Aspero near Supe, five parallel bands of white clay were found applied to a wall of the central room of the so-called Huaca de los Idolos (Feldman, 1978, p. 24). Highland architecture of this time is almost unknown. Walls were painted there also, but there is no particular evidence of painted decorative elements (Bueno Mendoza and Grieder, 1979).

THE INITIAL PERIOD

The earliest mural painting so far known dates to the Initial Period. There are two images discovered by the investigators from the University of Tokyo who excavated the ruins of Kotosh (department of Huánuco). One figure, found on the northeast stairway of the outer corner of the Temple of the Crossed Hands, probably represents a stylized serpent (fig. 1). The motif is very small (30 × 5 cm) and simply executed in white paint. Culturally it belongs to the Mitu Phase (Izumi and Terada, 1972, p. 140, fig. 82). The second figure from this period is a human figure painted in white with its hands raised, the right hand raised and extended while the left is raised and bent over the head (fig. 2). Apparently, judging from the published drawing (the figure does not show in the published photographs), only the upper part of the body was represented and measures barely 12 × 12.5 cm. This outline was on the south wall of a small niched room in the so-called White Temple (Izumi and Terada, 1972, p. 160, fig. 94, pl. 29e).

THE EARLY HORIZON

We have more information regarding the Early Horizon, although almost all of it comes from the coast. The characteristics of Early Horizon structures vary regionally and according to function. While stone was used on the coast, the primary building material was clay made into adobes of the most varied forms. Common dwellings had no outstanding features; they were simple and unplanned, with roofs of some perishable material. In contrast, ceremonial structures related to religion had well-defined traits, primarily in the form of terraces and stairways. But remains have also been found of temples built of adobes and finished with clay plaster, upon which religious motifs were painted in bright colors. The temple of Garagay near Lima is a good example of early coastal ceremonial architecture. There is a great

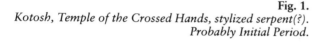

Fig. 1.
*Kotosh, Temple of the Crossed Hands, stylized serpent(?).
Probably Initial Period.*

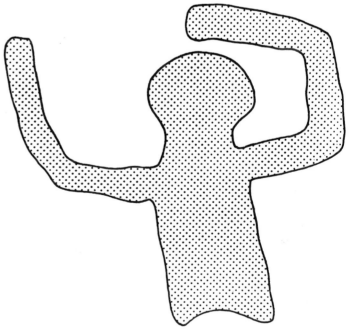

Fig. 2.
*Kotosh, White Temple, human figure contemporary with
the serpent of fig. 1. Probably Initial Period.*

U-shaped structure in which, around 1955 or 1956, a wall was found decorated with elements typical of the Chavín culture in flat relief painted in four colors (Rogger Ravines, personal communication, 1974). In 1974, under the direction of Rogger Ravines, work was initiated at the site that has so far uncovered a number of low reliefs and clay sculpture painted in red, pink, gray-blue, purple, and yellow, which represent mythical beings and conventional motifs (fig. 3). These elements precede the appearance of the Chavín style on the central coast, since they lack the iconographic conventions distinctive of that style, and may be contemporary with the early part of the sequence at Chavín de Huántar, possibly related to Phase AB in Rowe's stylistic sequence (Ravines and Isbell, 1976; Rowe, 1962).

Referring to monuments of the first phases of Ocucaje on the south coast, Engel mentions "Chavinoid traits surviving in the Paracas-Cavernas style . . . in the decoration of some walls made of unfired clay. These walls were sometimes ornamented with polychrome paintings that could well have been transposed from the Chavinoid sites in the northern valleys" (1976, p. 149). This information is interesting, since we have little data regarding these phenomena on the south coast, but the reference is excessively vague. In 1982, Sarah Massey found, near Callango in the Ica Valley, a Paracas temple with incised, but unpainted, decoration on the walls. The designs are Phase 9 of the Ocucaje style, dating to Early Horizon Epoch 9 (Massey, ms.). Toribio Mejía Xesspe also mentioned to me in 1974 that he recalls having seen in Ocucaje in the same valley, about 1930, the remains of a mural near an altar made of conical adobes. He was struck by the fact that the clay of which they were made had been mixed with a great quantity of grass, and also that there were many trophy heads at the foot of the altar. Mejía was able to recognize interlocking geometric motifs in the remains of the paintings on the ground. We cannot, however, date the mural positively on the basis of these data.

The Casma Valley

The site of Cerro Sechín in the Casma Valley (fig. 4) is a special case and requires detailed treatment. The only firsthand data on this monument are to be found in the works of Tello (1956), Samaniego Román (1973), and Jiménez Borja and Samaniego Román (1973). Apparently, besides the carved stone decoration of the outer wall, there were paintings and a profusion of color on the walls of the interior complex. Tello states that all the walls of the inner shrine were finely plastered and painted (1956, pp. 248, 252), and also notes the presence

> in the excavated soil removed to expose the stones, especially when the excavation is deepened near the base of the standing stones, of the remains of plastered mortar painted in white, red, bright brick-red, gray, blue sometimes almost black, yellow, red-brown and orange-yellow, which correspond to relief figures similar to those which, as arabesques, adorn the walls and altars of the temple of Cerro Blanco in Nepeña. Among these fragments are considerable portions of complex figures derived from the common representation of the Chavin feline. (Tello, 1956, p. 143)

The walls of the central section of the complex were made of conical adobes and painted blue on the interior and pink on the exterior, a color scheme repeated in the central chamber, now called the "sacred chamber," and the enclosure in front of it, as well as in the "vestibule" and the stairway (Samaniego Román, 1973, pp. 21, 43–48; Jiménez Borja and Samaniego Román, 1973, p. 14).

More recent work has revealed those decorated elements in clay that Tello reported only as fragments. Thus, a pillar in one of the rectangular chambers located in front of the central one bore a motif representing a man upside down. According to Samaniego Román, the figure is in low relief,

> [painted] red, blue, orange and other colors . . . he is semiclad in a loincloth; his right arm is dropped, while the left is raised with the palm of the hand outward; his little finger is missing. The face and nose are aquiline; details of the ear are suggested by a hook; the eye is simply an arc with the ends pointing up; the mouth [is] poorly preserved and, finally, falling back from the head is a sort of turban or cap in the form of an S. (1973, p. 44 and unnumbered photo; see Jiménez Borja and Samaniego Román, 1973, fig. 2, p. 19; Samaniego Román, 1980, p. 317)

This motif is important because of its stylistic relationship to those on the carved stones of the outer structure.

On the side walls of the double stairway there are two representations of fish outlined by incision (fig. 5; see also Samaniego Román, 1973; 1980, figs. 6, 7; Jiménez Borja and Samaniego Román, 1973, fig. 3, p. 20). Although I have personally seen only the eastern motif, since the western one was covered when I visited the site, it is perfectly clear from photographs that the two have similar details, although the western one is much more damaged than the one on the east side; only the proportions vary.

Briefly, the representation is that of a stylized fish with

Fig. 3.
*Temple of Garagay, Lima, part of polychrome frieze
adorning the atrium of the main structure. Chavín deity
painted yellow, gray, white, black, and red.
First epochs of Early Horizon.*

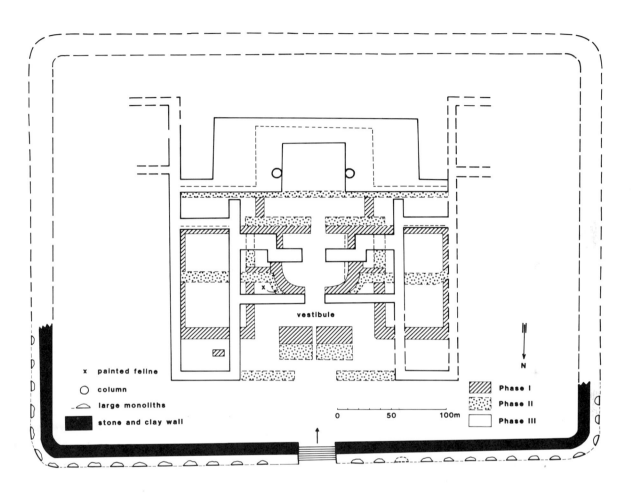

x   painted feline
○   column
⌒   large monoliths
■   stone and clay wall

vestibule

N

0   50   100m

▨ Phase I
░ Phase II
□ Phase III

Fig. 4.
*Cerro Sechín, Casma, simplification of Tello's schematic
plan of the temple, showing location of carved monoliths
and central structure. Scale approximate.*

one element that appears to be a foot and two, like tassels, at the union of head and body. The figures were executed in deep incisions, which were then filled with black paint for emphasis. I could see that the figure, although very faded, had been painted in a blue tone all over, except the eye, which was represented by two concentric circles, the outer one white, the inner blue; the appendage and mouth were painted red. I did not see any yellow, though it is mentioned as ground color by Samaniego Román (1980, p. 318). The general treat-

ment is Chavinoid, reminiscent of the technique used on the temples of Cerro Blanco and Puncurí in the Nepeña Valley, which are assigned to the same period (cf. pp. 24–30). There are also traces of geometric decoration in several places in the Cerro Sechín temple (Samaniego Román, 1973, p. 46).

Between 1969 and 1974 this monument was restored by Arturo Jiménez Borja and Lorenzo Samaniego, and the result of this "improvement" of the monument has been the destruction of much of the ancient evidence.[1]

Fig. 5.
*Cerro Sechín, the eastern of two incised fishes found
during restoration work on the inner structure.
Early Horizon.*

14 _____ *Mural Painting in Ancient Peru*

The extent of the destruction can be seen from a careful comparison of the reconstruction with evidence from the earlier excavation.

On the outer wall flanking the entrance to what Tello called the "inner shrine with conical adobes" there is now on each side a partial representation of what may be assumed to be felines (pl. 1; Samaniego Román, 1972b, cover and p. 34; 1973, unnumbered photo). The front and back paws and belly appear on both figures, while on one the tail is also represented. Elements that may be interpreted as claws appear on the front paws, two above and one below, and in reverse on the back paws, with one claw above and two below. The painting was executed in three colors: black, yellow-orange, and pure white. The figures were outlined in black and the same color was then used to shade in the body outline; the paws were filled in in yellow-orange while the claws are black with white tips.

Careful examination of these figures reveals two significant facts: the painting is recent, and both figures are identically incomplete, so that elements lacking on one are also lacking on the other except that the right-hand (western) figure shows the remains of a tail.[2] It is hard to believe that such symmetry resulted from natural destruction.

Tello (1956) provides us with the only information on the original state of these figures, but is vague and contradictory, adding to the confusion. Referring to the shrine of conical adobes, he says: "[its] inner and outer faces are plastered and painted. It was also found that the central compartment has a narrow entrance 1.64 meters [wide] and that its north façade is adorned with large jaguar figures (plates XVII D, E)" (Tello, 1956, p. 248). No details are visible in the published photograph of the north façade to which he refers. Later, speaking of the same building, he adds: "in the very center . . . is the façade of a rectangular building with rounded angles, with a doorway in the middle of the front, the sides of which are adorned with two large painted jaguars" (1956, p. 251). And that is all the information that Tello provides.

If we analyze these statements together with the illustrations, however, certain inconsistencies appear. In the text, both "large jaguar figures" and "two large painted jaguars" are mentioned. Nevertheless, Tello shows only the eastern jaguar in his figure 109 (fig. 6) as well as in his figure 131, which is an isometric reconstruction of the Cerro Sechín temple. However, in figure 130, an elaborate artist's reconstruction of the eastern section of the temple, Pedro Rojas Ponce shows felines on both the

Fig. 6.
Cerro Sechín, drawing published by Tello of eastern feline; the only known drawing, made during the 1937 excavations.

eastern and western sides. The only photograph of the feline that Tello published (1956, pl. XXVII F), shows only the eastern "jaguar" (compare figs. 6, 7, and 8).

The surest means of resolving these contradictions seemed to be to consult the people who collaborated directly with Tello during the work at Cerro Sechín in 1937. Toribio Mejía Xesspe explained that when they cleared the eastern side of the central-structure (inner) temple they found the "jaguar," but there was no figure at all on the opposite side, that is, the other side of the entrance of the same building, because that part of the wall had been destroyed by treasure hunters who had penetrated the building from above (personal communication, 1973). He further explained that the mention of two animals and the use of the plural in Tello's book are the result of deduction or analogy; that is, it was surmised that there were two "jaguars" and that only one was found. Pedro Rojas Ponce confirmed Mejía's statement and admitted that his own reconstruction was idealized; he deduced from symmetry that there must originally have been two animals, although there was evidence for only one (personal communication, April 1973).[3]

Donald Collier, who was excavating in another part of the monument when Tello cleared the doorway, remembers some details of undeniable importance and dependability. He was in charge of photography during the excavations and took the photograph that was published in the aforementioned work of Tello dealing with Sechín. Collier wrote me the following comments in a letter dated May 22, 1974:

> My recollection is that the western half of the entrance was badly destroyed, and that also there was a sufficient remnant to suggest architectural symmetry, there were no traces of a painted feline. I think Tello assumed there was bilateral symmetry of the painting and done so he accepted the assumption as a proven fact. I don't have color notes. The wall of the portada was painted rose color, I recall (and so it looks in the photo) that the feline was black with white claws.

Thus Collier fully corroborates Mejía Xesspe's and Rojas Ponce's statements.

Donald Thompson, who worked with Collier in Casma some years later, mentions two "jaguars" in one of his works (1964, pp. 208–209). In response to my query on this point, he told me that his information was secondhand and that he never actually saw the figure himself. He wrote me: "if I am not mistaken, the jaguars had disappeared or perhaps they were covered by rubble, at the time we excavated there" (personal communication, November 1973).

In July of 1974 Collier generously sent me three photographs of the eastern feline taken during the 1937 work, two of which I have reproduced here (figs. 7, 8). Comparing these images to the drawing Tello published (fig. 6; Tello, 1956, fig. 109), it can be seen that the reproduction is quite faithful to the original. The body of the animal is almost complete, with a long tail, partly destroyed, and part of the head with a clearly visible ear and an eye that seems to have been white. The eye is very indistinct in the photograph in Tello's work. The forepaw is not present. Some very revealing details can be seen in these photographs. In the first place, the image was exposed to weathering for a long time before being covered by the earth from which Tello and his collaborators cleared it. Only the lower part of the wall was covered, protecting the two lower claws of the hindpaws, which can be seen to have bright, perfectly preserved colors. All the rest of the figure is very faded with few visible details. One can gather that the artist first outlined the figure with a very sure and even broad line and then filled it with color. Only the part of the paw that, in the reconstructed version, is painted yellow-orange seems to have been originally delineated by an incised outline.

If we compare the Collier photographs to the eastern figure now visible at Cerro Sechín (fig. 9), it is evident that the current one has been entirely repainted and even modified in some details, giving its form a greater softness and symmetry. There is a striking similarity between this eastern figure and the one now seen on the western side of the doorway (fig. 10), for which there is no firsthand information or illustrations. Everything suggests that one of the figures is copied from the other, and copies are not common in prehispanic art. Even in cases where figures of the same theme are repeated, there are differences in execution from figure to figure simply because the work was always done freehand and without patterns. The Collier photos also show, in spite of weathering, the remains of a black color that covered the entire animal. The western image that exists today has no trace of color in the body section, although there is some, curiously, in the hindquarters and tail.

Also visible in the Collier photographs is a clear line marking the division between the portion exposed to weathering, with faded paint, and that protected by being covered with rubble. The line is not horizontal but slanted, higher to the east with a marked slope to the

Fig. 7.
Cerro Sechín, 1937 photograph of feline painted on east wall of inner structure; the only hard evidence known for this painting. Early Horizon.

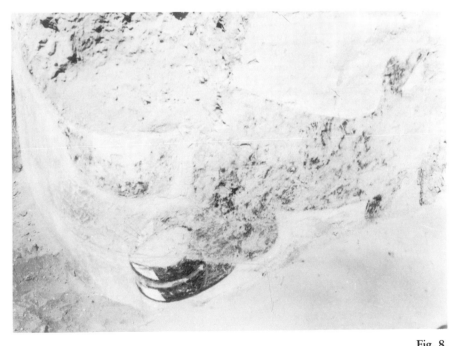

Fig. 8.
Cerro Sechín, detail of painted feline shown in fig. 7.

Fig. 9.
Cerro Sechín, painted eastern feline as seen today; modern retouching is clearly visible.

Fig. 10.
Cerro Sechín, western painted feline as seen today; note hindquarters and tail. There is no evidence from Tello or his coworkers for this figure. Similar photos have been available since October 1972.

west. Might we not suggest, therefore, that the entire western side of the structure was exposed to weathering, thus resulting in the partial destruction of the wall upon which the figure was painted? While this suggestion is purely hypothetical, the illustrations do reinforce Collier's position, and that of the others who support it, and agree with Mejía Xesspe's statement that part of the monument was destroyed by looters.

When I consulted Arturo Jiménez Borja, who was in charge of the restoration at Cerro Sechín, regarding these matters, he stated categorically that both figures had been found in the course of clearing (personal communication, April 1974) but conceded that they were in such poor condition that it was decided to retouch them. In initial tests it was found that using brushes for retouching left linear tracks that were not visible in the original. After several attempts, he found that the technique originally employed must have been rubbing, which spreads the pigment uniformly. The colors used in the reconstruction were obtained from soot for black, ground and calcined sea shells for white, and various ochres found in the nearby hills for the other colors. For application, these materials were mixed with a dilution of the juice of a columnar cactus in water, and once the retouching was terminated, the entire surface was covered with this liquid to fix the pigments. Jiménez Borja did comment, and correctly, that in the drawings illustrating Tello's book, there is an error in the placement of the designs, which are too high above the original floor.

The authors of the reconstruction have set forth their position in several publications. Thus, Jiménez Borja and Samaniego Román, referring to the "sacred chamber," as they call it, state "that it has a guardian feline painted on each side"; the figure they illustrate is that of the western feline with its tail complete (fig. 10; Jiménez Borja and Samaniego Román, 1973, p. 16 and fig. 1). In Samaniego's first published report on the work carried out at that time, he describes "two gigantic felines," the only illustration being a photograph of the western motif, with tail. He further states that "the feline of the west side is better preserved" (Samaniego Román, 1973, pp. 43, 49, and unnumbered photo). When I queried him he reiterated that they had found two figures, but admitted that both were very poorly preserved and the outlines had therefore been retouched (personal communication, May 30, 1974).

In 1980 Samaniego reaffirmed that there were "two great felines," adding that "they were briefly seen by Tello in 1937" (1980, p. 315), which is incorrect according to the people I quoted earlier who were present during Tello's fieldwork. Samaniego provided a single description for both figures, implying that they are identical, although I have already indicated that the western figure includes some elements not present on the eastern one. In the single illustration Samaniego provided of these paintings, only the western one is shown, together with the statement that it was "discovered by the author" (1980, pp. 326, 332 photo 2).

Today, following the repainting, it is impossible to differentiate the original portions of the figures from the modern ones. Moreover, elements that are illustrated by Tello with a photograph, such as the tail and an element that may have been the animal's ear, have disappeared from the figure on the east side, while the western figure does have a tail. Even in the reconstruction drawing by Rojas Ponce, which shows both felines, this tail is not shown (Tello, 1956, fig. 130). The clear impression one receives is that the western figure, for which there is no firsthand documentation, is a recent copy of the eastern motif as it was presented in Tello's book.

Were it necessary, still further evidence of the falsification perpetrated at Cerro Sechín can be found in a series of photographs of the western feline published in 1972 and 1973. Two photos of this figure, one in color and one in black and white, were published by Samaniego in May 1972 (Samaniego Román, 1972b, cover and p. 34). Both show the figure with only the back paw delineated and no continuation of the body or tail; in fact, no trace of those elements can be seen on the plaster (fig. 11). In October of 1972, however, another color photograph of the same figure appeared in a popularized history of Latin America, issued in fascicles and sold on newsstands (Anonymous, 1972, p. 46). Although the color reproduction is poor, the details are clear and the figure appears with the long tail and hindquarters that are visible today. A similar photograph was published by Samaniego in black and white in his 1973 report and another in his 1980 article (p. 332). From this sequence of photographs, one can infer that the painting of the western feline is recent. In other words, against the most basic scientific principles, a false image was created, destroying forever all evidence of one of the earliest mural paintings in Peru. The question of whether an original western figure ever existed must remain in doubt, since Mejía, Rojas, and Collier all state that there was none at the time that Tello discovered the temple. The fact that no one has disputed my contentions regarding the falsity of the western figure since 1974, when the first edition of this book appeared, indicates tacit acceptance of these allegations.[4]

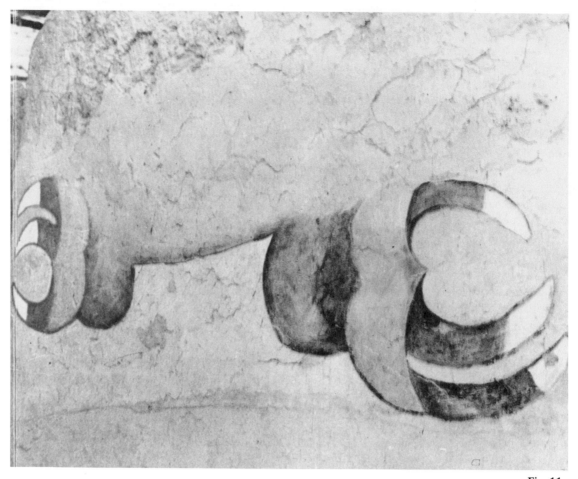

Fig. 11.
Cerro Sechín, western feline as of May 1972, showing no traces of the rear or top portions that appear in fig. 10.

There is a further problem regarding Cerro Sechín, namely its chronological placement. Theoretically there are two approaches to the resolution of this problem, the first through archaeological association, the second by stylistic analysis of the decorative motifs on the monument. There is, however, disagreement among specialists on the interpretation of these elements.

In 1956 Collier again worked in the Casma Valley assisted by Thompson. Collier said positively, "There is at present no proof of ceramic association with the carved monoliths or the adobe construction in the temple interior" (1962, p. 414), while Thompson observed, "The dating of Cerro Sechín Temple remains uncertain, but all presently available information tends to favor a date shortly following the Chavín horizon" (Thompson, 1962, p. 246). Later, on the basis of investigations in the vicinity of the monument, Thompson restated the uncertainty of the dating, adding that probably "the only ceramics of a Formative type found at the site were those belonging to the early form of the Patazca style" (1964, p. 208).

Although Donald Proulx did not work at Cerro Sechín, he did investigate, among other things, the problem of the Early Horizon in the nearby Nepeña Valley. There he ascertained that Tello's sequence at both Cerro Blanco and Puncurí is basically sound, in the sense that the earliest occupation is doubtless Chavín, as evidenced by architectural superposition (Proulx, 1968, pp. 26, 54, 76; 1973, p. 15). His final comment on these sites relates to our problem: "there do seem to be parallels in the construction found in Cerro Sechin and Moxeke in the Casma Valley" (1973, p. 15).

Nevertheless, some archaeologists consider the Cerro Sechín complex to antedate the spread of the Chavín style on the coast. Their contentions are not convincing. Lanning, for example, provides two reasons for assigning a probable Initial Period date to the Cerro Sechín structures. First he states that Collier argued for such a placement in his 1962 article. In fact, however, besides his statement regarding the lack of ceramic association quoted above, Collier says only: "My guess is that the monoliths, which lack Chavín stylistic elements, are contemporary with the Gualaño style, and the adobe superstructures with Patazca. Alternatively, they both date from Patazca times, toward the end of the Late Formative, and are contemporary with Mojeque" (1962, p. 414)—hardly a strong argument for an Initial Period date. Lanning also presents a stylistic argument according to which the carved stones of Cerro Sechín represent the antecedents of the Chavín style, a very debatable opinion (Lanning, 1967, pp. 93, 101). Willey simply states that he concurs with Lanning in following Collier (Willey, 1971, p. 112).

Lumbreras takes a similar position: "this complex . . . antedates the spread of the Chavín style" (1973, p. 81), there being "very clearly a pre-Chavín occupation that is shared by the immense site of Las Aldas to the south of the valley and the temple of Sechín with its engraved slabs, its paintings . . ." (p. 85). In support of these statements he refers only to an article by Bueno published in 1971, but attentive reading of this source fails to support Lumbreras's statement. Bueno defines Sechín I as "pre-Chavín" (Bueno Mendoza, 1971, p. 205) but specifies that it corresponds to a time "before the first buildings were erected at Sechín" (1971, p. 206). He then expands this statement: "it is clear to this point that the first occupation of Sechín occurred in ceramic times; we still lack evidence of the direct association of Sechín I pottery with the buildings of the site"; and "we still lack direct pottery association with the carved stones . . ." (p. 207). He later adds: "At Sechín, Stratum 2, from bottom to top, defines the Chavín occupation. The nucleus of conical adobes, plastered and painted to represent the feline motif, should correspond to this occupation, since it lacks antecedents in the vicinity" (1971, p. 218). Of Stratum 1 Bueno and Samaniego had earlier stated: "the pre-Chavín type found by us at Sechín is especially similar to Cahuacucho. Nevertheless the association with the monoliths is not direct; the pottery appears on the outside of the face with the carved stones" (Bueno Mendoza and Samaniego Román, 1969, p. 34). However, on the same page the authors also said,

"we are sure that the people who carved the stones and made the structure did not use Chavín pottery . . . ," which not only raises some doubt regarding the preceding assertion, but conflicts with Bueno's later writing. In the face of his positive and unqualified statements, it appears that this phrase may be an error.

Bueno is evidently very confused, since we later find him in a glaring contradiction. He repeats his 1971 position regarding the lack of ceramic association with the carved stones, stating: "at Sechín there is so far no clearly diagnostic pottery to place the monoliths temporally. We are sure that the people who carved the stones and made the structure did not use Chavín pottery, but are not yet in a position to state that they used Aldas II–Cahuacucho pottery of the lower Formative" (Bueno Mendoza, 1975, p. 146). He also notes that "the inner nucleus of conical adobes, plastered, painted is still poorly known" (p. 146). Bueno nevertheless concludes emphatically that "the crucial problem of Sechín has always been its chronological placement . . . its pre-Chavín nature is now indisputable" (1975, p. 155).

But another statement made by Bueno flies in the face of logic. "In Casma," he says, "it is important to note that structures of conical adobes always appear set inside large architectural units of an earlier tradition, made of stone" (1975, p. 159). That is, the clay temple, which is not at all intrusive, is later than the structure of carved stones that contains it. Bueno clearly believes this when, partly repeating his 1971 statements, he says: "At Sechín, Stratum 2, from bottom to top, defines the Chavín occupation. The nucleus of conical adobes, plastered and painted representing the feline motif, must correspond to this since antecedents are lacking in the entire vicinity. Thus, the conical adobes sustain the Chavín style ornaments and they always go together in structures containing that style" (Bueno Mendoza, 1975, p. 160). I do not understand how the inner temple of conical adobes can be Chavín and the structure with carved stones pre-Chavín. A statement to this effect displays a faulty interpretation of the unquestionably very complex stratigraphy of the site.

Samaniego attempted to establish a chronology in 1973, but his data are not persuasive. He states firmly, "the clay structure . . . is earlier than the stone one" (1973, p. 47), which I do not doubt in the least. He considers there to have been three construction phases for the clay nucleus. The first comprised the sacred chamber, a vestibule, two rectangular rooms with wide entryways formed by pillars, one of which bears the representation of a person upside down, and, in front of the vestibule, a low wall communicating with the exterior by means of a stairway. The second phase was a horizontal and vertical enlargement, in which the structures of the first phase were covered and a stairway built leading to the second level. Finally, growth in the third phase was horizontal, with a stepped wall divided by two new stairways. It is on these last structures that the fish are represented (Samaniego Román, 1973, pp. 86–87). Samaniego adds, "the complex . . . antedates Chavín in the Casma Valley" (1973, p. 71), assigns it a tentative age of 1500 B.C. (p. 72), and insists that it is of "pre-Chavín fabrication" (p. 73), older than Puncurí and Cerro Blanco (p. 82). To support his hypothesis he explains:

> There is no pottery recovered to date properly associated with the stone structure; but the next group to occupy the site, partly disfiguring the earlier building, left in its refuse small, incomplete, baked clay figurines . . . which at Aldas are associated with the first Chavín manifestations. On the other hand, the style of the architecture and sculpture differs from that known for Chavín, although slight similarities may be noted. Thus it is reasonable to place Sechín in the Early Formative Period. (1973, p. 89)

He expresses the same ideas in his 1980 article (p. 322). Now, if "the next group to occupy the site" (to use Samaniego's own words) used elements that can be associated with "Chavín manifestations," and "There is no pottery recovered to date properly associated with the stone structure" (I suppose there is also none associated with the clay structure, since Samaniego never mentions it), it seems to me that there is no proof whatsoever that the complex is earlier than Chavín.

Samaniego made and repeated one statement that he attributes to Tello and that should be corrected since it is totally erroneous. He says that Tello wrote that the structure "of stone antedates the clay one" (Samaniego Román, 1972a, p. 38; 1980, p. 311). Doubtless Samaniego misunderstood Tello. In his report, Tello essays a trial historical reconstruction including several diagrams, clearly expounding his ideas (1956, pp. 282–87, figs. 124–29). He propounds the existence in Chavín times of an edifice with carved stones, closer to the river, which was destroyed by a flash flood. On the base of the hill (where it is today) another complex was raised later, in which, besides the carved stones, conical adobes were used as well as "the technique of plastering and painting on the walls of the chambers *built within the wall of carved stones*" (Tello, 1956, pp. 283, 285; emphasis

mine). This structure was covered by a landslide, upon which there are much later post-Chavín occupations. Nevertheless, Tello understood perfectly that there were several building phases in the structure that has been left to us. Moreover, his figure 108 (fig. 4) seems to indicate that he considered the earliest structure, with conical adobes (his Phase I), to be earlier than the wall with the monoliths, which he seems to relate to his Phase III. In spite of the fact that Tello's excavation was not exemplary, there is no doubt that his genius for intuition and his experience combined to give him a substantial understanding of the fundamental elements of the stratigraphy at Cerro Sechín.

The feline motifs cannot be dated stylistically. One diagnostic element, the mouth, has disappeared. The treatment of the claws is not typical. Nevertheless, it is undeniable that the figure as a whole recalls the Chavín style. In the case of the fish representations, we do not know if the structure on which they are found is contemporary with the one bearing the feline paintings or later. Samaniego considers it later, assigning it to his third phase (1973, p. 87; 1980, p. 321). Although Tello does not say so, one can infer that he thought it corresponded to Phase II of the building construction (Tello, 1956, fig. 108). As far as the style of the fish is concerned, here also there are no elements that lend themselves directly to a relative date. While in general in Chavín-style sculpture late elements are abstract, we do not know if this norm is valid for clay (Rowe, 1962, p. 17). Moreover, in terms of the published chronology of the style, fish are secondary figures and so not the motif best calculated to resolve a chronological problem (Rowe, 1962).

It is difficult to reach a conclusion regarding the figure of the person represented upside down, which, according to Samaniego, should be associated with the feline paintings (1973, p. 86; 1980, p. 321). But its stylistic similarity to the motifs on the stones of the outer edifice is evident, which should indicate that they are all from a single tradition.

I consider the treatment of the Cerro Sechín fish to be similar to the representations of the same element found on the Tello Obelisk and the Yauya Stela, although the style of the Sechín figure seems later. Both the Tello Obelisk and the Yauya Stela belong to Phase C in Rowe's stylistic chronology, contemporary with phases 4 and 5 of the Paracas sequence. If this placement is correct and Samaniego's sequence is correct, the feline paintings might be assigned to the first phases of Rowe's Chavín sequence. That is, temporally the paintings of the Cerro

Sechín temple would fall at the beginning of the spread of the Chavín style to the coast, and their contemporaneity with the Aldas-like figurines found by Samaniego at Cerro Sechín would be correct, too.

Regarding the temporal placement of the carved stones, I am entirely in accord with the position taken in 1968 by Lathrap, who wrote, refuting Lanning: "In a number of specific details the Cerro Sechín carvings suggest a rustic rendering of the EF segment of Rowe's (1962) chronology for Chavín rather than a precursor of Chavín AB" (Lathrap, 1970, p. 236; 1971, p. 74). This opinion supports my hypothesis regarding the antiquity of the paintings as well as the one that the monoliths are a final expression of the Chavín style, assuming that the stones were erected later than the first temple construction phase.

Writing on the Cerro Sechín stone carvings, Bueno stated that it is in the Lanzón "more than any other example of the Chavín style that one finds the borrowings of Sechín" (1971, p. 216), repeating the statement in the article written with Samaniego (1969, p. 33). This assertion strikes me as stylistically untenable but, if true, it would support Lathrap's contention and my own that the monoliths are late in the style, since we know that the Lanzón, or Great Image as Rowe calls it, belongs to the first or second phase of the Chavín style. Moreover, if we accept Tello's conjecture, which seems correct to me, that the monoliths originally belonged to another structure and were simply reused in Cerro Sechín (Tello, 1939b, p. 242; 1956, p. 121), the outer structure would be substantially later than the central complex.

Peter Roe, in his review of the chronological problem of Chavín, accepts the Cerro Sechín monoliths as corresponding to Rowe's Phase EF (Roe, 1974, pp. 33–36), a position also espoused by Proulx (ms., p. 5). Fung Pineda and Williams León (1979, pp. 139, 140 note 7) display some confusion in holding that the Cerro Sechín monoliths are post-Chavín but basing their argument (although with certain errors in citation) on those works of Jiménez Borja, Bueno, and Samaniego to which I have just referred, and in which the author's position is quite different.

Evidence of other paintings at Cerro Sechín (Samaniego Román, 1980, p. 318) opens the possibility of future clarification of the problem.

There is another important monument in the Casma Valley that, according to most specialists, also dates to the Early Horizon, although there are serious doubts in this regard (see Fung Pineda, 1969; Fung Pineda and Pimentel Gurmendi, 1974). I refer to Chanquillo, also called Chancaillo and Castillo de las Calaveras. While the site has very special architectural characteristics, except for some traces of paint reportedly still visible on its plastered walls (Fung Pineda and Pimentel Gurmendi, 1974, pp. 72, 74), only one author has reported the existence of mural decoration there. Squier, speaking of the inner rectangular buildings located on the upper part of the monument next to the circular structures, notes: "The walls throughout appear to have been stuccoed and painted. On the stucco in the passage-ways and other protected parts are traces of figures in relief, of paintings of men and animals, and what are apparently battle-scenes" (1877, p. 212). This statement is important, since it refers very concretely to decorations that have either disappeared forever or have been buried under rubble on some wall that has not yet been cleared. On the other hand, we do not know whether the reference represents firsthand knowledge or is simply the repetition of reports, since, as we shall see, Squier also mentions the decorations of Paramonga, in spite of the fact that he seems not to have visited that monument. Tello's reference to "high and low reliefs [which] were painted in bright colors" (Tello, 1933b) seems to be based on Squier.

In her discussions of this complex Rosa Fung mentioned only some motifs incised in the wall plaster that appear to be late. One of these motifs has been published and seems to correspond to the Middle Horizon (Fung Pineda, 1971, cover).

Aside from Cerro Sechín and Chanquillo, other important early monuments in Casma are distinguished by their decoration, although none of them has been completely described. For example, painted low reliefs were found in the Sechín Alto complex (Samaniego Román, 1973, p. 79). Furthermore, at the site of Moxeque there is a great terraced structure whose façade had six niches, each containing a clay figure. All the figures were partly destroyed when discovered. These sculptures, representing a feline, a serpent, and a human torso, had been painted in various colors. Some columns and floors were also handsomely painted in red, white, blue, black, green, yellow, and gray (Willey, 1951; 1971, p. 92; Tello, 1956, pp. 56, 59, 66). The clay sculptures are always mentioned in connection with Moxeque and are obviously the most outstanding elements of the monument. Only Willey notes that on the terrace walls between the niches there were decorative elements outlined with deep incision. Our knowledge of these elements is limited to the fact that they were "curvilinear designs painted white" (Willey, 1951, p. 119). Willey had apparently not seen them, basing his description on information provided by Donald Collier.

The Nepeña Valley

The Nepeña Valley is probably as important as Casma. It contains architectural remains of the Early Horizon so outstanding that Larco Hoyle considered the valley to be the original center of the Chavín culture. Puncurí and Cerro Blanco are important sites, even though we have almost no information concerning them. What there is comprises an interview with Tello (Anonymous, 1933), three news articles Tello wrote himself (Tello, 1933a;

1933b; 1933c), and yet another newspaper article by Antúnez de Mayolo (1933). A plan and elevation of Puncurí (figs. 12, 13), as well as some photographs, were published by Larco Hoyle (1938, figs. 18–23) but without further discussion. Bennett's comments on the sites (1939, pp. 16–17) were entirely secondhand, a simple summary of the newspaper accounts. Indeed, even Tello's articles contain little information, an understandable result of their being written under pressure to respond to the negative bias of a commission named to scrutinize his work.

It is of historical interest to note that the painted remains of these monuments had been known in the valley

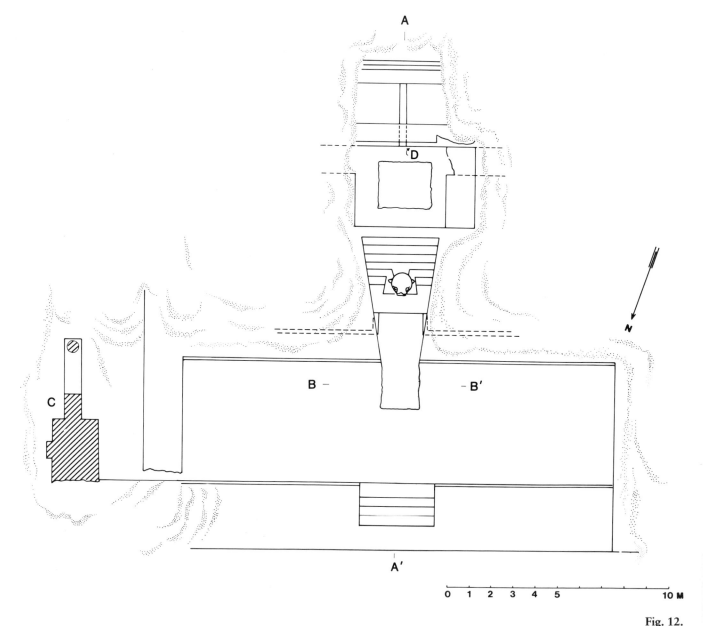

Fig. 12.
Puncurí, Nepeña, plan of the cleared portion of the temple as of September 24, 1933. Scale approximate.

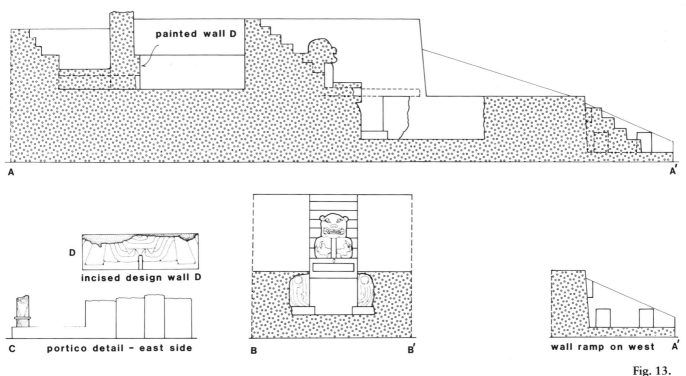

painted wall D

D
incised design wall D

C portico detail - east side

B B'

wall ramp on west A'

Fig. 13.
Puncurí, elevations and decorative details of the temple.

for some time, since Tello himself mentions having been invited on several occasions "to see . . . certain painted walls" (1933a, p. 4). He further recounts that he asked to be taken to the sites after seeing the reliefs in a photograph album shown to him by John B. Harrison, administrator of the Negociación Agrícola Nepeña Limitada (1933a). Tello here, as well as in the published interview, attributes the original discovery of these monuments to Harrison. On the basis of these sources, Cerro Blanco was discovered in 1928 and Puncurí in 1929. Tello did not visit them until 1933, when they had already been partly destroyed.

Speaking of Puncurí, Tello first mentions the discovery of the famous idol of painted clay (figs. 14, 15), in front of which there was a clay stairway painted gray as well as two columns, painted and with reliefs, placed on each side of a doorway. He also notes that there was a platform reached by a stairway on the north side of the building. Behind this platform there was a wall "adorned with large panels in painted relief" (Anonymous, 1933, p. 13). No detailed report on the work at Puncurí was ever published, and in a later article Tello mentions only "an idol made of stone and mud, representing in high relief the figure of a feline painted in different colors"

(1943a, p. 137). John B. Harrison recalls that the colors of this idol were white, black, red, and ochre (personal communication, 1971). He adds that he saw a sort of tunnel or passageway, which Tello knew of but never mentioned, that was located at the side of the main structure; on its walls were a number of figures in relief and in color.[5] Although Tello never wrote about these features, when he mentions the Chavín structures in the Nepeña Valley, he says: "The wakas are . . . connected by galleries . . ." (1939b, p. 235), which may be a reference to them. We also know that there is a superposition of construction at the site. Moreover, according to Kauffmann Doig, the structures of the "lower and middle floor" had clay-plastered surfaces, and "on them were scratched Chavinoid motifs [which were] then painted" (1970, p. 254). On wall D (see fig. 13) there is an elaborate incised design (Larco Hoyle, 1938, figs. 19, 22), which, according to Kauffmann Doig (1970, p. 255), was also painted. Although Larco Hoyle published a plan and elevation of the temple made in the course of Tello's excavations, as well as several photographs of details, he does not discuss this material at all (1938, pp. 32–37).

There is, however, one very well-known figure at-

tributed to Puncurí, which was not only exhibited in the Museo Nacionàl de Antropología y Arqueología, Lima, but also published several times (e.g., Kauffmann Doig, 1970, p. 255, fig. 338). It is a stylized bird with very specific traits (fig. 16). This bird is depicted fullface with circular eyes outlined by an element that recalls falcon markings. The mouth is large with triangular teeth. The curved wings rest on the middle part of the body. The feet are anthropomorphic, and from the central part of the body issues a large feathered tail. Enclosed by each wing is a figure that could be either fish or bird; on the lower part of the body, symmetrically arranged, are two

monkeys and two figures, each with head, feet, and tail, which Kauffmann for some unknown reason identifies as "guinea pigs or vizcachas" (1970, p. 255). In the center of the bird figure is a simple geometric motif.

I began to doubt the authenticity of the figure because of an evident contradiction between the presumed replica, which was in the Lima museum until 1973, and the text accompanying an illustration of it published by Tello (1943b); the museum replica was in low relief, while Tello referred to a "fresco," suggesting that it was a painting. Further information has led me to the conclusion that the "reproduction" that was in the Museo

Fig. 15.
*Puncurí, clay idol originally painted white, black, red, and
ochre-yellow. Early Horizon.*

Nacional de Antropología y Arqueología in Lima was
an "artist's deception."

In the first place, I was informed by Mejía Xesspe,
who saw the original, that it was oriented horizontally, a
sort of frieze at the foot of the monument, whereas the
imitation was oriented vertically. Moreover, what was
found was only half of the figure in the museum. Ccosi
Salas, the perpetrator of the deception, considered it
more aesthetically pleasing to orient the figure vertically,
and he then completed the original figure symmetrically,
thus transforming it into imaginary decorative form.
Mejía recalled that it was not possible to determine

whether the figure had really continued on the lower
part, and if so, whether the elements there would have
been exactly symmetrical to those that were found (personal communication, 1968). We see, then, that Kauffmann errs in writing that "the destroyed side is completed" in the museum reproduction (1970, p. 255),
since further evidence renders it unlikely in the extreme
that such a side ever existed.

Bennett's comments on the find are apparently from
indirect and rather vague information (1939, pp. 16–
17). He refers to a wall on the back edge of the platform
upon which there is a "painted design," and, citing
Antúnez de Mayolo, enumerates its colors: orange, light
yellow with red daubs, yellow, dark blue, lighter blue,
purple, violet, gray, white, dark green, and black. This
list of colors is disorganized and probably not very reliable. Of the motifs, he refers to "a rather realistic
monkey, a small animal, a fish with stylized head, and
various stylized figures" (p. 16). He then mentions the
passageway through this decorated wall that leads to the
stairway where the clay idol already mentioned was
found. At the top of this stairway there was apparently a
chamber, and on its "south wall is an incised and painted
design of a stylized condor in yellow, blue, red, violet,
and white" (p. 16), probably a reference to the design
shown here in fig. 13 (Larco Hoyle, 1938, fig. 22). Also,
the statement "One column seems to have a low relief
design at the base" (Bennett, 1939, p. 16) most likely refers to the column shown in fig. 13 and a photograph
published by Larco Hoyle (1938, fig. 20).

I have not been able to see the photographs taken at
the time of discovery that should be in the Archivo Tello
at the Universidad de San Marcos, nor is there any evidence concerning the original colors. I assume that the
colors reproduced were more or less faithful, and hope
that note was made of them before the reproduction was
destroyed.

The final evidence regarding this figure is to be found
in an article published in *El Comercio* by Antúnez de
Mayolo (1933), to which Bennett refers. I had no opportunity to read the article before writing the first edition
of this book, but it entirely confirms the conclusions I
drew on the basis of other sources. Antúnez de Mayolo
included a drawing of the figure in question, and it shows
only the right half, which is oriented horizontally so that
the eye appendage and the foot are on the bottom, and
the center line of the figure at the top (Antúnez de
Mayolo, 1933, p. 17).[6] The colors he mentioned are
those listed by Bennett, and the caption reads: "wall in
high relief" (Antúnez de Mayolo, 1933, p. 16). Antúnez

Fig. 16.
Falsified Puncurí motif as exhibited for many years in the Museo Nacional de Antropología y Arqueología, Lima.

spread wings" (p. 16), neither his figure 11 nor the other illustrations resemble a condor, even with the exercise of considerable imagination. Rather the motif may depict the clothing of some personage.

Regarding the chronological placement of the remains, Bennett comments: "In both Cerro Blanco and Punguri, the incised, or low relief, and painted wall designs, the modeled cat, and the incised stone artifacts are unquestionably of Chavín style. Only the many-colored fresco at Punguri seems to be somewhat doubtful of identification" (1939, p. 17). Indeed, while we now know that the temple corresponds to the Chavín style (Proulx, 1973, p. 15), the relief motif, if the few illustrations we have are accurate, is evidently related to that style, although the majority of its elements are strange, calling for more detailed analysis. It could be a later element applied to an older structure.

Roe thinks that the monument can be assigned to Rowe's Phase D or EF, although the relationship that he notes between the relief feline of Puncurí and the painted one from Sechín seems forced (Roe, 1974, pp. 37–38, Chart 1).

There are many similarities between the case of Puncurí and that of the small temple of Cerro Blanco, considered to be one of the most important and distinctive examples of Chavín religious architecture on the coast (fig. 17). This site, as noted, was also discovered by Harrison and was cleared by Tello in 1933, but again Tello's notes remain unpublished and we have only vague comments and numerous worthless citations based on the newspaper information from the time of the clearing. Moreover, the site has suffered severe damage that may prevent the verification of many facts.

This temple is probably best known from a spurious reconstruction that stood until 1973 in the main courtyard of the Museo Nacional de Antropología y Arqueología, Lima (see Museo Nacional, 1948, unnumbered photo replacing title page). This "reconstruction" included various extraneous elements, including some from Puncurí.

Tello explains, in his most important work, that at Cerro Blanco there was a superposition of structures belonging to at least four epochs (although in the descrip-

de Mayolo thought that, for symmetry, the same figure should be found repeated on the opposite side of the stairway, but there is nothing to indicate such a repetition. This article provides definite grounds for saying that Ccosi Salas's work was spurious. It also clarifies the initial contradiction; we now know that the figure was not a painting but a relief treatment, so that Tello (1943b) was in error, while the legend exhibited so many years in the Lima museum was correct.

Antúnez de Mayolo's article also indicates that the painted condor to which Bennett referred was not a painting but a "flat relief" (Antúnez de Mayolo, 1933, p. 16). The photograph of the motif, as well as its caption, however, clearly demonstrate that the figure was simply incised and painted (Larco Hoyle, 1938, fig. 22), even though the labels on the elevation and architectural details of Puncurí are somewhat confusing on this point (fig. 13, wall D). It appears that Bennett had not seen the article, the photograph, or the plan, since, although Antúnez de Mayolo does mention "a condor with out-

Fig. 17.
Cerro Blanco, Nepeña, frontal section of the temple immediately after it was cleared in August 1933. Early Horizon.

tion he mentions only three). The first had "high reliefs with cutbacks, finely plastered and painted in red, yellow, pink and white," while the second layer was not painted (1942, p. 115). Bennett disagreed with Tello regarding colors, and is incorrect (1939, p. 16). Regarding the third building stage, which was inferior in quality to the rest, Tello says that there were plastered and painted walls and that "pictorial decoration replaces plastic," though the themes are still typically Chavín (1942, p. 115). I have not seen these decorative motifs, nor do I know what colors were used. Curiously, in Tello's earlier writing he did not mention the painted reliefs (1939b, p. 234); his later report adds nothing (1943a, pp. 136–37). Proulx writes that part of the wall decorations, the building façade, and other remains of the structure are still preserved (1968, pp. 26–27, 77). He further notes that the lowest platform of the mound provided access to another platform "enclosed by three walls painted with feline motifs" (1973, p. 15).

This oft-illustrated monument (e.g., Tello, 1942, lám. XV), which should correspond to the building with Tello's "lower floor" (1942, pp. 114–16), was originally assigned by Rowe to Phase C of the Chavín style (Rowe, 1962, p. 16). Kauffman Doig placed it in Phase EF (1970, p. 256), while Peter Roe argued for a position "at the very end of C, or perhaps early D" (1974, p. 37). Rowe himself now holds for a placement in Phase D, with the second building phase probably in EF (personal communication, 1982).

Department of La Libertad

The most beautiful recorded example of mural painting in the Chavín style is that illustrated by Kosok, unfortunately only in a rather poor photograph of which the painted portion of the structure is only a detail (fig. 18; Kosok, 1965, p. 109, fig. 32). His text provides no information about the site. The caption says it was a *huaca* but gives neither its name nor its exact location, only the fact that it was within the boundaries of the former Hacienda Casa Grande in the department of La Libertad. The structure was intentionally destroyed (when, is not known) by the personnel of the hacienda, shown hard at work in Kosok's figure 31, which also shows a mound cut in two and two cylindrical columns that seemingly formed part of the temple. The structure was built of conical adobes. In the closeup photograph the lower part of the column shows the remains of polychrome decoration that must have originally covered the entire column. The other column may have had the same

Fig. 18.
Casa Grande, La Libertad, remains of painted column destroyed many years ago. Early Horizon.

characteristics. The motif is typically Chavín; in spite of the size and quality of the reproduction the feline mouth with its typical prominent fangs is clearly visible. It brings to mind two themes, also painted but on cloth, one illustrated by Rowe (1962, fig. 30) and another similar one in the Reynaldo Luza collection (Anonymous,

30 _____ *Mural Painting in Ancient Peru*

1973, top right; Nakamura H., 1973, p. 16 top). These textiles are stylistically late in the Chavín style and belong to Rowe's Phase EF. The column in question must have dated to that phase. This painted column is the only elaborate Chavín mural painting we know so far, especially with such marked stylistic characteristics. It is a pity we know nothing of its technique and coloration.

There is also evidence for the former existence of a decorated monument of the same period in the lower Santa Valley. Fragments of reliefs painted in green, red, light blue, black, white, and orange or yellow have been found in the fill of the Huaca Ureña and on the remains of conical adobes (Mercedes Cárdenas, personal communication, 1980).

Several important monuments belonging to this period have been found in the Moche Valley. The Huaca de los Reyes in the Caballo Muerto complex near the Hacienda Laredo is a typical monument of the Chavín culture: very complex, U-shaped, with plazas, platforms, and mounds. The monument is decorated with sculptural elements in low relief and incised motifs. There are human figures, profile heads with prominent fangs, and feline figures with claws. There was white painting on the base, and, "Although no definite painted fragments or painting in other colors were found at the site, evidence from other huacas in the complex suggests that the friezes might have been extensively painted at the time they were in use" (Pozorski, 1976, pp. 242–44). The monument is related, according to Pozorski (1976), to the northern development of Chavín known as Cupisnique, and might be an early development of the style near the end of the Initial Period. Yet another monument in the Cabello Muerto complex, discovered in 1972, is known as Herederos. It also has the classic U shape, and on the south wing are remains of white paint, which seems to have formed vertical bands; I do not know whether or not they formed a more complex design (Claude Chauchat, personal communication, 1975). Only ruins remain of the Early Horizon monument known as Huaca Sacachique or Cañahuaca, which seems to have had a decoration in red paint (Alvarez M., ms.). Finally, in the same valley there is some information about very poorly preserved Early Horizon paintings on the Huaca de los Chinos (Cristóbal Campana, personal communication, 1980).

La Leche Valley

An important discovery of paintings was recently made at the Huaca Lucía in the Batán Grande complex of the Leche Valley in the department of Lambayeque, by a team of archaeologists from Princeton University under the direction of Izumi Shimada (Shimada, personal communication, 1981). There a remarkably large and distinctive temple was found, today known as the Temple of the Columns. The temple stands on a rectangular, two-level platform mound, oriented north-south and measuring fifty-two meters east-west. On this mound is a U-shaped, walled enclosure decorated on the exterior with "largely obliterated polychrome murals" (Shimada, 1981, p. 39). To the north of a three-level platform that spans the width of the enclosure are twenty-four columns in three parallel rows.

Shimada considers this temple to be the "earliest known monumental construction in the Lambayeque Valley Complex," and says that it "symbolizes the emergence of a corporate religion in the Batan Grande region" (1981, p. 41). He also observes: "Associated ceramic and polychrome mural fragments indicated that it belonged to the Cupisnique culture, an early North Coast culture associated with monumental religious architecture and an iconography characterized by feline features. Its relationship to the important highland Chavin culture . . . is still unclear, although there appears to be a strong ideological connection" (Shimada, 1981, p. 39).

A tracing of the remains of this painting (fig. 19) leaves no doubt of its Cupisnique affiliation, although, because of its poor state of preservation, it is impossible to reconstruct the original motif. The remaining elements seem to be related to the typical feline terminals of Chavín iconography. The mural fragment measures approximately 1.60 m long by 0.72 m high. The wall was first plastered and the motif then painted in red, outlined by a broad black line, on a dark blue-gray ground. An intriguing feature of the temple is the fact that "its architectural features [were] carefully 'entombed' in thick layers of pure white sand" (Shimada, 1981, p. 39), leading Shimada to suggest that it represents a sort of "ritual burial" (1981, p. 40). The association of the Huaca Lucía with the Cupisnique style makes it one of the earliest examples of mural painting on the Peruvian coast during the Early Horizon.

The Highlands

Regarding art in the highlands in the Early Horizon, with the exception of the temple of Chavín de Huántar, we know very little, and even there the evidence is poor. Engel notes that some buildings at Chiripa, in the south-

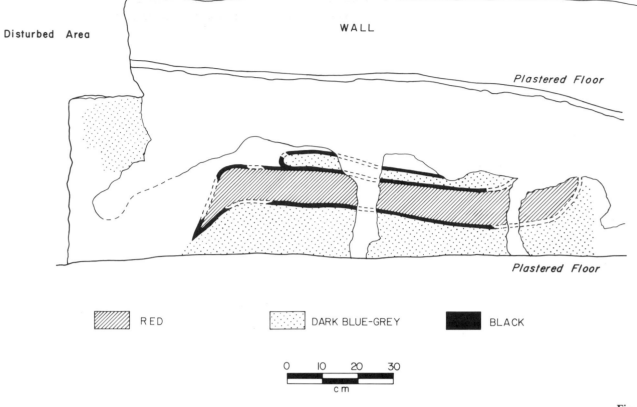

Disturbed Area
WALL
Plastered Floor
Plastered Floor

RED   DARK BLUE-GREY   BLACK

0   10   20   30
cm

Fig. 19.
Huaca Lucía, Lambayeque, fragment of painting.
Early Horizon.

ern altiplano, "were built with unfired clay bricks painted red, green, and white . . ." (1976, p. 116).

Chavín de Huántar, the most important known monument of the Chavín culture, evidently had painted areas in its buildings that made it even more impressive than it is now. Tello suggested the existence of decoration when he wrote:

> At present the walls of the galleries are bare; but it may be surmised that they were originally plastered, perhaps decorated with polychrome frescoes and reliefs like those of the temples of Punkurí and Cerro Blanco . . . and Moxeque . . . judging from the great quantity of clay on the floors and the remains of red and yellow paint that appear on some side walls and by the pieces of burned clay in the rubble of the galleries and upper buildings of the principal temple. (Tello, 1960, p. 92)

In his study of Chavín art, John Rowe noted that besides the well-known stone sculpture at the site of Chavín de Huántar, there had also been painted clay plaster reliefs (1967, p. 72). He further stated: "There are traces of painted plaster on the walls of these [interior] passages, and in one of the rooms three of the slabs forming the ceiling have traces of low relief carving, now badly damaged" (1967, p. 74). Later, Lumbreras reported very briefly on incised figures painted in red, green, and blue that represent a fish and a group of four probable crustaceans (perhaps crayfish [*camarones*]) found on the roof slabs of the eastern section of the Galería de las Columnas (1970, p. 117). He also noted several layers of clay plaster with orange paint in the Great Pyramid and suggested that all the interior and exterior walls were plastered and painted in yellow, red, and white (1970, p. 132). We have no further details.

Muelle suggested in 1937 that the renowned Raimondi Stela was originally painted. He argued that "the execution of the engraving technically compels one to see in it a polychrome drawing, that is, it forces one to hypothesize a pictorial experience" (Muelle, 1937, p. 140). The idea is suggestive, and if correct, as some recent evidence intimates, would admit the notion that many stone sculptures in ancient Peru received the same treatment. When Muelle wrote his article, however, it was mere speculation, inspired, perhaps, by Greek art.

Before concluding this discussion of the Early Horizon, I wish to make one observation and one correction. The observation relates to the pattern of temples with columns. This pattern is repeated in several important monuments of the Early Horizon, including the Huaca Lucía, Chavín de Huántar, and the temple with columns that Kosok illustrated. It clearly merits careful analysis in the future.

The correction is to a caption published by Federico Kauffmann Doig, which reads: "Chavinoid fresco from the Ica region made known by A. Kroeber" (1970, p. 244, fig. 308; and subsequent editions until 1978, when the error was corrected). Although he cites no specific work of the North American author, the illustration that the caption accompanies is from Kroeber's synthesis of Peruvian archaeology in 1942, plate 11, lower right, which is accompanied by a description reading: "part of a large receptacle, of leather, heavily sized, and then painted" (Kroeber, 1944, p. 40, with a similar description on p. 146). Further comment is unnecessary.

► Plate 1. Cerro Sechín, Casma Valley, paintings on entryway of inner structure as they appear today; eastern feline on the left. This photo, taken in November 1972, shows the western figure already complete (compare fig. 11). The left-hand figure and the structure bearing it are from the Early Horizon.

▼ Plate 2. Cerro Culebra, probably Stumer's Panel 1. Lima style, Early Intermediate Period.

Plate 3. Cerro Trinidad, Chancay Valley, murals as found when Ravines studied them in 1963. Panel A is to the left. Lima style, Early Intermediate Period.

Plate 4. Cerro Trinidad, detail of Ravines's Panel B with typical interlocking motifs of the Lima style.

▶ Plate 5. Huaca Cotón, Pacasmayo, detail of mural fragment found in 1981. Early Intermediate Period.

▼ Plate 6. Pañamarca, mural A, detail of large scene of two people fighting. Visible are one arm of each antagonist and the face of the right-hand figure. Moche style, Early Intermediate Period.

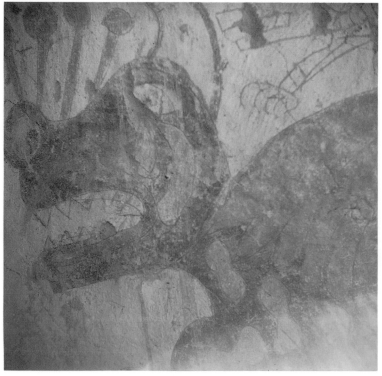

▲ Plate 7. Pañamarca, mural B, "feline snail" facing into corner; note traces of mural D on adjoining wall.

◀ Plate 8. Detail of "feline snail." Moche style, Early Intermediate Period.

▲ Plate 9. Pañamarca, mural C, portion of great "procession" Schaedel found in the plaza. The center figure was the last exposed for his study; the ones to its right were uncovered later.

▼ Plate 10. Detail of new figure in plate 9. Moche style, Early Intermediate Period.

Plate 11. Pañamarca, detail of mural E, discovered in 1958. Portion of scene of ritual human sacrifice; the large figure is an attendant of the "great priestess"; behind him are two prisoners. Moche style, Early Intermediate Period.

► Plate 12. Pañamarca, detail of mural E, including one prisoner and a guard.

▶ Plate 13. Pañamarca, mural F; this feline representation was apparently part of a larger context now destroyed. The date of its exposure is unknown; the author first saw it in 1974, when it was already badly damaged. Moche style, Early Intermediate Period.

▼ Plate 14. Huaca de la Luna, Moche Valley, large preserved fragment of second of three murals found on platform 1a. Middle Horizon.

▶ Plate 15. Huaca de la Luna, detail of third mural of platform 1*a*, principal personage shown in fig. 68. This part of the mural was not exposed in 1955 but found only in 1972.

▼ Plate 16. Huaca de la Luna, part of mural first described in 1955 and re-excavated in 1972. It is the third stage of repainting of the wall on platform 1*a*. Middle Horizon Epoch 3. For combination of plates 15 and 16, see plate 17.

Plate 17. Huaca de la Luna, third mural of platform 1*a*, detail showing two motifs that repeat in checkerboard fashion (compare fig. 68).

Plate 18. Huaca de la Luna, detail of second mural (platform 1*a*) showing surface and technique.

Plate 19. Pampa Grande, detail from south end of mural, showing a typical Moche "warrior." End of Early Intermediate Period or beginning of Middle Horizon.

▲ Plate 20. Huaca Pintada, Lambayeque, painting of mural details made in 1916 for Brüning. The complete panel represents Schaedel's figure 2 (fig. 75); to the right are examples of the four background motifs, showing color alternation. Handwriting is Brüning's. Middle Horizon Epoch 2.

▼ Plate 21. Túcume, Lambayeque, decorated doorway photographed in 1953 when it was found. Late Intermediate Period.

Plate 22. Huaca Corte, Lambayeque, mural detail showing border of interlocking step frets and an unidentifiable jagged element. End of Middle Horizon 4.

Plate 23. Chornancap, detail of mural from right side of west wall, showing personages 29 and 30. Middle Horizon 4?

Plate 24. Chornancap, detail of mural on right side of west wall, including personages 36 and 37. Middle Horizon 4?

Plate 25. Chornancap, portion of mural from south wall, including personages 1–5. Middle Horizon 4?

Plate 26. Chornancap, portion of mural on right side of west wall, including personages 28–33 and half of 34. Middle Horizon 4?

Plate 27. Chornancap, detail of mural from right side of west wall, including half of personage 37, personages 38, 39, and half of 40. Middle Horizon 4?

Plate 28. Chornancap, detail of mural from right side of west wall, showing personage 33. Middle Horizon 4?

Plate 29. Temple of Pachacámac, Muelle's "bench of wall C" with plant representations (see fig. 106). This 1938 image is probably the first photographic documentation in color of Peruvian archaeological remains. Late Horizon.

Plate 30. Temple of Pachacámac, 1938 color photograph of Muelle's wall C to the right of bench shown in plate 29. Late Horizon.

Plate 31. Huaca de la Centinela, room on south end of Inca structure with remains of mural painting on its south and west walls; distant mound is the Huaca Tambo de Mora.

Plate 32. General view of mural.

Plate 33. Fish motif.

Plate 34. Fish motif.

Plates 32−34. Huadca, Lima, murals found in 1962 and destroyed the same year. Late Horizon.

— 3 —
Further Developments

THE EARLY INTERMEDIATE PERIOD

During the Early Intermediate Period remarkable changes took place in architecture, not so much in the materials employed, which remain fundamentally the same, but rather in the monumental nature of public works, a change that is especially marked on the north coast. Patterns differed between the highlands and the coast, perhaps because of differences in building materials; but the coast is not entirely uniform either. All the sites seem to represent settlements that might be characterized as towns. On the south coast the first cities were born. The Early Intermediate Period is especially important in terms of mural painting, not so much for the quantity, although that is remarkable, as for the quality displayed.

The Rímac Valley

A good example is to be found at Cerro Culebra, a small mound located on the right side of the Chillón

River, a few kilometers from its mouth, on the lands of the former Hacienda Márquez. When archaeological work was undertaken there, the area was still uninhabited. Today it is not only bordered by housing but irrevocably destined to disappear.

Excavations by Louis Stumer carried out in 1952 disclosed a superposition of structures. Unfortunately, the published descriptions of the results, and especially of the decorated walls, which must have been the most interesting, are very general and not very well illustrated (Anonymous, 1952; Stumer, 1954; 1955). The decorations to which I shall refer were found on the lower structure, corresponding to the earliest occupation of the site. They comprise polychrome paintings executed on a wall that was damaged when it was covered by walls of the second occupation period. The portion of the paint-

ing that survived was in a magnificent state of preservation and clearly represents the finest example of mural painting so far known from the central coast (pl. 2, figs. 20–24). Clearing this painting was complicated by the fact that the decorated wall supported another of *tapia*[1] of the later period, and was covered by a layer of clay.

The painted wall was also of *tapia*, to which a very fine yellow clay plaster had been applied. Stumer does not specify whether the clay was naturally yellow or had been mixed with pigment; the latter would appear to be the case. The total wall length was 65 m; we do not know its original height, but it was more than 2 m, since the wall was later cut above that height. This wall formed one face of the quadrilateral main building and was apparently protected by a roof. Stumer could not determine whether the remaining walls were also painted or

Fig. 20.
Cerro Culebra, Chillón Valley, mural detail, probably Stumer's Panel 1; motifs are similar to those of Cerro Trinidad. Lima style, Early Intermediate Period.

Fig. 21.
Cerro Culebra, Panel 2, showing Stumer's "ugly deity surrounded by serpents." Early Intermediate Period.

Fig. 22.
Cerro Culebra, Panel 3, showing interlocking motifs difficult to relate to Stumer's description. Early Intermediate Period.

not. The design occupied only about 26 m of the middle of the wall, the end sections beyond that portion being light yellow. The design was executed in seven colors: black, white, brown, purple, orange, and two shades of red.

The painted design was divided into six sections, marked by changes in theme, each section about 4.5 m wide.

> The three easternmost sections are representations of a highly simplified and geometric anthropomorphic or feline head. The first two show this ugly "deity" surrounded by stylized serpent attributes [pl. 2, figs. 20, 21]. The second section [fig. 21] shows the god's serpent arms; the serpent heads are his hands. In the third section [fig. 22] he is in the center, surrounded on all sides by smaller heads symmetrically arranged, perhaps representing trophies. The three remaining sections are less geometric and simplified; they make use of more colors and are more difficult to interpret. The first [figs. 23, 24] has a central anthropomorphic standing figure, its arms upraised, holding a trophy head in each hand. This being is flanked by a lizard or fish and various obscure geometric figures. The next section is badly damaged and only some geometric figures can be identified. The final panel has an anthropomorphic or feline face flanked by a balanced design of attributes. These appear to include a serpent or fish motif and are especially interesting since they alone use curved lines. (Stumer, 1954, p. 227)

This description is lacking in detail, and Stumer did not illustrate Panel 1 (pl. 2, fig. 20), so it is difficult to get a concrete idea of the feline motif he mentioned, which should have been the most important of the mural.

From the photographs, the decorations at Cerro Culebra are extremely similar to those discovered by Uhle at Cerro Trinidad, which will be discussed below. Stumer compares the Cerro Culebra designs stylistically to similar designs in the Recuay style of the Callejón de Huaylas, but the comparison strikes me as somewhat farfetched. According to Stumer, the structure upon which the paintings were executed corresponds to the Playa Grande style, which stratigraphically underlies the Maranga style and is dated between 600 B.C. and A.D. 600. The motifs of interlocking snakes, or fish, are typical of what we now call the Lima style, specifically its Phase 5 according to Patterson (Patterson, 1966; Bonavia, 1966, pp. 30–31).

Fig. 23.
Cerro Culebra, Panel 4. Early Intermediate Period.

Stumer's final observation is of some interest. He believes, on stylistic grounds, that the mural was the work of at least two artists who must have worked simultaneously. He bases this inference on the fact that the first three sections differ greatly from the other three, not only in the preparation of the surface upon which the paintings were placed, but also in the colors, composition, execution, and feeling (*sic*). It even appears that the artist who painted the right-hand sector had to compress the left part of his/her first section in order not to overlap the painting of the right-hand sector. And while the painter of the right-hand sector was more inventive, less neat, and less sure in composition, design and use of color, the left-hand artist was more self-assured. These two expressions could represent "a prehistoric version of traditional and modern" (Stumer, 1954, p. 228).

Sometime around 1970 personnel of the museum of the Universidad Nacional Agraria de Lima and the Instituto Nacional de Cultura re-exposed this mural. Since they failed to recover it properly, it fell prey to the curious, who uncovered it again and left it exposed to the elements. It is now in very poor condition. There is a color replica of the mural, apparently natural size, in the aforementioned museum.

The Chancay Valley

North of Lima, at the entrance to the Chancay Valley, is Cerro Trinidad, one of the most important archaeological sites for understanding the Lima style. The site is on a hill, part of which was modified by architectural additions. There, in the early 1900s, Max Uhle discovered a handsome mural to which he first referred in 1904 (in Kroeber, 1926, pp. 302–303), later publishing an illustration with a very brief mention (fig. 25; Uhle, 1910b, pp. 356 and 358 fig. 6; 1935, p. 27, fig. 13), although the illustration does not give an exact idea of the mural's quality. Kosok reproduced a drawing of parts of this illustration (1965, pp. 232–33), and the replica published by Rogger Ravines in a Lima newspaper is important because it is based on the original (see Bonavia, 1965b). These references gain significance since the mural no longer exists and they are the only evidence left to us. There is also a tracing of the mural made by Ravines and deposited in 1963 with Manuel Chávez Ballón, then a functionary of the Patronato Nacional de Arqueología. In that year Ravines, foreseeing that the mural was bound to disappear under urban expansion, decided to clear it for study with the help of some students of the Department of Anthropology of the Universidad Nacional

Fig. 24.
Cerro Culebra, detail of Panel 4.

Mayor de San Marcos (pls. 3, 4); at the end of the work it was reburied. Ravines wrote an important report on the project, which is still unpublished (Ravines, ms.). I consider it of sufficient interest to present the pertinent section verbatim, with the author's kind permission:

> *Huaca* located to the SW of Cerro Trinidad was, at the time of the study, a badly damaged, dissected, and amorphous mound no more than 100 m long and about the same in width, totally covered by windblown sand, soil, refuse, and ancient and modern rubble. . . . the structure upon which the paintings are found represents one of the few visible walls in that shapeless pile of earth and refuse. It is oriented 325° North. It is 29 meters in a straight line from the left gutter of the road to the Port and rests on a thin stratum, 12 cm thick, of very fine sand resting, in turn, on a gravel bed mainly composed of laminar fragments of reddish slate each no more than 5 or 6 cm long, which apparently formed a platform 7 meters high measuring from the present level of the highway. . . . The type of painting that adorns this wall is what is today known as painting in distemper. . . . the walls in general seem to have been plastered in very fine clay about 0.5 cm thick that has erased the traces of the joints, providing a smooth and uniform surface, then washed with an ochre-yellow paint upon which the decorative motifs in question were then drawn.
>
> The cleared portion of the *huaca* shows the aforementioned wall which extends to the southwest. Shortly after beginning our clearing we encountered another

Fig. 25.
*Cerro Trinidad, Chancay Valley, mural discovered by
Uhle. Lima style, Early Intermediate Period.*

wall transverse to it extending northwest for 2 meters, where it changed direction and continued parallel to the larger wall. For descriptive purposes, we have arbitrarily designated the panels A and B [pl. 3], and although both are integral parts of the same structure and they are stylistically complementary, the division is valid.

When we visited the site Panel A was almost totally visible, thus most subject to environmental and human attacks, with only one extreme covered by a thick layer of refuse. Seen from the road, the wall appeared to extend longitudinally inward. The visible part is composed of about 4000 adobes arranged in 20 courses of 32 elements [*sic*] giving a maximum height of 3.9 m and a maximum length of 4.9 m. The design presently occupies the middle and upper part of the face. There, on an ochre ground there are still remains of a totally linear and geometric design. Small triangles outlined by black lines appear on the lower part, while red and white lines also outlined in black follow one another alternating, suggesting a repetitive rhythm.

The upper part is totally flaked off, as are those portions preceding a motif of elongated vertical shape next to the transverse Panel B. This figure is also composed of triangles with its vertical development based on two triangles, the vertex of the lower one joined to one extreme of the base of the one above. This motif is clearly different from those of Panel B. It could be called stepped triangles to differentiate it from those of B, because it lacks a lineal union through the cathetus. The figure is not explicit, so we cannot agree with Uhle when he says that this is a conventional fish motif of ancient Ica art (Uhle, 1910a, p. 341). The painting is similar to that of Panel B in its range of color (white, ochre, Indian-red, scarlet, and black), except that the fragments of scarlet over red, which are very rare on Panel B and always in the same position, occupy a larger area on Panel A. They probably represent a color that covered the red in the entire design, although the fact that the red color adheres so firmly and is so carefully applied suggests that it was only a later retouching [fig. 26, pl. 4].

Panel B, because of its apparent frontal position within the complex framed by two walls, its slight height and the hard floor that supported it, gives the impression that the wall containing it represents the facing of a platform which is today totally destroyed and filled with refuse and rubble of later pre-Columbian periods. This painting, when we examined it, was covered and preserved by a thin layer of very clean sand under a shapeless heap of soil and broken adobes. When cleared for reproduction, the surface presented serious breaks and cracks that penetrated to the heart of the wall itself, perhaps resulting from the pressure that it was supporting, although the drawing preserved its design integrally.

The colors used in its composition are the same used in Panel [A]. The base paint is an ochre, which, as we mentioned earlier, may have covered the entire structure, at least this is suggested by the walls of Cerro Trinidad. On this color the motifs are outlined with black lines, apparently made in a single stroke, although later widened and retouched to a width of more than 3 cm with quite visible strokes [pl. 4]. The white paint was applied last and, although the pigments have not yet been chemically analyzed, this color seems to have been produced from chalk or calcium carbonate. It must have been difficult to obtain and its adhesion even more so, since it is the color which flakes off most easily, so that there has been constant retouching as shown in the irregular texture visible today.

The particular effect of the Indian-red results from the underlying ochre-yellow base, although later it seems to have been retouched until it forms a thick scarlet film, a color to which we referred above. The black outline, which has the same thickness as the red and is sometimes seen to have been applied after the other colors, has lasted very well; it may have a manganese base. . . . This design composition cannot be called overlapping or interlaced or even interwoven . . . its true technical name is "interlocking." . . . Associated with these paintings were numerous fragments of pottery of the well-known Baños de Boza and Playa Grande

Fig. 26.
Cerro Trinidad, detail of drawing of Panel B cleared by Ravines in 1963. Lima style, Early Intermediate Period.

styles. But turning to the purely chronological and stylistic aspect of the paintings, we find ourselves in serious difficulties in trying to place them within a specific phase of the style, above all when "from Playa Grande 1 onward, Early Intermediate phases of the central coast all have interlocking elements in the designs" (Lanning, 1963, [p. 53]). Nevertheless, the simple interlocking designs are antecedent to those with rows of dots and rings, thus permitting us to place the designs of Panels A and B respectively clearly in Playa Grande Phase 4 or later, but never in 3 or earlier, and contemporary with Nasca 7 (A, B, C) on the south coast and with Moche IV, which is equivalent to a radiocarbon date of 655 ± 80 years A.D., in the north.

A closer comparison of the Uhle mural with the one recorded by Ravines suggests that they are not, in fact, the same panels (compare fig. 25 and pl. 3). Even the

small fragment remaining of panel A is sufficient to establish that it is not the same as the portion reproduced by Uhle. While Uhle's mural was doubtless in the same sector of the structure, it must have already been totally destroyed by the time Ravines and his team reached the site. Such an interpretation would resolve the disagreement between Uhle's description of the design and Ravines's observations.

Department of La Libertad

The antecedents of the Moche culture on the north coast are unclear. Indications today are that these origins are not necessarily to be found in the area between Virú and Chicama, as has been thought. The Gallinazo culture was doubtless influential in the process but apparently not a primary element. Gallinazo developed basically in the Virú Valley, but its influence was felt beyond the frontiers of that small drainage. An important expression of that influence, in my opinion, is the Huaca Licapa, also known as Licape or Huaca Mocan, located in the Chicama Valley, district of Paiján, department of La Libertad (fig. 27). The *huaca* was discovered in 1954 (Horkheimer, 1965, p. 27), when a wall was exposed adorned with flat relief motifs representing stylized interlocking serpents very similar to motifs that characterize the Lima style. The serpents were painted white (A-81, Cailleux and Taylor),[2] while the sunken portions forming their background and eyes were of a very intense red tone (E-16, Cailleux and Taylor) (see Hagen, 1976, color pl. X).

There is no study of this monument, and some writers have suggested that it should date to the Moche era (Garrido, 1956b, p. 2; Horkheimer, 1965, p. 27; Benson, 1972, p. 98; Donnan, 1976, p. 20; Hagen, 1976, caption to color pl. X). I believe that it belongs to the Gallinazo culture (see Schaedel, 1957, fig. 2; Bonavia, 1965b), since its structural characteristics are not precisely those of the Moche culture. The wall bearing the flat relief is of *tapia*, and only in the upper part were there adobes. This fact was observed by Mario Florián and Oscar Lostaunau, who were the first to reach the site after looters uncovered the monument (Florián, 1954, p. 10), and I was able to confirm it personally in 1955. In his article, Florián made an important observation regarding the Huaca Licapa adobes, which were "rectangular (made in cane [*caña brava*] molds, with visible mold marks on all sides of the brick), being distinguished from the others of Mochica stamp by this detail since adobes made in cane molds are not very common" (Florián, 1954, p. 2).

In the first place, *tapia* walls are not a Moche tradition, but they are Gallinazo. The use of *tapia* is, in fact, a local Virú tradition that begins in the Preceramic and lasts into Bennett's Gallinazo I phase. It then disappears, reappearing with slight modifications only slightly before the advent of the Incas (Bennett, 1950, pp. 105–106). In the second place, adobes with deep cane marking are also characteristic of Gallinazo; thus, when Hastings and Moseley studied the adobes of the Huaca de la Luna in Moche, they wrote: "Deep cane marks are found in some bricks of the preceding Gallinazo phase. Marks of the Moche phase are often shallow, faint, and difficult to distinguish" (Hastings and Moseley, 1975, p. 198). Third, the decorative technique of flat relief is not a Moche but a Gallinazo tradition (see Bennett,

1950). Fourth, while it is indeed true that the motif of interlocking serpents appears in Moche (although not frequently; see Schmidt, 1929, p. 187 and Rowe, 1974, fig. 389b), especially in Phases I and II, this motif is one of the distinctive characteristics of the Gallinazo style, and the Licapa motifs are more similar stylistically to the Gallinazo ones (e.g., Bennett, 1950, p. 27). Moreover, when the decorated wall of Licapa was exposed by the looters, it was covered by a layer of clay (see fig. 27), as Florián noted at some length (1954, p. 2). We find the antecedents of this custom in Gallinazo (Bennett, 1950, p. 39).

Bennett attempted to establish a chronology based on a sequence of construction techniques found in the Virú Valley (1950, pp. 64–65). The earliest phase of this sequence, Gallinazo I, contained *tapia* constructions, while adobes made in cane molds belong to Gallinazo III. Thus the decorated wall of Licapa would be contemporary with Gallinazo I and would have been completed or remodeled in the course of Gallinazo III. This interpretation agrees with Bennett's statement that decorated walls in the Virú Valley are characteristic of Gallinazo I and perhaps II (1950, p. 107).

I have heard of some paintings that, since they are not exactly Moche, I prefer to include here in spite of their intimate relationship to that culture. One of them was found at the site of Loma Quemada (on Cerro Oreja, whose exact location I do not know, but it is in the Moche-Chicama region), where there was an occupation during the Early Horizon (Cupisnique) and the Early Intermediate Period (Moche). Cristóbal Campana (personal communication, 1980) saw remains of "friezes" that could well belong to a late Gallinazo or early Moche style. On fragments found in the rubble there were clearly visible remains of motifs in Indian-red, black, white, and ochre. The paint was on a layer of plaster applied to cane; clear traces of the cane remained on the back of the fragments.

Campana also recalls having seen on the esplanade located near the back of the Huaca del Sol (in Moche), some 200 meters toward the sea from the *huaca* at a location called Jusape, the remains of mural paintings in the Gallinazo style, with red, cream-white, and black colors (personal communication, 1980). There was a personage with open arms reminiscent of the similar motif so common in Middle Horizon representations, but that forms part of a tradition that was probably born in the Early Horizon.

At the end of October 1981, Lima newspapers reported the finding of a polychrome mural of the Chimú

Fig. 27.
Huaca Licapa (or Mocan), Chicama Valley, wall with flat relief painted white and red. Gallinazo style, Early Intermediate Period.

culture in Pacasmayo. These reports referred to the remains of paintings in the Huaca Cotón, district of Pueblo Nuevo, province of Pacasmayo, department of La Libertad, uncovered by Víctor Castro Talledo early in May of 1981. The Instituto Nacional de Cultura in Trujillo learned of the matter from an archaeology student[3] and decided to undertake minor cleaning and consolidation work on some parts of the wall and to cover the one with the painting to avoid greater damage. This work was carried out on June 19, 1981, so I had no opportunity to see the new find. Reports are on file in the Instituto Nacional de Cultura, one in the Trujillo branch (Morales Gamarra, ms.b) and another in Lima (Campana, ms.). In comparing Campana's report with Morales Gamarra's (Morales was in charge of the work carried out at the monument), I perceived serious errors in the Campana report, and that observation was confirmed by an interview with Morales Gamarra (February 17, 1982). Thus Campana's report should not be taken into account.

The monument is small, set between rice fields and in a bad state of preservation. On its upper part are the remains of a wall that was apparently in front of a now-destroyed room. This wall contains the remains of a doorway and, on one side of that, the vestiges of three niches (Ricardo Morales Gamarra, personal communication, January 30, 1982). The painting is on the right-hand side of the door below the line of niches. It measures 2.37 m long by 0.62 m high. It "also extends to the partition walls separating the niches" (Morales Gamarra, ms.b, p. 2), but is there almost entirely destroyed. Still according to Morales Gamarra, the state of preservation is very bad and the colors very faint (personal communication, 1982). Information from local looters suggests that on the lower part of this wall, which was not exposed, there are more paintings of another kind.

The motif represents stylized serpent heads treated in a linear fashion and clearly showing the eyes and mouth (pl. 5). The body has been reduced to a simple band that is joined to the side of the following head. The mural fragment is small, but the motif seems to repeat. The heads are painted black with the eyes round and white with black pupils. The bands indicating the bodies are wide and white, outlined by a narrow black line. The space between the head and the band marking the body has been filled in with an ochre-red color. There is no evidence of a band delimiting the lower edge of this motif, while above it are traces of red and black, which may have formed alternating bands. It is clear that the painting continued above, but impossible to discern whether

it formed a design or simply painted areas. Both Campana and Morales Gamarra think that the motif represents a stingray. I believe, however, that it is stylized serpents.

Campana states categorically that "the frieze is clearly of early Chimú manufacture," while Morales Gamarra more cautiously indicates no cultural affiliation but suggests that the painting could correspond to the Late Intermediate Period (ms.b, p. 1). Campana's report provides no archaeological evidence to support his contention. According to Morales Gamarra, no cultural remains were found during the work he effected that could, by association, supply a clue to the chronological placement of the complex (personal communication, January 30 and February 27, 1982). The motif clearly resembles the serpents in the flat relief of the Huaca Licapa (fig. 27) and bears some similarity to the incised motifs that Bennett found on walls in Virú (1950, p. 27), as well as to motifs that appear with certain frequency on Moche ceramics. I consider it impossible to give a definitive opinion, but from the stylistic viewpoint, I am more inclined to place this painting in the Early Intermediate Period than in the Late Intermediate Period. It might be related to late phases of the Gallinazo style or the first periods of Moche when these two traditions may have mixed.

The colors used are "blue-gray as a ground color; on this the ochre-yellow, red and white were applied (although white is infrequent in all the mural)" (Morales Gamarra, ms.b, p. 3). There are no incisions outlining the motifs, which leads me to think that this painting does not belong to the Moche school.

The Highlands

In the highlands of northern and central Peru, where it was customary to deposit the dead in tombs excavated in the rock, which are commonly known as "little windows" (ventanillas), there is a different use of color. The inner and outer walls of the cavities were often painted in several colors. All of these "little windows" seem to be contemporary with phases III/IV of the Cajamarca style (Anonymous, 1967, p. 7).

THE MIDDLE HORIZON

The Middle Horizon, marked by the expansion of the Huari empire, is one of the most complex cultural phenomena to occur in the Andean region, and culminated in the first imperialistic movement in South America. The concepts of the city and of planning, born from a syncretism of the Nasca and Tiahuanaco cultures that converged in the Ayacucho area, soon diffused throughout the territory, lending some peculiar characteristics to architecture. On the coast there are great buildings with high *tapia* walls, presumably used for public gatherings, although their exact function is not known. There are also small settlements with defensive walls. In the highlands there are great fieldstone structures with high walls that are generally plastered and painted a solid color, as in the structures at Canta in the Chillón Valley (Cirilo Huapaya, personal communication, 1976) or at Rúpac in the same area with interior color and possibly designs (Peter Kaulicke, personal communication, 1981). In 1974, in the course of building a road through the site of Huari, bulldozers discovered and subsequently destroyed houses that were plastered and painted white. There are also occasional underground structures made of very well-cut, great stone slabs. Remains have also been found of semisubterranean one-room houses with clay-plastered and painted stone walls and beehive roofs of large stone slabs.

This period doubtless saw the continuation of the tradition of architectural adornment, although there is little archaeological evidence for such practice. Some years ago I made some observations in a cemetery dating to the final epochs of the Middle Horizon at the site of El Alamo in the Huarmey Valley (department of Ancash). There, on the inner finish of some looted tombs, were traces of red and yellow (E-16 and A-82, Cailleux and Taylor; Bonavia, 1965b). In 1976, during my most recent exploration of the Huarmey Valley, I again found tombs painted yellow in a Middle Horizon cemetery near the Quebrada Posuqui; while in the intermediate portion, in the El Castillo cemetery of the same period, were tombs painted red. In the Manache area of the lower valley there was a group of tombs that are probably Moche, bearing the remains of yellow coloration, and many tombs in nearby cemeteries of the Middle and Late horizons displayed evidence of having been plastered and then painted red or yellow. These data are important not so much for their aesthetic as for their cultural import, since they are among the few indications we have regarding tomb painting.

We know almost nothing of Middle Horizon painting in the Huari style. There are paintings from the Middle Horizon on the north coast, but all are in the Moche tradition.

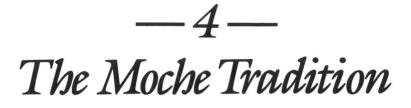

—4—
The Moche Tradition

Moche mural paintings are the best-known expression of this Andean art. They must have abounded in the area influenced by that culture, although few examples have survived to our time. Larco Hoyle, who knew as did few others the history of the Moche people, wrote of the architecture: "Both exteriors and interiors of the palaces were decorated with symbolical figures executed as frescos and polychrome murals in relief. Adobes with decorative geometric stucco motifs were used in the building of palaces and temples" (1946, p. 164). I do not know what Larco meant by "polychrome murals in relief" and "geometric stucco motifs," since to my knowledge, neither existed in the Moche culture. He was probably correct in general terms, since Moche monumental architecture was always ornamented somehow, either painted a solid color or with volutes and many other motifs outlining doorways and entrances (e.g., Donnan, 1976, pp. 72–77, figs. 56–58, 61–62). But depictive mural painting, which is the most relevant to this art style, has remained virtually unknown, with the exception of a few widely publicized examples that are mentioned repeatedly (e.g., Benson, 1972, p. 98; Donnan, 1976, p. 20; 1978, p. 22).

Moche temples are outstanding for their size and beauty. They are great stepped platform mounds ascended by straight or zig-zag ramps, often calling to mind Sumerian ziggurats. Almost all these Moche structures were adorned with multicolor paintings. The complexes most renowned for such paintings are Pañamarca in the Nepeña Valley and the Huaca del Sol and Huaca de la Luna in the Moche Valley.

THE NEPEÑA VALLEY

Today we know that the Moche culture expanded as far south as the Huarmey Valley, but the Nepeña Valley doubtless has the most important large southern occupation of this culture. One of the most impressive buildings of the period was erected there. It is also one of the best preserved, in spite of having suffered considerable damage, with numerous works of art that could still be saved. I refer to the temple of Pañamarca (fig. 28). Its excellent state of preservation can be seen by comparing

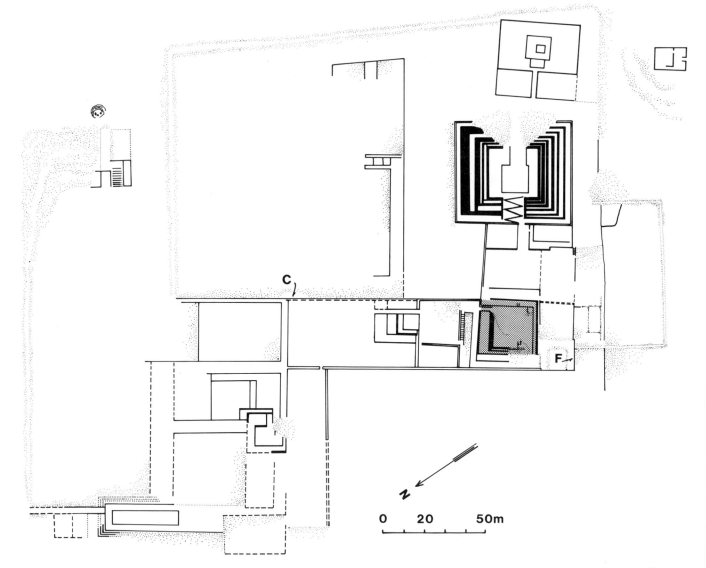

Fig. 28.
Pañamarca, Nepeña Valley, site plan. C *and* F *mark mural locations. Scale approximate.*

the monument as it is today with the drawing published by Squier in the second half of the nineteenth century (Squier, 1877, p. 201). I shall not discuss the site in detail, since it has been the object of study by several specialists and there is an extensive bibliography on the subject (Bonavia, 1959b).

To date Pañamarca is unquestionably the architectural monument with the greatest number of mural paintings, which are also probably the most elaborate from the technical standpoint. Some of these murals are presently visible, naturally somewhat deteriorated but still in a condition to be saved; others have disappeared forever. To my knowledge none has been specifically sought and excavated by an archaeologist; they have been found by farmers, looters, or by thrill-seeking tourists. Only four of the paintings have been studied and published, and of these only one was analyzed in any detail, that being precisely the one that no longer exists. Besides the murals, the walls of Pañamarca were carefully plastered and painted in red and yellow (Bennett, 1939, p. 17).

All the paintings I shall mention are found either in a sector of minor structures adjoining the main structure or in the great temple plaza (figs. 28, 29, 30). The technique used in all these murals was the same. Once the wall on which the paintings were to be executed was completed, it was carefully plastered and the white ground color applied while the plaster was still fresh. This was allowed to dry and then the designs were outlined with incisions and subsequently filled in with different colors.

Richard Schaedel (1951; 1967b; 1970) reported on a large scene of two individuals fighting (pl. 6, figs. 31, 32). They are represented face to face, each grasping the other's hair. This design is on a wall that must have been part of one of the earliest structures of the complex. This wall was, for unknown reasons, later covered by other more recent ones, so that the painting was covered. At the same time another wall was apparently built in front of the decorated one and the space between filled with rubble and adobes. When this part of the fill was removed, the painting in question could be seen, although it is very difficult to view in its entirety and almost impossible to photograph, given the narrowness of the artificial passage thus formed. I should emphasize that the known portion that Schaedel reproduced is only a fragment of a much larger mural. This painting is located in the very nucleus of the structure, on the side where the zig-zag ramp leading to the top was originally placed (fig. 29, A). Recently a large part of the personage located on the outer side was damaged and has disap-

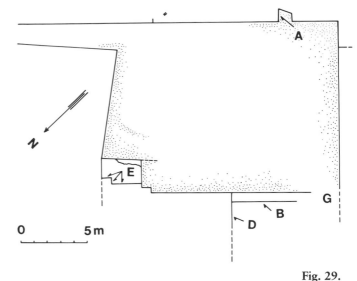

Fig. 29.
Pañamarca, detail of portion of site shaded in fig. 28; A, B, D, and E mark mural locations; G is an exit.

peared. The colors employed, in the terminology of Cailleux and Taylor, were: white, A-81; red ("light red"), H-26; yellow ("yellow-brown"), between E-66 and E-64; and blue-gray ("gray"), E-90.

I do not know the meaning of this scene, but it has a long tradition on the Peruvian coast. I have studied many sculptural representations in ceramics that represent the same activity: two individuals standing, clad only in breechcloths, hair well dressed and tied back; they are face to face, leaning slightly toward each other, and each grasps the other's hair at the forehead in his right hand while holding his left hand with the clenched fist upward at the height of the other's shoulder. Outstanding examples are found in the collection of the Banco Popular del Perú. One specimen (cat. no. 627; Banco Popular, 1979, p. 40) is of the Vicús culture, and another (cat. no. 826; Banco Popular, 1979, p. 41) is a beautiful Moche I–style vessel from Vicús. They may well represent some type of ceremonial contest.

Schaedel studied a second painting, also incomplete, on a wall that had been cut so that only the lower part

Fig. 30 (overleaf).
Pañamarca, partial view of great plaza with long mural (fig. 28, C) studied by Schaedel in 1953 in foreground; note how top of wall was cut off, probably in the Middle Horizon. Moche style, Early Intermediate Period.

Fig. 31.
*Pañamarca, mural A, showing two people fighting,
grasping each other by the hair. Moche style,
Early Intermediate Period.*

Fig. 32.
Mural A, drawing of entire scene.

remained. The entire section in front of the figure was missing, and the other side of it, in which some traces of color indicated a continuation of the pictorial work, had not been cleared (fig. 29, *B*). In this case there was a single figure that I have been calling the "feline snail," since it represented a snail with feline characteristics (pls. 7, 8, figs. 33, 34). It was fairly large, and a photograph of it was published in the Spanish translation of Schaedel's work (Schaedel, 1970, p. 315). Schaedel also mentions "an anthropomorphic bird figure" next to the feline snail, or "cat-demon" as he calls it (1951, p. 153; 1967b, p. 113); that figure had already disappeared in 1958 (figs. 35; 29, *D*). The feline snail has also been destroyed.

The third mural studied by Schaedel is the largest of all (pls. 9, 10, figs. 30, 36–38). It is located on the lower part of one of the walls forming the great plaza of the

Fig. 34.
Drawing of mural B.

Fig. 33.
Pañamarca, mural B, fragment showing a "feline snail."
Moche style, Early Intermediate Period.

Fig. 35.
Pañamarca, drawing of mural D. Schaedel published a photo of this little known painting, calling it an "anthro-pomorphized bird." Destroyed before 1958, it was located only centimeters away from mural B. Moche style, Early Intermediate Period.

temple (fig. 28, C). The section he described measured 12 m, but the entire composition was evidently much longer, showing a great scene. It extended farther on both sides, and one part of the wall is still buried. The wall was cut in prehispanic times, although we do not know exactly when (Schaedel suggests during the Middle Horizon). Of all the murals studied by Schaedel, this is the most deteriorated. He reburied it once and I did likewise later, but others have re-exposed it, and at the moment it is open to weathering and to damage from carelessness.

The portion of the mural unearthed by Schaedel showed eight large figures, with a maximum height of 1.5 m (fig. 36). He notes that the composition seems to center around a central figure, suggesting some kind of procession or ceremony (Schaedel, 1951, p. 153; 1967b, p. 113). He also conjectures that the three figures on the left and the last one on the right represent warriors, differentiated from the other figures by the lack of tassels on their tunics and the presence of knee markings. Because of their raised feet and joined hands, he suggests that the warriors on the left are dancing. The individual to the left of the central one and the two to its right lack knee markings and have tassels "trailing from their shirts or tunics"; Schaedel assigns them to a somewhat higher order of importance and refers to them as "'priests' if for no other reason than to avoid calling them 'figures'" (1951, p. 154; 1967b, p. 114). He continues:

It will be noted that both the priests and warriors have a semi-lunar knife suspended from their belts by two thongs. On the basis of Mochica pottery scenes we can safely say that this knife was used principally for decapitation, and figures prominently in what might be interpreted as scenes of sacrifice. The typical offensive weapon of the Mochicas was the mace, the defensive the shield. The principal figure, whom we are calling henceforth the high priest, is shown in front view and wears a tunic with three serpentiform figures. He is the only man in the group not shown with the knife. (Schaedel, 1951, p. 154; 1967b, p. 114)

He goes on to suggest that the lower small figure on the left of the central one might represent an "anthropomorphized knife in its sheath" and that the tiny upper figure on the left represents part of a background scene, the rest of which has been destroyed (1951, p. 154; 1967b, p. 114).

Following Schaedel's work, anonymous hands cleared either side of the paintings, exposing new figures that have not been described, although one side was partly published in a poorly reproduced photograph taken in 1967 (Kauffmann Doig, 1970, fig. 457). There is a new figure immediately to the right of the farthest right figure described by Schaedel. In May 1972 I made a quick visit to Pañamarca and was able to see this figure and one more to its right (pl. 9). At that time the remains of a figure in front of the farthest left personage studied by

Fig. 36.
Pañamarca, somewhat reconstructed drawing of mural C. Moche style, Early Intermediate Period.

Fig. 37.
*Pañamarca, detail of mural C showing the first four figures
on the left of fig. 36.*

Schaedel could also be seen. These two additions form the extension I mentioned above. The following description is based on photographs and on notes taken on the spot in 1972, when some details were visible that cannot be seen in any of the photographs.

In 1972, when I saw the new personage to the right of the last described by Schaedel, it was visible only as far as the legs, which were covered by sand. The upper part of the head was in very poor condition and the rest more or less well preserved. But the lower part is shown to the ankles in photographs (pl. 9), so that we have a more or less exact idea of the personage represented, which is important since it is the only one in the scene whose

head was partly preserved; the upper part of all the other figures was destroyed when the wall on which they are painted was cut. The ground, technique, and colors employed are those described by Schaedel, evidently the work of the same artist who painted the remainder of the panel.

Judging from the legs, the body of this individual was facing left, but the head is facing right. The facial portion is almost totally destroyed, though traces of the yellow used as flesh color remain, and I noted that the nose is round, the chin effectively nonexistent, the eye almond shaped, and the mouth barely indicated. Part of the headdress is also preserved. What can be seen is a

Fig. 38.
*Pañamarca, detail of mural C showing the last two figures
on the right of fig. 36.*

large circular red element with a large blue dot in the center and, attached to the right edge of this element, an essentially trapezoidal yellow element from which emerge three rather narrow, curved blue bands, probably representing feathers, which sweep upward to the right. Below the headdress, resting on the figure's left shoulder, is an oblong black element, which might represent hair or might be more of the headdress. Unlike the other figures in the procession, this one has both arms reaching in the same direction, the direction the body is facing; they too are yellow. The figure's right arm is bent at the elbow, the forearm pointing straight up, while the left forearm is extended across the body.

Neither hand is visible, but both wrists appear to bear red-and-blue bracelets. The left hand may have been grasping a white element that crosses part of the body.

The body is garbed in a tunic divided into three broad horizontal bands, each covered with two horizontal rows of large white dots. The topmost band is blue and has sleeves or sleevelike extensions that reach the right elbow and to just above the left elbow. The center band is red, with slightly smaller dots than those on the blue portions. The bottom band is very confused. According to my notes it has two blue elements that occupy almost the entire area, of the same hue used above. They seem to be two similar faces that represented a serpentiform mythological animal with circular white eyes. There were other motifs, also white, that cannot be identified. The garment terminates in a much narrower solid red band, which may have been divided in two sections by a thin line of a lighter color. There is another relatively narrow red band at waist level immediately below the left forearm. This element is crossed by vertical white stripes. Pendent from the right side of the lower blue band on the tunic is a great trapezoidal tassel, which reaches to just below the personage's knees.

Three white tabs are attached to the outline of this figure: one to the left (front) side near the top of the central broad red band, one to the right (back) extreme of the white-striped red band at the waist, and a third near the center of the right (back) side of the broad band of the tunic. These tabs are like those shown on the left sides of the upper portion of the garments of the second and third figures to the right of the central personage in fig. 36.

The legs, which are painted yellow with black knee spots, are more sharply bent than those of any of the other figures, perhaps explaining the lower position of the head. They are rather carelessly drawn, but otherwise treated like those of the other figures, and are visible only to the ankles.

Immediately to the right of the figure just described are the remains of yet another of approximately the same size and depicted in the same colors. This personage is facing in the opposite direction from the last one. Nothing can be seen of its head or feet, and only a small portion of its right arm can be discerned extending to the right of its body. The top portion of the figure's tunic is dark blue with large white dots, and a red sash marks the waist. Pendent from the sash is a central zone painted dark blue and stepped on each side, with the narrowest portion at the bottom; the two side areas thus delineated are red. Down the figure's back, apparently suspended from the neck, hangs a red serrated element similar to those worn by Schaedel's central figure and the three he calls priests (fig. 36). Immediately below this element is one essentially identical to those Schaedel refers to as a "semi-lunar knife," here colored yellow, and issuing from its lower edge are two red bands, perhaps representing the terminations of the serrated element. There may be two white tabs attached to the right edge of the upper part of the tunic, but it is very difficult to distinguish details in the available photographs.

Finally, to the left of the first personage in Azabache's drawing published by Schaedel (fig. 36) are the remains of another very badly damaged figure. In truth, the only

visible part is the legs from the knees to the ankles. They are in an attitude of movement and indicate that the figure was facing left. The legs are painted yellow, the knees marked in blue (for an interpretation of these elements, see Bonavia, 1959b), and the feet are also blue. The thigh of the left leg can barely be discerned. There is evidence of a great red tassel hanging in back. In front of this personage were other elements, to judge from the remains of yellow and blue paint, but it is impossible to determine even the forms represented. The colors used were white, red, yellow, blue, dark brown, black, and gray.

I believe Schaedel is mistaken in his interpretation of the object hanging behind the three personages to the right of his central figure and the first and fourth to its left. He calls this element a "semi-lunar knife." I think Muelle (1936) adequately demonstrated that this is not a knife, as commonly noted, but a large rattle worn suspended from the waist of Moche warriors. Schaedel is correct, however, in noting that there are basically two types of personage in this scene: warriors and others of higher rank, probably great chief-priests. The smaller figures, in the spirit of Moche art, were evidently personages of lower rank and secondary in importance. In fact, the three that Schaedel reproduced appear to be assisting the other personages, who are, doubtless, more important from the standpoint of rank.

Schaedel suggested that the warriors to the left of the central figure "seem to be engaged in a dance" (1951, p. 154; 1967b, p. 114). Muelle earlier identified as representations of dances depictions on ceramics of lines of people linked by their hands (Muelle, 1936), and, more recently, Donnan has related to dancing several scenes with similar lines of people, but linked by a long ribbon (Donnan, 1983, figs. 8–12). The warriors to the left of the central figure in the mural would appear to be such a ribbon-linked group, but because of the destruction of the mural, the ribbon is visible only where it crosses the chest of the last figure on the right in fig. 36 (in the original it is seen as a curved white band), and again where it terminates on the body of the newly exposed figure (pl. 10) after probably passing through the figure's left hand, just as the ribbons joining dancers end in Donnan's illustrations. The raised hands of the other three warriors to the right of the central figure could well have held such a ribbon. Groups of dancers like these are often separated by larger, more important personages like the central figure in the mural. Thus, it is reasonable to interpret the entire known mural as representing two groups of dancers, the one to the left linked by the hands, the one to the right by a ribbon. This interpretation was suggested to me by Patricia Lyon after she had read Donnan's manuscript, and I agree that it is probably correct.

Another Pañamarca mural is still better known through having been reproduced many times. It was discovered in 1958 and I studied it that year (Bonavia, 1959a; 1959b; 1961). I should point out that Tabío's version of the discovery is erroneous (Tabío, 1977, p. 236). This mural is now totally obliterated; the few vestiges still remaining were destroyed by the earthquake in May 1970. There are, however, two replicas drawn at one-half natural size. One, which should be in the hands of UNESCO in Lima, is the work of Félix Caycho Quispe (fig. 39); the other, in the Museo Nacional de Antropología y Arqueología, Lima, was made by José Velásquez.

The principal scene measures 1.5 m wide by 1.54 m high. It was painted on a high wall near the scene including the feline snail (fig. 29, *E*), on the upper part of the structure and at a much higher level than the other Pañamarca paintings (fig. 40). It showed a religious procession and is apparently a scene of ritual human sacrifice, with the officiating great priestess aided by two acolytes and, behind them, toward the immolation, three prisoners in the care of a guard. There are also animals from Moche mythology in the representation, as was the custom at that time.

At the head of the procession is a great priestess garbed in a long feather mantle and many other adornments as well as an elaborate headdress (figs. 41–43). She is walking and has a goblet in her hand. I should emphasize the fact that a female personage is included in this Moche ceremonial scene, whereas it has been said that women in Moche culture were always relegated to domestic tasks and the second ranks. I direct the reader to the work of Hocquenghem and Lyon (1981), in which the authors demonstrate not only the female gender of this personage but also the need for more careful analysis of Moche sceneography.

The priestess is followed by two acolytes of smaller size. The first is an anthropomorphized feline, evidently one of the helpers of the great priestess (pl. 11, figs. 44, 45). In its right hand it bears a recipient holding something that could be a human heart; in the left hand is what appears to be a knife. The feline is richly garbed and wears a helmet with a chin strap. Between this figure and the priestess is the small figure of a snail with a serpentiform head (pl. 11, figs. 44, 45, 46). The other personage of the same category as the feline seems to be an anthropomorphized bat (figs. 47, 48). In its right hand it holds a goblet, into which it appears to be putting something with the left. Immediately behind these acolytes are three nude males, each with a rope about the neck (pls. 11, 12, figs. 45, 46, 49–51). They are seated and, at the height of the right shoulder, bear something strange that could be a receptacle of a kind commonly used in Moche sceneography to collect prisoners' blood. These three men are guarded by a fourth, who bears something like a whip in his hand (pl. 12, figs. 49, 50). In the scene there also appears a great serpent with a head that could be that of a fox with a forked tongue, and above that figure is an object shaped like a spherical segment with three artifacts resembling goblets on top of it (fig. 51).

The top of the mural is defined by a broad band terminating in a series of triangular elements with dentate volutes ending in bird heads (fig. 39). This motif is similar to what Sawyer calls "the nose plume motif" (1954, p. 26; see also Bonavia, 1959b, p. 38). There is another broad band at the bottom, under which is a band of pendent wave designs. Finally, at one end there is a very large-scale weapon bundle comprising typical offensive and defensive Moche arms: a club, a shield, and a third element that might be a cloth belt.

The colors employed in the scene are, on a cream-white ground: gray-white, dark orange, dark brick-red, red-brown, dark sky-blue, and blue-black. The weapon bundle is differently colored: light orange, rose-beige, ochre-red, a dark sky-blue different from the one just mentioned, and a dark sepia. (For color dictionary definitions of the hues, see Bonavia, 1959b, lám. V.)

In his analysis of Moche sceneography, Donnan concluded that, in spite of its apparent richness, Moche art actually contains a restricted number of themes, of which a basic series can be identified (Donnan, 1975; 1976; 1977; 1978). One of these, which he calls the "Presentation theme," contains seven major and nine minor personages, each of different rank and position within the group. These personages are not only found together but can also be identified in isolation. One example of this "Presentation theme" is the Pañamarca mural just described. Donnan has tried to reconstruct the Pañamarca painting as it was originally seen (1976, pp. 117–29, figs. 108–109), arriving at a scene that is very interesting, although still hypothetical, as he admits (Donnan, 1976, p. 125).

In fact, the mural continued beyond the weapon bundle on the right, but was covered by an abutting wall. It was never possible to study the continuation,

Fig. 39.
*Pañamarca, mural E, one of the finest examples of Moche
mural art, representing a ritual scene of human sacrifice;
rollout painting based on tracing by Félix Caycho Q.,
original size of mural 2.8 × 1.5 m. Moche style,
Early Intermediate Period.*

Fig. 40.
*Pañamarca, view of architectural context of mural E, dis-
covered in 1958 and destroyed in 1970.*

Fig. 41.
Pañamarca, mural E, "great priestess" of ferocious mien.

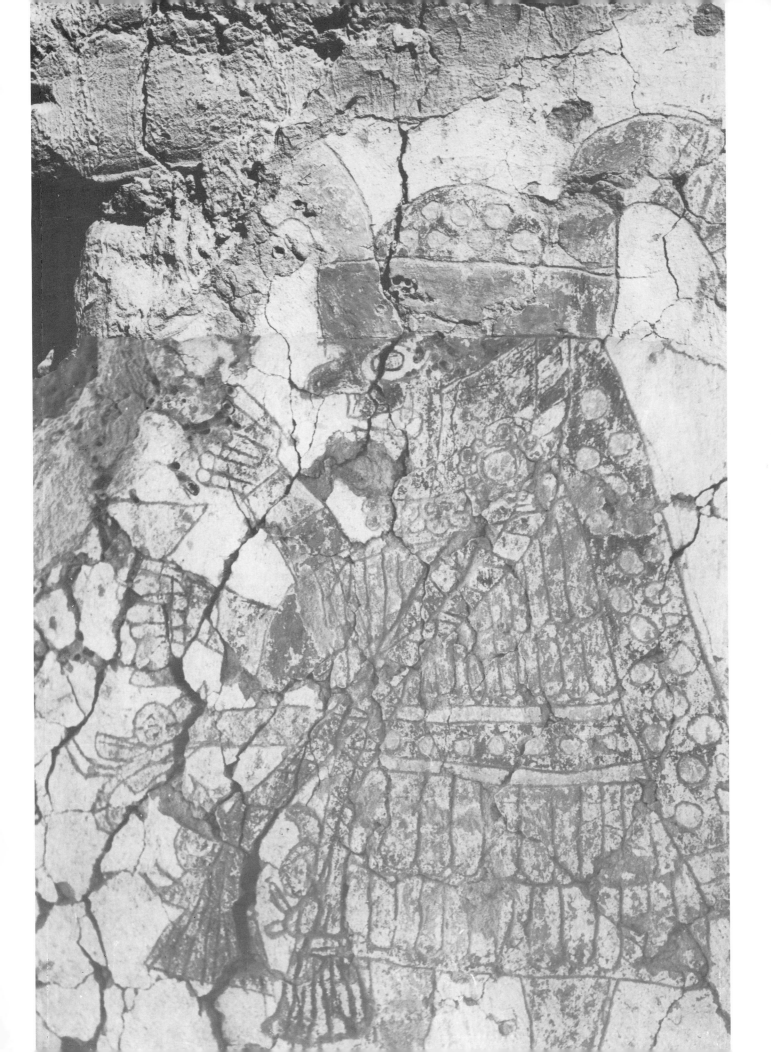

Fig. 42.
Pañamarca, mural E, photograph of the "great priestess" taken immediately after the mural's discovery.

Fig. 43.
Detail of Caycho replica showing "great priestess."

and now it is destroyed. We do not know what scene was there, but it may be that the "Presentation theme" is more extensive than Donnan has suggested (Bonavia, 1981, pp. 242–43).

In any case, Donnan's work represents the principal endeavor in the study of Moche art since the pioneer publications of Larco Hoyle (1938; 1939; 1948), and its originality cannot be denied. It strikes me as still too speculative to pronounce so firmly on the limited number of basic themes in the Moche scenic world. Nor am I entirely sure that the components of each theme appear only in that particular context and not mixed with others, in which case we would have a great many possibilities, immensely enlarging the small universe posited by Donnan.

As I have discussed elsewhere (Bonavia, 1981), the version of this last Pañamarca mural that Donnan illustrates in color (1976, pl. 2b) is not a photograph of the original but rather a photomontage based on the drawing made by Félix Caycho. Donnan later published the same photograph in black and white (1978, fig. 39, p. 22). Finally, the version of this same mural published by Lumbreras (1977, p. 93, lám. 43) was not done by

Fig. 44.
Pañamarca, mural E, attendant of the "great priestess," represented as an anthropomorphized feline. The small figure in front of this personage is a snail with a serpentiform head.

Fig. 45.
Detail of Caycho replica including anthropomorphized feline, snail with serpentiform head, and prisoner.

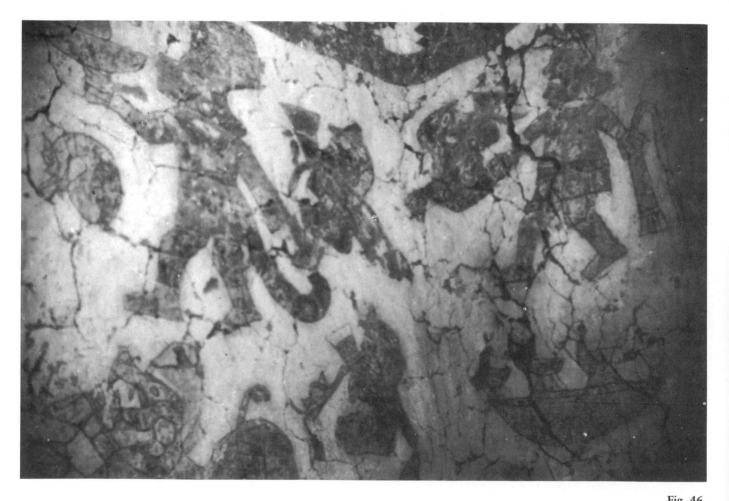

Fig. 46.
Pañamarca, mural E, photograph taken at time of discovery showing a corner of the mural including the anthropomorphized feline, prisoners, and guard.

Fig. 47.
Pañamarca, mural E, anthropomorphic bat, attendant to the "great priestess."

Fig. 48.
Detail of Caycho replica showing bat attendant.

Félix Caycho, as erroneously credited, but is rather the work of José Velásquez on exhibit in the Museo Nacional de Antropología y Arqueología, Lima.

In the same sector of the ruins that contained the painting I studied, southwest of and not far from the exit labeled G (fig. 29), is a small quadrangular structure. Around it several sections of wall were uncovered in 1974, all showing the remains of paintings. With the exception of one located on the wall facing northeast (fig. 28, *F*), all are so badly damaged that one cannot even guess at the motifs. The figure that can be seen, although in poor condition, can still be identified as a schematic profile feline (pl. 13, fig. 52). Details of the face are lost; the body is spotted and its male sex is indicated; the tail is raised and curved forward to the middle of the body; and each paw has three disproportionately large claws. The figure measures about 51×32 cm. In front of this feline was another element, probably of the same size or a bit smaller, but impossible to interpret. In this mural the same colors were used as in the one de-

Mural Painting in Ancient Peru

Fig. 49.
*Pañamarca, mural E, prisoner and guard; the prisoner is
nude, a common Moche convention.*

Fig. 50.
Detail of Caycho replica showing prisoner and guard.

Fig. 51.
Pañamarca, mural E, detail of Caycho replica including serpent with a head that might be a fox's, a prisoner, and a spherical segment surmounted by three goblets(?).

scribed by Schaedel showing the two personages fighting. That is, in Cailleux and Taylor's terminology: red ground, H-26; outline in blue-gray, E-90; body yellow with spots of the same hue but a different intensity, E-66 to E-64.

Proulx mentions a "new mural" on the west wall of the room that I studied. "It is an elaborately dressed human figure, perhaps in procession like those in the courtyard. The extent of this mural is unknown because it too was covered by later construction" (Proulx, 1973, p. 42). In my most recent visit to the site I could not locate this painting.

A comparison of the various Pañamarca murals leaves no doubt that they are the work of several artists. Grouping them on the basis of treatment and execution of motifs, I think I can identify at least two groups with no chronological implications: one group comprises the paintings of the two individuals grasping each other's hair and the plaza paintings; the other contains the feline snail and the religious scene on the upper part of the structure. The first group has a rough and somewhat careless execution; the second is very elaborate, made with great care and even, I might say, certain finesse and greater artistic sensibility. The profile feline would belong to the latter group.

Stylistically, I believe that all these paintings belong to Moche Phase IV or a transition to Phase V (for the stylistic subdivisions of Moche ceramics, see Larco Hoyle, 1948). The plaza murals and the scene in the central structure (the two persons fighting) may be slightly earlier than the feline snail and the representation of the religious cortege, a suggestion based on analysis of the superposition of the Pañamarca structures. The feline is reminiscent of Middle Horizon representations and might belong to the latest Pañamarca occupations toward the end of Phase V. Proulx, who has studied the Moche occupation of the Nepeña Valley in considerable detail, touches very lightly on the chronology of these paintings. In his first report he is vague: "The style of the murals is identical to the motifs on the figure painted vessels of the Moche III and/or IV periods . . ." (Proulx, 1968, p. 27). As will be seen, I do not totally agree with this contention, since it would appear that the potters were restricted by other conventions and also by the limits of the medium itself; the wall offered greater freedom of action. There is no basic disagreement with my position regarding the chronology, but I posit a longer occupation at the site. Moreover, without touching on this point specifically, in Proulx's second publication he supports the position I took several years previously re-

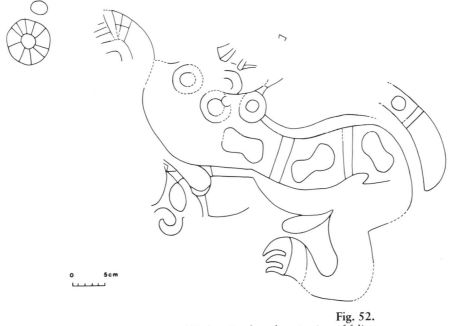

Fig. 52.
*Pañamarca, mural F, drawing based on tracing of feline
shown in plate 13 and associated designs found on wall of
small structure. Moche style, Early Intermediate Period.*

garding the Pañamarca paintings on purely stylistic grounds. In fact, after visiting twenty sites of different types with Moche occupations, Proulx found them all to belong to Phase IV of the Moche style (1973, p. 1). And while he suggests that the first occupation of the valley by the bearers of this culture may correspond to Phase III, that occupation was so slight that it has left no clear traces (see also Rowe, 1974, p. 305; Proulx, 1983). Since Donnan found a similar phenomenon in the Santa Valley, the proposal is logical (Donnan, 1973; Proulx, 1973, pp. 48–49). Nevertheless, Rowe thinks that the scene of the persons fighting belongs to Phase III (1974, fig. 310), a position with which I am not in accord.

My work has indicated that there are many murals yet to be discovered at Pañamarca (Bonavia, 1959b). If an extensive study were made there, it might be possible to establish an interesting stylistic sequence. The Pañamarca complex is without doubt one of the most important of the Moche culture as far as mural painting is concerned. Nevertheless, its state of preservation is more and more precarious; the pace of destruction has increased tremendously in recent years, and the future is dark.

As a final note, Tello, referring to the Nepeña Valley in general, mentions "stepped pyramids associated with other structures having large rectangular rooms, built of adobe, and adorned in part with polychrome frescos representing scenes of war or mythology similar to those adorning Muchik vessels" (1939b, p. 235; also 1943a, 1943b and 1970). There are several reasons why this comment is interesting. While there are references to Pañamarca before 1939, there is no mention of the paintings I have described because they were unknown. Bennett's discussion of Pañamarca in 1939 cites Squier's reference to paintings but adds, "no decoration can be seen today" (Bennett, 1939, p. 14). Why then did Tello use the plural? Did he see paintings that the North American archaeologist did not see that were later entirely destroyed? More curious still is Tello's reference to "pyramids," which leads one to ask if there were other monuments similar to Pañamarca in the Nepeña Valley that were somehow destroyed. It seems unlikely that there would be no record of such a fact, but not impossible.

THE SANTA VALLEY

The Santa Valley also had an important Moche occupation that was investigated by Donnan. Apparently, in their epoch of splendor the Moche palaces there were also decorated, since Donnan mentions in a general comment on Moche architecture in this area "some sites where portions of the plaster suggest that the walls were painted either in solid colors or with polychrome murals . . ." (1973, p. 53). He then notes: "One further medium for artistic expression should be mentioned, and that is the possibility of polychrome murals on the walls of some of the structures. . . . Murals apparently were restricted to large adobe structures, however, and have never been noted in the domestic architecture" (1973, p. 128). Apparently the most remarkable site in this sense was Castillo, which had a Moche III occupation. There, "A few of the walls had traces of clay plaster with red, yellow, and white pigment adhering to their exterior surfaces. No design could be recognized, but it is quite possible that these had originally been polychrome murals" (Donnan, 1973, p. 40).

THE MOCHE VALLEY

One of the most important Moche ceremonial centers is found at the site of the same name located a short distance from Trujillo in the department of La Libertad and comprising two great structures in the form of truncated stepped platform mounds, often called pyramids. This site is the most spectacular architectural monument remaining from the Moche era as far as volume is concerned.

I have already referred to the smaller of these structures, abutting Cerro Blanco, as the Huaca de la Luna and the larger one, on the left bank of the Moche River, as the Huaca del Sol; and they are known by these names in the scientific literature. Evidently these are not the original names, and we do not know exactly when or why they were applied to the monuments. In 1877 Squier, following local usage, called the Huaca de la Luna "Temple of the Sun," and, referring to the present Huaca del Sol, he says, "sometimes itself called *El Templo del Sol* (the Temple of the Sun)" (Squier, 1877, pp. 129–31); but in one of his two illustrations (p. 131), he labels it "the Great Pyramid of Moche" and in the other simply "Pyramid," a term he does not apply to the Huaca de la Luna, which he does not illustrate at all. A much earlier statement than Squier's provides yet another name for the Huaca del Sol. In a document dated 1565 in the notarial archives of Trujillo, the *huaca* is referred to as the temple of Pachacámac (Netherly,

1978, pp. 321–22 and p. 271, fig. 6.1). The reference to Pachacámac, coastal creator god, could lead to important research on the subject. The designation might possibly go back to the time of the Huari invasion, when the sanctuary of Pachacámac was immensely influential and Huari expansion reached north to the Lambayeque Valley. However, to avoid confusion and misunderstandings, I shall continue using the present names, which are the best known.

While mural paintings are abundant in the Huaca de la Luna, only one has been recorded for the Huaca del Sol, in a report mentioned by both Udo Oberem (1953, p. 250) and Heinrich Ubbelohde-Doering (1967, p. 137), although the latter does not identify his source. The account, by Antonio de la Calancha, relates that about 1602, while the author was in Trujillo, a resident Spaniard named Montalvo and some colleagues were engaged in dismantling the "great huaca of Trujillo," using water to achieve their ends.

> One day an entire wall face fell and revealed silver vessels, bells, and small sheets of low-grade gold, as well as a figure in the round made of very fine gold, a span high from the waist up, in the form of a Bishop from the middle of the body up, with his miter and lappets, his garment, a dalmatic, all with propriety and considerable likeness: he had ears like those of the Inca Kings. . . . [A second thing] that was seen is the most admirable. I already said that one wall is next to another as one piece of paper covers another or canvases or plates that are joined by shoving them together. An entire wall face was exposed and on it, roughly drawn in crude colors, many armed men on horseback, with hats, swords of flat discs [? *espadas de rodajas*], jousting lances in their hands, and beards indicated on their faces. . . . With these paintings appeared the Bishop. . . . (Calancha, Lib. II, cap. XXXV; 1638, p. 486)

Unfortunately, we cannot tell what scene Calancha viewed, since his description is obviously influenced not only by his European background but also by his desire, manifest throughout his book, to prove the preconquest presence of Europeans in the New World. It is clear, however, that some sort of large mural was painted on at least one wall of the Huaca del Sol. I remember seeing traces of paint on some of the walls of the Huaca del Sol, and Kent Day found yellow paint on one of the oldest façades of the Huaca de la Luna (personal communication, 1973). Santiago Uceda reports having seen red coloration on the third platform of the Huaca de la Luna, and in one place older walls that had come to light with remains of orange and white, as well as the remains of red on the walls of the Huaca del Sol (personal communication, 1979). Shades of white and red on the plaster of the Huaca de la Luna have also been reported by Morales Gamarra (ms.a, p. 2).

As in the case of Pañamarca, reports on the murals of the Huaca de la Luna are neither exhaustive nor detailed. On the basis of published information, we know that Eduard Seler discovered and studied a painted wall in 1910, which he then described in summary form and illustrated partially. In 1925 another painted wall was uncovered, which, to judge from its location (fig. 53, A) and style, may be a different section of the same one studied by Seler. This painting was examined by Alfred L. Kroeber in November 1926. There is a more or less extensive description of it and three reproductions of its details, as we shall see below. Of all the murals of the Huaca de la Luna it is the best studied to date, although

some points remain obscure. In 1955 a third mural was exposed by unknown hands and briefly described by José Eulogio Garrido; a reproduction was made, which is housed in the Museo de Arqueología of the Universidad Nacional de Trujillo. In 1972 this mural was again cleared in the course of the work of the Chan Chan–Moche Valley Project of Harvard University and was found to be superimposed on two others, previously unknown (fig. 53, B).

Bennett, in his synthesis, mentions the Huaca de la Luna paintings and even lists the colors used there. Curiously, however, he not only refers to the mural studied by Kroeber but says: "There are traces of fresco painting at other sites too, and also walls decorated with relief clay arabesques" (1946, p. 100). It is a pity there is no further information, since Moche artists did not use re-

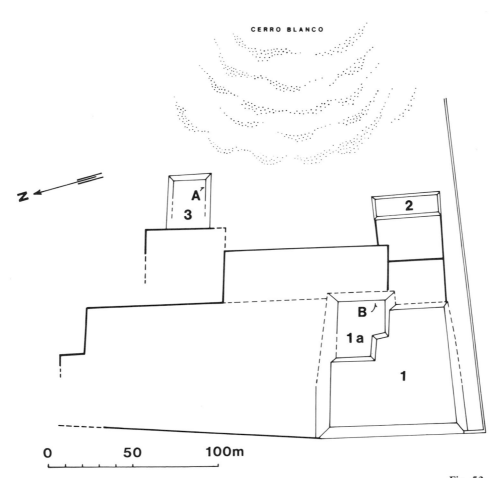

Fig. 53.
Huaca de la Luna, Moche Valley. 1, 1a, 2, and 3 are platforms;
A and B indicate approximate location of murals.

liefs to decorate walls. Nonetheless, such decoration was mentioned, without specific location, by Larco Hoyle (1946, p. 164) and later by Schaedel (personal communication, 1973), who also recalls a Moche-style deer-hunting scene in painted clay relief in a small monument on the road to Galindo before reaching the Cerro de la Virgen, at the boundary between the vegetational zone and the desert sand.

At present only a few insignificant traces remain of the murals of the Huaca de la Luna, except the ones studied by the Chan Chan–Moche Valley Project, which were buried to prevent damage. Tello wrote that when he visited the site at the end of 1919, "the fresco" illustrated by Seler had already disappeared (1923, p. 376). In 1932 Ubbelohde-Doering photographed part of the mural studied by Kroeber and published a brief description of its condition. The photograph (Ubbelohde-Doering, 1967, fig. 148) includes the two central figures shown here in fig. 59d. The author comments:

> Remnants of *wall-painting in Mochica style* are preserved on the ruins of a small building near the Moche moon pyramid. The incised outlines of the legs of two running figures are visible painted in white, yellow, dark ochre, brick red, pale blue and black. The remaining portion measured 2 ft. 6 in. high by nearly 4 ft. wide in 1932. I have no idea how it has fared, lying exposed to the weather, the sea-wind and to tourists. (Ubbelohde-Doering, 1967, p. 137)

We know that traces still remained in 1935 (Pedro Rojas Ponce, personal communication, 1973), but seem largely to have disappeared by the end of the decade, when, probably on the occasion of the twenty-seventh International Congress of Americanists in Lima, the site was cleared by Hans Horkheimer. "When, in 1939, we cleared the site, which was totally covered by sand, the greater part of the painted wall had collapsed, and on the remaining part the sand had erased the traces except the incised outlines that delimited the previously colored planes . . ." (Horkheimer, 1944, p. 28, n.82). He rewords the same information in the caption to his figure 70 (p. 75) and adds: "In some planes of reduced size are still seen the remains of the seven colors of this frieze, which probably illustrated the legend of the revolution of the implements and arms against man." Imbelloni visited the site in 1939, probably shortly after its clearing, and confirmed Horkheimer's observations, saying that the murals had "almost entirely disappeared" (Imbelloni, 1943, p. 266), although Garrido found a few traces still visible in 1956 (Garrido, 1956a, p. 30). Of course, Tello's statement that he and Kroeber discovered the

painting is inaccurate, since the discoverer was really some unknown, and Tello simply accompanied Kroeber while he carried out his study in 1926 (Tello, 1933a).

As noted above, Seler's description is brief and not very informative (1912, pp. 217–20; 1923, pp. 368–70). He apparently saw the remains of painting, which led him to clear a wall upon which he found the mural (figs. 53, 54).

> Somewhat behind and up the hill from the north end of the Huaca de la Luna, masonry had been exposed at the time we visited the ruins that looked like the back wall of a large hall. At a certain distance from this wall we found at one end a rectangular, walled depression, and farther off, massive blocks of masonry. On the back wall as on the faces of these blocks there were still preserved on an imposing expanse, the remains of a thin clay-lime plaster, showing traces of painting. . . . In the excavated soil next to the cleared, walled depression, we found potsherds from vessels of the boldly modeled, red-and-white painted style (Typus Chimbote). (Seler, 1912, p. 217)

This description is especially interesting because of the report of associated pottery, which, from the description, is doubtless of the Moche style.

Seler had already studied Moche pottery and had noted the presence of scenes of combatants, whom he called "warriors," among whom he distinguished two groups on the basis of their clothing and arms. Seler concluded that they belonged to different tribes (1912, p. 218; 1923, p. 368).

> My attention was drawn to the weapon worn by the adversary of the better dressed, and apparently more civilized of the aforementioned peoples; a sort of club but with a quite remarkable head and with a bunch of long stiff feathers standing out from the lower half of the club handle. Now, in the painting in the rooms on the hill behind the Huaca de la Luna I recognized such a battlescene with adversaries who bore the same singular weapon, only in place of the principal warrior there is drawn a club in the form of a small man. (Seler, 1912, pp. 218–19)

This then was the scene painted on the wall; the colors are not reported. And the figures are, of course, the "humanized objects" that also appear in the mural Kroeber studied. The photographs published by Seler (1912, Abb. 9, 10) do not show much detail, but they show enough to identify the wall painting with the drawing he also published (fig. 54; Seler, 1912, Abb. 13; 1923, fig. 3), which is little known. They also show that the figures were located at a corner of the structure, one at right

Fig. 54.
*Huaca de la Luna, drawing of mural fragment discovered
by Seler in 1910 and related to the mural Kroeber
studied later in the same building. Moche style,
Early Intermediate Period.*

angles to the other, so that the drawing is not entirely accurate with respect to their relative positions. This mural was located on what Mackey and Hastings have called Platform 3 of the Huaca de la Luna (fig. 53, 3; Mackey and Hastings, 1982, p. 294).

The painting is clearly Moche, as Seler indicated when he wrote that it belonged to Uhle's "Proto-Chimú" epoch. Moreover, I am inclined to believe that it is Phase V of the style rather than Phase III or IV as suggested by Mackey and Hastings (1982, Table II, pp. 310, 311).

The only real information regarding the mural discovered in 1925 comes from Kroeber (1930). All else is repetition, often lacking the basic information. Such is the case of Garrido (1956a), who provides an incomplete list of the colors, which could be misleading to anyone not consulting the original source, and the anonymous article that appeared in the same journal (Garrido, 1956b). Kroeber and Tello visited the Moche monuments in 1926, and it was then that Kroeber carried out his study. The paintings were already visible, and the structures, which were partly filled with sand, were simply cleared in order to see the figures better, so

that several meters of a beautifully ornamented wall appeared (fig. 55).

According to Kroeber, the Moche artist first outlined the figures on walls that had been previously prepared with white plaster. This outline was made with incisions that were then filled with black (see figs. 55, 56, 57). Finally, areas of the completed outline were painted in various colors. Comparing the style of the motifs to those represented on pottery of the same period as the murals, Kroeber noted: "The frescos give a freer rein to fancy than is usual in vase paintings. The strokes . . . are vigorous and unhesitating, the conceptions of form definite if somewhat conventional; the execution shows both imagination within the traditions of a school and skill based on practice" (1930, p. 71). From Kroeber's plan (fig. 58), it can be seen that the paintings cover both the

Fig. 55 (overleaf).
Huaca de la Luna, part of platform 3 with murals discovered in 1925 and studied by Kroeber in 1926. Moche style, Early Intermediate Period.

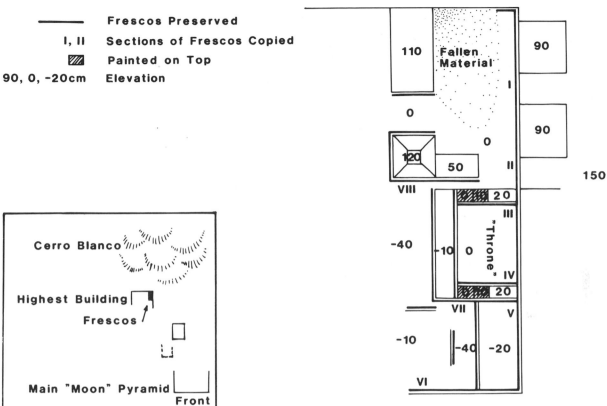

Legend:

─── Frescos Preserved
I, II Sections of Frescos Copied
▨ Painted on Top
90, 0, -20cm Elevation

Cerro Blanco
Highest Building
Frescos
Main "Moon" Pyramid
Front Face

150 150

110 Fallen Material
90
I
0
90
0
120 50
II
VIII 150

20
III
-40 "Throne"
-10 0
IV
20
VII V
-10 -40 -20
VI

40

Fig. 58.
Huaca de la Luna, Kroeber's plan showing location of murals he recorded in 1926; corresponds to platform 3 of fig. 53.

Fig. 56.
Huaca de la Luna, detail of mural studied by Kroeber, segment to left of the "seat," comprising at least part of his section II.

Fig. 57.
Huaca de la Luna, sections III and IV of mural studied by Kroeber, immediately to the right of the portion shown in fig. 56.

outside and partition walls as well as other internal structures of the room. The same can be seen in fig. 55 and the fine photograph published by Willey (1971, p. 138, fig. 3–61). Kroeber traced only a small section of these murals (fig. 59) and clearly states that there were more decorated sections of the same structure (a statement confirmed by the later finds). Of interest is the fact that in one part of the mural (the left part of Kroeber's section I, fig. 59a), the figures were simply outlined without being filled with color, causing Kroeber to think that for some reason the site, or at least the work, was abandoned before it was finished.

The room with the murals was painted on repeated occasions, and, judging from the position of the designs, it would appear that they were not limited to the small area in which they were found. Toward the middle of the wall there was "a seat or elevation similar to a throne"; this seat was flanked by low stepped walls, the two lowest steps of which were painted on the top as well as on the sides (fig. 55). Kroeber suggested that the niche between the stepped salients contained an altar, idol, or seat. The total height of the mural nowhere exceeded one meter and it was less on either end (see fig. 58).

The plaster upon which the paintings were executed was first whitewashed; the outlines of the figures were then delineated with firm and sometimes long strokes. In the middle section the incisions are V-shaped in section, neither very wide nor very deep, although in some cases they penetrate to the underlying adobes. Occasional crossed lines were left that way, showing that the execution was freehand without attention to fine detail. The fact that these lines generally meet cleanly is clear proof of the practice and skill of the Moche artist. The incisions were later painted black, thus achieving a sharp outline without overwhelming the colored areas.

The colors were seven, including black and white. The most common were red, yellow, and light blue, with pink somewhat less frequent. Black was used especially for the feet or "shoes" and, as on the pottery, to paint the knees. White provided the background and only occasionally entered the design. Brown is seen in only a few small areas and served to represent the artifacts; it seems to be the natural earth tone of the adobes. Kroeber surmised (there was no analysis made of the pigments) that the red and yellow were based on natural earths, the pink a mixture of red ochre with the white of the plaster, the blue a strong dilution of the black with the same white, and black based on charcoal (1930, p. 72).

There were at least two reproductions made of the painting. The one that was in the Field Museum of Natural History in Chicago was made by Kroeber (fig. 59). The author of the other (fig. 60), in the Museo Nacional de Antropología y Arqueología, Lima, is unknown. Although the personnel of the Lima museum know nothing definite about it, Mejía Xesspe thought it was the work of José Eulogio Garrido, made at Tello's behest (personal communication, March 1974). This datum may seem insignificant but is nevertheless of considerable importance because of the impossibility of comparing either reproduction with the original. The mural has been published several times in various places, sometimes in the Kroeber version and others in that of the Lima museum. The problem is that the two versions do not agree. Imbelloni drew attention to this fact at the International Congress of Americanists in 1939, although in his fig. 4 (1943, p. 266) the illustrations were inadvertently reversed and the one called the "Lima version" is actually the "Chicago version" and vice versa. The whereabouts of Kroeber's original tracings is not known.

The replica in the Museo Nacional de Antropología y Arqueología (fig. 60) has not previously been published in its entirety. It appears to be an independent rendering, since it includes details not published by Kroeber, including the damaged areas. The artist did not understand Moche iconographic conventions as well as did Kroeber, and the damaged areas are not very accurately delineated, as can be seen by comparing the drawing to photos that must have been taken at about the same time that the drawing was made (figs. 56, 57). Moreover, the Lima drawing includes only the material from one wall of the room, while Kroeber includes elements from the internal structures and possibly from other walls.

There are two other published versions that might be taken as originals but are actually of no evidential value. In 1937 Bennett published a very partial and inaccurate one showing only two personages (Bennett, 1937, p. 37). The other (fig. 61), published by Díaz (1940), is clearly an incomplete and inaccurate copy of the Lima version.

We obviously do not have a complete version of this mural from the Huaca de la Luna, although there may

Fig. 59.
Huaca de la Luna, Kroeber's drawings of the mural.

a. *Kroeber's section I with motifs outlined but not filled in.*

b. *At least part of Kroeber's section II, and all of III and IV (see figs. 56 and 57).*

c. *Kroeber's section V (left) and possibly section VI (right).*

d. Left, *Kroeber's section VII from wall flanking the "seat" (see fig. 55); right, probably Kroeber's section VIII.*

REPLICA DE UN FRESCO QUE ADORNABA UNA DE LAS CAMARAS DEL TEMPLO DE LA LUNA. MOCHE - VALLE DE CHIMU. EXPEDICION ARQUEOLOGICA DE 1926.

Fig. 60.
Huaca de la Luna, painted version of the mural studied by Kroeber as exhibited in the Museo Nacional de Antropología y Arqueología, Lima, and labeled "Replica of a fresco that adorned one of the chambers of the Temple of the Moon. Moche—Valley of Chimú. 1926 Archaeological Expedition." It differs in detail from Kroeber's drawings, most notably in the presence on the extreme left of five vertical elements and an anthropomorphic figure not present in Kroeber's version, and in the presence of facial details on the figure on the extreme right of Kroeber's fig. 59a as well as the inclusion of the complete figure that is grasping this personage by the hair. It is not clear why Kroeber did not include these elements if they really existed.

be one among Kroeber's papers. All the published versions are incomplete, and details found in one are lacking in the other. As noted above, Kroeber's is the most correct but, in spite of his statement that it is a tracing, details are lacking that can be seen in the photographs that he himself published in 1930 (pl. XVI, 3,4).

Krickeberg was the first to suggest that Seler's fragment (fig. 54) might represent part of an American myth called "the revolt of the objects" (Krickeberg, 1928, pp. 386–88). He relates it to the Popol-Vuh from Guatemala and to some myths collected by Avila in the sixteenth century in Huarochirí (Peru). Kroeber applied this interpretation to the mural he studied at the Huaca de la Luna and wrote:

> The subject of the Moche frescos is evidently a battle between human beings and personified implements. Krickeberg has recently shown that this "revolt of the

artifacts" was a Peruvian as well as a Mexican myth, that a Chicama stirrup mouth vase in Berlin depicts this contest, and that the Moche fresco described by Seler evidently had the same scene for its subject. Seler's principal figure of a personified war club is similar to that in portion IVc of my reproduction, but not identical. Seler's frescos are evidently also from the same part of the same ruin, but their precise situation was not fixed by him. The vase painting shows a dozen or more implements already victorious, two human prisoners, and a third besieged indoors. The frescos depict the battle itself, in a series of individual combats, with the artifacts winning; a helmet, a shield, a club, are smiting their armed but helpless human opponents. (Kroeber, 1930, p. 73)

Imbelloni also dealt with this subject, referring to Krickeberg and to various chroniclers and to the Popol-Vuh. Discussing the scene described by Francisco de Avila, he writes:

Fig. 61.
Huaca de la Luna, the mural studied by Kroeber as illustrated by Díaz, clearly a poor and incomplete copy of the version in fig. 60.

The scene to which Dávila refers and which so distresses him is no more than an authentic American representation preserved intact from European influence and corresponding one hundred percent to native concepts and feelings. Properly ordering its component elements we find a description of a period of darkness signalling the end of an Age of the World; the human beings who lived under the sun which ceased to shine are condemned to die and shortly a new group will replace them; meanwhile a revolt of the animate and inanimate beings who were at the service of these doomed men takes place. Of course the men have now lost all their power and the domestic animals rise up against them to insult and destroy them. Especially striking are the kitchen utensils, among them mortars and pestles, which revolt against their masters in retribution. . . .

. . . [At Moche] among the inanimate objects there are several easily recognizable items of adornment and clothing, weapons, a belt and warrior's helmet as well as a quadrangular artifact with its surface decorated with crossed lines which appears to be a beater or other wooden implement. Regarding the men whose figures appear in several scenes of the fresco, they are represented already fallen to earth or on the point of collapse. The implements and utensils are grasping them by the hair and beat them with heavy clubs or they are riddled with darts (last scene of the fresco). The will and vitality animating those in the battle is expressed by the addition of a human face, eyes, arms and legs; moreover, they are dressed in human garb; . . . (Imbelloni, 1943, pp. 264–65, 266)

The author essentially repeats himself in 1963 (pp. 225–26), where he illustrates part of the reproduction from the Lima museum.

Patricia Lyon has analyzed these interpretations using not only the archaeological evidence of the paintings of the Huaca de la Luna and various scenes painted on Moche ceramics but also the oral traditions that have come down to us (Lyon, 1981). These traditions were gathered between the sixteenth and twentieth centuries in Guatemala, Peru, and Bolivia; not all were known to Krickeberg. Lyon concludes that "there is virtually no point of correspondence between the oral traditions and the scenes from the Moche culture," but there is a relationship among the various oral versions, and she contends that: "the scenes represented in Moche art, although related to one another, surely refer to some mythical happening other than the rebellion of the objects to which they have so long been linked. More than a simple rebellion of objects against human beings, the painted representations show a battle between two groups of warriors" (Lyon, 1981, p. 107).

It should be noted that scenes such as this one, although they do appear in Moche ceramic sceneography, are not common. Nonetheless this scene must have been especially important and significant to be placed in a ceremonial site like the Huaca de la Luna. There are two magnificent examples of a very similar scene that evidently refer to the same theme and are found on ceramic vessels.

In the first case, mentioned by Krickeberg (1928, pp. 386–88) and Kroeber (1930, p. 73), there is a series of humanized objects (among which predominate pieces of warriors' arms and equipment) who have caught two human prisoners, represented in classic Moche fashion as nude and with ropes around their necks. A third individual is shown inside a low hut under the care of at least two of the humanized objects. Each of these objects has been converted into a warrior, that is, not only has it been provided with lower and upper limbs but it holds a weapon, usually a club. A good example of this treatment is a club, which is very clear in Schmidt, drawn with legs and arms and holding another club in its hands (see drawing in Krickeberg, 1928; Berezkin, 1972, fig. 5; photo in Schmidt, 1929, p. 197 left).

In the second case the scene is much more complex; it represents a fight between Moche warriors, mythical beings, and humanized inanimate objects. The position of the mythical beings is not clear, but they seem to be neutral, while the real fight is carried on between the other two bands. In this case the humanized implements not only fight fiercely but some also drag Moche warriors by the hair. In some cases these warriors retain all their accoutrements but with the clubs turned upside down, and in others they are nude with ropes around their necks. While the animated objects in this scene belong to several categories, most of them are humanized clubs (see photograph in Ubbelohde-Doering, 1936, pl. 5 right; Benson, 1972, fig. 3–15; Donnan, 1978, fig. 270; drawing in Kutscher, 1950, Abb. 43; Berezkin, 1972, pl. 2; Donnan, 1978, fig. 270).

The vessels upon which the scenes appear belong to Moche Phase V. Kroeber already noted that the painting is "Early Chimú," that is, Moche in present terminology. Given the stylistic similarity between some elements of the scenes represented on the pottery and this Huaca de la Luna mural, I think the mural should belong to the same phase as the vessels.

José Eulogio Garrido reported on a third painting found at the Huaca de la Luna (1956a), but the article is not very useful. This mural was apparently discovered accidentally by looters in February 1955, when their perforations caused the collapse of a wall that covered the one bearing the painting. News of the discovery reached the personnel of the Museo de Arqueología of the Universidad Nacional de Trujillo, who visited the site eight days later. The painting studied by Kroeber, you will recall, was located in a sector of the Huaca de la Luna next to Cerro Blanco (fig. 53, 3), while this third mural was found toward the east-northeast side on an upper level (1a) of the principal platform (fig. 53, B). When Garrido reached the site, he found the painting incomplete. The wall upon which it was executed was part of a narrow rectangular room and the part lacking was the painted corner oriented to the northwest. According to Garrido, this chamber had an opening, which may have been either a door or a window, into a courtyard on the southeast.

In 1972 the Chan Chan–Moche Valley Project of Harvard University again exposed the murals mentioned by Garrido (Michael Moseley, personal communication, 1972). They were associated with the later building phases and could not be seen, since they were covered by later structures. The archaeologists were able to establish clearly that the walls bearing these paintings had no relation to the early building phases of the platform. The data I used regarding these paintings in the first edition of this book were supplied by the codirectors of the project, Michael Moseley and Carol Mackey (Bonavia, 1974, pp. 86–92). Mackey later reported on these findings at the Annual Meeting of the Society for American Archaeology in San Francisco in 1973, but I had no access to her paper (Mackey, ms.). Then, in 1980 the Trujillo branch of the Instituto Nacional de Cultura, at the request of the Comisión Técnica Calificadora de Proyectos Arqueológicos, re-exposed the paintings to clarify some details and provide greater protection, and Ricardo Morales Gamarra wrote an important report on that work (Morales Gamarra, ms.a). Finally, in 1982 Mackey and Charles Hastings, who supervised the Huaca de la Luna excavations of the Chan Chan–Moche Valley Project, published a report. It is on the basis of these reports and many photographs from several sources that I have been able to study these paintings. We now know that there was a sequence of murals. The one illustrated by Garrido (1956a, p. 29, and color plate facing p. 28) was only the upper part of the third phase, corresponding to the repainting of the interior of the courtyard wall.

The first mural was decorated with fullface anthropomorphic motifs repeated in rows of units 3.4 m wide by 2.4 m high separated from one another by vertical bands 34 cm wide. Each unit has, in turn, a 3.5 cm grid (Mackey and Hastings, 1982, p. 294). The remains of these images are badly damaged, so that the motif can be only partly reconstructed (fig. 62). It was executed with very regular rectilinear lines and is doubtless copied from a textile pattern. It represents a personage seen fullface, with the arms open and holding in each hand an element like a staff, terminating at the top and bottom in two stylized, apparently feline, animal heads (interpreted by Mackey and Hastings as serpents). The head and upper body of the central personage are totally destroyed. The bottom of the design was bordered by a straight narrow band and each side by a vertical row of double frets. The original is not as regular as represented in the drawing made by the staff of the Chan Chan–Moche Valley Project (fig. 63).

The mural was executed on a white ground in red, black, and yellow; the body is red and yellow while the hands and staffs are red, black, and white. The serpent heads are also red, yellow, black, and white (Mackey and Hastings, 1982, p. 296). According to the Munsell color chart, the colors are: white, 10 YR chrome value 8/2 (approximately); black, 2.5 Y chrome value N2; cadmium yellow, 7.5 YR chrome value 6/8; and red, 10 R chrome value 5/4 (approximately) (Morales Gamarra, ms.a, p. 5).

In the second phase of remodeling, an entrance was opened in the back part of the courtyard, damaging a section of the paintings. That section was repainted with a new series of motifs, which alternate in a checkerboard (pl. 14, fig. 64). The motif is a stylized face with anthropomorphic characteristics, from which issue a series of appendages terminating in bird heads, repeated symmetrically on each side (figs. 65, 66). The units were painted alternating red on white and yellow on blue, in both cases with black eyes. The units repeat diagonally and measure 34 cm wide by 26 cm high; they are separated from one another by some 5 cm (Mackey and Hastings, 1982, p. 296). The Munsell color identifications here are: white, 10 YR chrome value 8/2 (approximately); red, 10 R chrome value 5/4; yellow, 10 YR chrome value 7/8; blue, 2.5 Y chrome value N4 (Morales Gamarra, ms.a, p. 8).

Moseley has published a black-and-white photograph and a drawing of the motif but with no special commentary (1978, figs. 40, 41, p. 57), and two good color photographs have appeared in a tourist magazine (Cisneros G., 1981). There are also two black-and-white photographs and a drawing in the Mackey and Hastings article (1982, figs. 3, 6, 7).

The third repainting is the one originally reported by Garrido (1956a), and it also has a checkerboard

Fig. 62.
Huaca de la Luna, earliest of the three murals cleared and studied in 1972 by the Chan Chan–Moche Valley Project. Probably first epochs of the Middle Horizon.

Fig. 64.
Huaca de la Luna, platform 1a, second mural above the earliest one, showing doorway that cut the original painting. Middle Horizon.

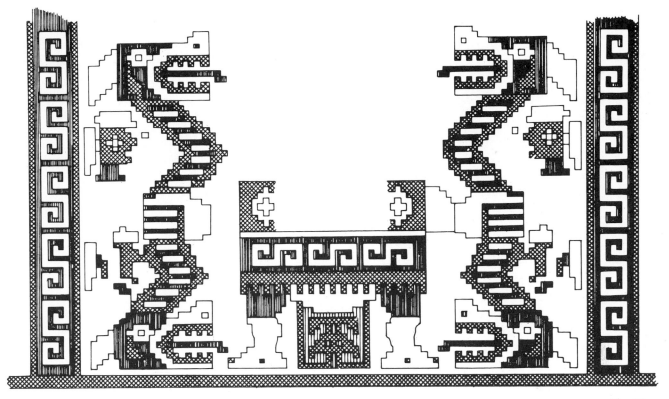

Fig. 63.
Huaca de la Luna, drawing of earliest platform 1a mural.

Fig. 65.
*Huaca de la Luna, platform 1a, detail of second mural,
probably representing a crab, painted over mural
bearing image shown in fig. 63 and later
covered by mural shown in fig. 68.*

format. Garrido's is the first description of this mural (1956a, pp. 28–30). He reported that the decoration was "painted flat, with two alternating motifs in squares, like a tapestry or mosaic." He noted that one of the motifs was a standing human figure with a turban of a crested serpent. The figure, which he interpreted as mythological, had a "masked . . . or perhaps simply painted" face and was framed by "two semi-coiled serpents . . . with three heads, two terminal and one central with a crest or ear." The ground color is described as ochre-yellow, the serpents Indian-red with black outlines and white teeth and eyes; the faces and thighs of the main figures are sienna, the "turbans" a slightly greenish blue, black, and white; tunics are greenish-

blue, and "stockings" black (pls. 15, 17). The alternating motif is a complex one of human and zoomorphic stylized heads on a "slightly greenish, blue ground. The colors used in this motif were ochre yellow, Indian red or sienna, white and black" (pl. 17). In the center of the square motif is a smaller white square bearing a symmetrical cross in sienna, its arms terminating in zoomorphic heads (pls. 16, 17, fig. 67). "The alternating squares were joined by broad bands of uniform Indian red. They measured 74 cm. by 72 cm. and the framing bands 11 cm." Garrido also states that "underneath the decorative painting there had been a previous layer painted white." He further notes that while the remains of painting could be seen in cracks in other walls of the

Fig. 66.
Huaca de la Luna, drawing of motif of second mural.

room, it was not possible to ascertain whether the decoration was the same or not.

This description is brief and imprecise. The author does not discuss the chronological placement of the mural. Moreover, the "stockings" he mentions are probably just an indication of the use of body paint, as is frequent in Moche art (Bonavia, 1959b, pp. 36–37). The photograph illustrating the description is very bad and does not show detail. The color "lithograph" Garrido published (1956a, facing p. 28) is interesting but should not be taken as reproducing the original state of the painting. It is, in fact, a copy by Manuel Sánchez Vera of a color reconstruction by Pedro Azabache (here reproduced in black and white as fig. 68), which was in turn based on tracings of the original. The entire wall had not been cleared and only fragments of the three rows were visible, according to the note on the back of the published drawing. The motifs in Azabache's version, though reasonably exact, are too regular and there is great symmetry and precision (compare fig. 68 to pls. 15, 16, 17 and figs. 69, 70); the colors, as published, are only approximate.

The checkerboard actually has motifs placed within squares 72 cm on a side, separated from each other by 15 cm and arranged in identical diagonal units. The motifs show two basic figures. One is anthropomorphic, represented fullface with the head in profile. It bears a headdress of wave forms terminating in the front in an

animal head. The personage has a winged eye and conspicuous teeth. The headdress is painted red, white, and black, the face red, and the area of the mouth black with white teeth. The color of the clothing varies from unit to unit, but the colors used are blue, yellow, black, and white. The legs are red and the feet black with the anklebone and clawed toes white. The hands have been replaced by two sinuous elements that end at the upper and lower extreme in serpent heads, while from the central part of each issues an appendage terminating in an unidentifiable animal head. This entire element is painted red with a thin black outline and white eyes. The ground color is yellow.

In the center of the second motif is a small square 21 cm on a side, which contains a design, apparently in imitation of woven patterns, representing four very stylized serpent heads joined in the center (fig. 67). The remainder of the motif surrounds this central square. At the top and bottom are two fullface anthropomorphic heads with a very strange treatment: from the upper head issue two appendages that terminate in bird heads, while from the lower one the appendages are the same but issue from the neck. On each side of the square is a serpent head next to which are two bird heads, one above and one below. Separating the anthropomorphic from the snake heads are four stylized diagonal elements that radiate from the central square (see pl. 17).

The illustrations upon which I have based this description are the drawing published by Mackey and Hastings (1982, fig. 5) and the Azabache version (fig. 68), and the two are very different. While the anthropomorphic heads at the top are somewhat similar, the

Fig. 68.
Huaca de la Luna, platform 1a, third and last repainting phase. While not a tracing, this reconstruction drawing by Pedro Azabache was made at the time of discovery and under the guidance of José Eulogio Garrido, so it should be more exact than the published version by Manuel Sánchez Vera (Garrido, 1956a), which was based on it. Middle Horizon Epoch 3.

Fig. 69.
Huaca de la Luna, platform 1a, 1955 photograph of detail of third mural showing fullface personage with head turned.

Fig. 70.
*Huaca de la Luna, platform 1a, complete view of exposed
portion of third mural shortly after its discovery in 1955.*

lower ones are very different, and the serpent heads at the sides are entirely different. The mural is now in very poor condition and the photographs I have seen show little detail. Nevertheless, they do show that the Mackey and Hastings version, although not perfect and clearly not a tracing, is the more accurate.

The background of this motif is blue, but the colors used in the design, always white, red, and black, vary in placement from unit to unit (Mackey and Hastings, 1982, p. 296). This variation is not reflected in the Azabache version, where the use of color is uniform.

One important detail still needs clarification. While Mackey and Hastings report "at least three rows" of motifs (1982, p. 296), thus agreeing with Garrido's earlier reconstruction, the report of Morales Gamarra presents a schematic drawing of the pictorial sequence in his Anexo 4, in which there are at least four rows of motifs.

Morales Gamarra reports the colors, according to the Munsell color chart, as: white, 10 YR chrome value 8/2 (approximate); blue or gray, 2.5 Y chrome value N4; ochre-yellow, 10 YR chrome value 7/8; red, 10 R chrome value 5/3; and black, 2.5 Y chrome value N2 (ms.a, p. 8).

Moseley published a drawing of the motif from this mural that represents the fullface personage with his head turned (1978, fig. 42). A comparison of this drawing with the photograph of the original and the Azabache version shows that Moseley's drawing is reversed so that the personage faces left rather than right. Moreover, the mouth detail is changed, with Azabache's much more similar to the original. On the other hand, details of the representation of the figure's shirt are more exact in the Moseley version. The drawings published by Mackey and Hastings, while probably not tracings, are quite exact and show both motifs. It is also worth noting that in Rowe's publication in color of a detail from the Sánchez Vera version, the publisher reversed the negative so that the entire plate is backwards (Rowe, 1974, pl. XXXV).

All these paintings are located on the interior of a large room or court in the northeast corner of the principal platform of the Huaca de la Luna (fig. 53, 1a). This is the "room" referred to by Garrido. The members of the Chan Chan–Moche Valley Project have differentiated three temporally significant construction stages. This room or court was built during the second stage, and part of it was preserved into the third. The murals, which were painted on three occasions, correspond to various remodelings of the space; all appearances indicate that it was used for a relatively long time. While the

wall upon which the murals were painted has been severely damaged by looting operations, there remains an eastern section 18 m long and a southern one of 4.4 m with an approximate height of 3 m.

The walls were plastered and painted white, but the North American archaeologists found no evidence for a roof. The space was used before the painting of the first mural, which was undertaken in the course of remodeling. After that mural had become somewhat weathered, further remodeling was carried out. A bench was constructed in the northeastern corner, and a doorway, which damaged the mural, was opened; the southern portion of the mural was repainted. In the northern zone the first mural was partly covered by the bench and the remainder removed and the second one painted in its place (fig. 64). Note that this second mural has been located only in the northern section, which suggests to Mackey and Hastings that there was a time when the first and second murals were in use together. Morales Gamarra agrees with this suggestion. The first mural began to deteriorate, but, before the second was worn, all walls were plastered over and the third mural was painted. When that one began to deteriorate, the plaza was filled in with adobes. There was no chronologically useful debris (Mackey and Hastings, 1982, pp. 300–301, 303–304).

Regarding the painting technique, we know that the same sequence was used in all three superimposed murals. In the first place the wall was plastered with a clean mortar rich in clay, varying in thickness from 1 to 2 cm. Then, while this plaster was still fresh, the motifs were incised, and a white ground color was applied either while the plaster was still damp or when it was already dry. The final operation was to color in the motifs (Morales Gamarra, ms.a, pp. 8–9) (see pl. 18).

Mackey and Hastings present a series of arguments to support their chronological placement of these murals (1982, pp. 301–11). They first state that the murals are within the Moche tradition with the addition of foreign elements belonging to the Huari culture, and point out similarities to Pañamarca represented by isolated elements such as the use of painted black legs, serpents, etc. This argument is totally unconvincing. In the first place, there is more than one painting at Pañamarca with stylistic and surely chronological differences among them, as I have noted. In the second place, using isolated elements for comparative purposes, one can establish similarities between any two styles. Taking context into account, there is no similarity between Pañamarca and the Huaca de la Luna. Equally forced and baseless are the comparisons with the Huaca Pintada and La Mayanga (which they call Huaca Facho).

The authors then suggest a relationship between the murals and a fullface anthropomorphic figure associated with a staff and serpent, which commonly appears on Moche III and IV pottery. The argument is very far-fetched. In the first place, the personage the authors illustrate in their fig. 9a is not the same one that appears in their fig. 9b. The first bears a knife in its right hand and in its left it probably held a trophy head, although the specimen is incomplete; it is clearly not holding staffs. The second figure, on the basis of its face and especially its feline teeth, is doubtless the famous Moche Sacrificing God. The only comparable figure in the Huaca de la Luna murals is the personage of the third mural (fig. 69; Mackey and Hastings's Motif IIIA), who has none of the characteristics of the two examples presented.

The authors also refer to the "hanging head motif" as a common Moche theme (Mackey and Hastings, 1982, p. 305), and compare it to the "hanging heads" of the second and third murals. I do not see, in the first place, how the motif of the second mural can be called a hanging head, and such an identification is very dubious for the anthropomorphic heads at the top and bottom of the other motif from the third mural, the one Mackey and Hastings call IIIB (pl. 16, pl. 17 right). In the second place, I do not see the relationship between the head motifs on the pottery and those in the murals. The treatment and context are so different that I see no way to establish relationships; the vessel presented by Mackey and Hastings in their fig. 10b shows the Sacrificing God, who has nothing to do with the mural, and the representation in their fig. 10a is totally different in its conception.

The position of Mackey and Hastings regarding the winged eye is correct, and I have noted for some time that it is found in Moche IV (Bonavia, 1959b). Donnan's suggestion, to which they refer, that this eye treatment is already found in Moche III is interesting and logical (Mackey and Hastings, 1982, p. 305). On the other hand, Mackey and Hastings state categorically that Huari influence on these materials is not great, a viewpoint with which I do not agree.

Numerous writers, including myself (Bonavia, 1974, p. 88) and Jorge Muelle, who mentioned it on more than one occasion, have noted that the personage with staffs shown in the earliest of these three murals can be traced back to the Early Horizon. But to go further and discuss similarities in religious ideology on the basis of few data and without an intensive and extensive study, which

Mackey and Hastings do not appear to have made, seems very speculative. The same can be said of invoking the mechanism of diffusion via textiles. It would be interesting, however, if Mackey and Hastings could demonstrate the transformation they propose of textile patterns into free forms. The idea of applying to rigid materials designs that derive from textiles and reflect the structural limitations of weaving has been discussed since Semper in 1878, who called such designs plectomorphic (see Muelle, 1959), and the concept has been attributed to various Peruvian styles. But I know of no one else who has taken the position, apparently espoused by Mackey and Hastings, that textiles could serve "as a mechanism for diffusing a Huari-derived concept of motif layout . . ." (1982, p. 308).

The effects of Huari influence on the arrangement of motifs, which Mackey and Hastings accept, was noted by Donnan (1972), and he is surely correct. The oft-mentioned lack of Huari elements has been averred by other archaeologists and is reiterated by Mackey and Hastings. That position is, however, baseless. If pure Huari forms and decoration are sought, especially in pottery, possibly they will not be found. But elements deriving from the Huari style are undeniably there. This is not an appropriate place to discuss the matter in detail, but these influences are evident in the murals of the Huaca de la Luna that Mackey and Hastings have studied, and are also manifest in the Uhle collections, as Menzel has clearly stated in a work cited but apparently ignored by the authors (Menzel, 1977).

In conclusion, the authors argue that the work carried out at the Huaca del Sol and the Huaca de la Luna at Moche indicates that the site was abandoned before the beginning of Moche V and that the brick seriation (Hastings and Moseley, 1975) supports this position. "Combining these architectural and stylistic lines of evidence, we consider the second half of Phase IV to be a best estimate of the antiquity of the murals" (Mackey and Hastings, 1982, p. 311).

Now I think that a relative dating of the paintings can be done on the basis of stylistic analysis. As I mentioned, the mural corresponding to the first stage is a copy of a textile model. In general concept, the figure is related to one of the oldest religious patterns of the Andean area. The divinity who appears early in the Chavín style, characterized in the Raimondi Stela, and then reappears with transformations on the Monolithic Gateway at Tiahuanaco, is copied in the Middle Horizon styles in a variety of truly surprising forms and later altered. In this particular case, because of its treatment, I relate the figure of the first mural to the Middle Horizon textiles, which could have been copied or could have served as inspiration to the artist who painted the court of the Huaca de la Luna (see for example, Rowe, 1974, pl. L). The feline heads of the staffs could be related to the stylized versions of this animal that appear on Moche ceramics, or rather, on the rare Moche textiles. There is some similarity to the figure on one of the textiles excavated by Ubbelohde-Doering at Pacatnamú (Ubbelohde-Doering, 1967, pp. 72–73). Nevertheless, the method of representing the nose and ears suggests a relationship to feline representations found on Recuay-style pottery from the Callejón de Huaylas. To my way of thinking, there is only one typically Moche element, and that is the shape appearing between the legs of the personage. This shape is a stylized serpent head, very common in Moche art, frequently associated with a bird motif (Larco Hoyle, 1939, p. 3; Lavallée, 1970, lám. 98B). Thus, while the earliest mural figure cannot be related directly to any known style, several of its elements can be related to different Early Intermediate Period styles joined in a syncretism peculiar to the Middle Horizon. In other words, it contains a grouping of local motifs from the northern coast and highlands that were amalgamated under the impact of foreign ideas, probably in the first epochs of the Middle Horizon (for the division of the Middle Horizon into epochs, see Menzel, 1964; 1968; 1969).

The figure created during the second painting phase doubtless represents an archaistic reference to the Moche style. The original motif had various treatments generating a series of variations all based on the same theme: the representation of a central element, a face with anthropomorphic characteristics and with appendages varying in number but almost always terminating in bird heads (Larco Hoyle, 1938, p. 30; Kutscher, 1954, lám. 17). Moseley has suggested that it may represent "crabs or spiderlike figures" (personal communication, 1974). The former idea seems correct to me (compare Lavallée, 1970, lám. 74B). Lavallée has identified the bird as the osprey (*Pandion haliaetus*) associated with a daemonic representation that she calls a "raptorial demon" (1970, pp. 134–36).

The paintings corresponding to the third remodeling phase of this room of the Huaca de la Luna are really two repeated figures, as noted above. In them we find a synthesis of the ideas that originally motivated the two previous murals. The figure that appears in the top left square of fig. 68 and is then repeated diagonally is, I believe, the same personage seen in the first painting to

adorn that wall. The two staffs have been converted into elements that could perhaps be considered serpentiform, with the addition in the central part of each of a head that may provisionally be identified as a fox. We do not know the position of the head of the central figure in the first painting; it may have been represented fullface, but in this third mural it is in profile and wearing a headdress. In both positions, however, the concept is very similar. In the center of the following image, the one alternating with the personage, we again see the motif of the stylized serpent head so commonly found in the Moche style and mentioned as appearing between the legs of the staff-bearing personage of the earliest painting, except that here it is repeated four times. Each of the elements surrounding this center theme is, I think, a modified elaboration of the figure that was painted in the second remodeling stage, which I have identified with the idealized and anthropomorphized crab combined with the osprey motif. The treatment of the feline elements, the toes and the eye of the personage with staffs, may be directly related to Middle Horizon styles. The division of the surface into squares, like a checkerboard, in the second and third stages of repainting reinforces my position, since this arrangement is foreign to the Moche style.

Moseley attributed the third remodeling stage to a very "late" period of the Moche style, perhaps the end of Moche IV, adding that "it could well be attributed to Moche V," in spite of the fact that the Chan Chan–Moche Valley Project found no evidence of Moche V occupation at either the Huaca del Sol or Huaca de la Luna, since the population could have been living at Galindo at that time (Moseley, personal communication, March 1974). Not only are there remains of the last Moche phase at Galindo, but there are even the remains of painted figures on the walls (see Conrad, 1974, cited in Mackey and Hastings, 1982, p. 293). Moseley and Hastings reiterated the Moche IV to early V placement for the murals in 1975, citing Mackey's 1973 presentation (Hastings and Moseley, 1975, p. 197). Later Moseley stated firmly that the paintings were Moche Phase IV, and that the Huaca de la Luna was abandoned during that phase (Moseley, 1978, pp. 57–58, caption to fig. 42, p. 57), and this is basically the stand taken by Mackey and Hastings (1982). I disagree with this position, since I find no reason for associating any of the three paintings with the last phases of the Moche style. Although they doubtless include some archaizing Moche elements, these have been completely reworked in a concept and spirit foreign to that style, one much closer to the canons of the styles of Middle Horizon Epoch 3.

This is the position I held when the first edition of this book was published (1974), and since then it has been supported by Menzel's work (1977) on the materials excavated by Max Uhle at Moche in 1899–1900. We now know that, in spite of the impact of the Huari conquest, the site of Moche, while losing importance, nevertheless continued as an important sanctuary. In fact, the top of Cerro Blanco, at whose base the Huaca de la Luna was built, was used as a ceremonial site for offerings in the Middle Horizon. And everything indicates that during the time of the Huari empire, the Huaca de la Luna, which was built at the beginnings of the Moche culture and later remodeled, continued in use but was replaced in importance by the Huaca del Sol, which became the most important shrine and ceremonial center of Moche. From the associated materials that Uhle left us, we know that the Huaca del Sol was used until Epoch 3 of the Middle Horizon (Menzel, 1977, p. 37). This fact contradicts the position taken by Moseley and by Mackey and Hastings that both the Huaca del Sol and the Huaca de la Luna were abandoned in Moche Phase IV.

From Uhle's research, we find that on top of Cerro Blanco there were important buildings with mural decorations in relief painted red and white, which should be related to those of the Huaca del Dragón at Chanchan, which was built at the end of the Middle Horizon. Menzel thinks that, although the capital of the Moche Valley was moved to Chanchan in Epoch 2 of the Middle Horizon, the Huaca del Sol continued to function even after Epoch 3, and the Cerro Blanco shrine may have been built to represent the new order in the valley as a sort of rival to the old Moche shrine of the Huaca de la Luna. Located in a more prominent position than the Huaca de la Luna but close to it, the Cerro Blanco shrine could serve to counteract any political influence that the old temple doubtless retained (Menzel, 1977, p. 40). The top part of the Huaca de la Luna was remodeled to reinforce this position in Epoch 3 of the Middle Horizon and the walls painted with the third mural.

It should be noted that Rowe also assigns this painting to Moche V (1974, pl. XXXV), while Morales Gamarra mentions "phases III and IV" (ms.a, p. 1). Neither writer, however, provides any basis for his opinion.

A detail of the Sánchez Vera illustration published by Garrido was republished by Kauffmann Doig (1970, p. 396, fig. 630) with an erroneous caption identifying it as "frescos found at Chanchan." The error was corrected in later editions.

There are several further problems raised by the Morales Gamarra report. He says that the team from the Instituto Nacional de Cultura in Trujillo did not work in the "central sector" of the Huaca de la Luna, but that on "the side adjoining the doorway, we found the profile of a floor and evidence of another mural of a type that does not correspond to those already described. In the restoration laboratory we have an adobe with remains of this decoration, which we found in the Harvard backdirt, resulting in a puzzle with no easy solution" (Morales Gamarra, ms.a, p. 15). I have seen slides of the adobe in question and there is no doubt that it bears the remains of a motif in black on a white ground that does not correspond to any of the paintings we have dealt with. Was there yet another painting that was somehow destroyed?

Morales Gamarra also reports that there is clear evidence of an attempt, perhaps successful, to detach a part of the paintings by the "strappo" method (ms.a, pp. 11–12). After examining his excellent documentation and discussing the matter with him at some length (February 27, 1982), I am sure that not only is there evidence of the use of a "strappo," but there is actually a part missing from the paintings cleared by the Harvard project. Moreover, I was informed by separate and reliable sources, first in 1977 and again in 1978, that a fragment of this painting comprising one complete motif was for sale outside Peru. The only sure means to discover the truth regarding this priceless work of art would be to compare the photographic documentation of the Chan Chan–Moche Valley Project with that in the archives of the Instituto Nacional de Cultura in Peru. Such comparison is even more desirable since it appears that the Harvard project personnel did not take adequate protective measures when reburying the paintings, but rather increased the destruction by carelessly filling in their excavations. Today very little remains of the paintings representing the final phase of repainting.

The report of the Chan Chan–Moche Valley Project has been awaited for many years. It is one of the few archaeological projects that not only had the means to carry out a complete study of ancient Peruvian murals, but did indeed complete the study of one of the most important examples of that art. Unfortunately, the Mackey and Hastings article has not fulfilled our expectations and suffers from grave defects: the description of the motifs is very general and lacking in detail; the color description is inadequate, no color dictionary was used, and the text descriptions do not agree with the color-keyed illustrations; there is no analysis of the painting process and the techniques employed, and the pigments were not analyzed; the stylistic analysis suffers from a simplistic and superficial approach; moreover, while the bibliography is reasonably complete, it was either poorly consulted or not used at all. For example, the original edition of this book is mentioned, and in it I took the same position I have expressed here regarding the chronological placement of the three painting phases at the Huaca de la Luna (Bonavia, 1974, p. 92). But in spite of my position being clearly at odds with that of the authors, they do not even discuss it in the text. In many respects the Morales Gamarra report is more detailed and complete.

As a final word on the study of the Huaca de la Luna, I was told by Christopher Donnan of the existence of another mural. He had only glimpsed a small part of it, and no further data are available (personal communication, April 1982).

THE CHICAMA AND JEQUETEPEQUE VALLEYS

Farther north, in the Chicama Valley, near the Huaca Licapa and on the lands of the ex-hacienda Chuin Alto, there was apparently a Moche ruin with a large Moche-style mural representing a warrior. Claude Chauchat, who was told of the mural by Gustavo Alvarez Sánchez, looked for the site but could not locate it (Chauchat, personal communication, 1975).

We also know that in the lower part of the Jequetepeque Valley, in the course of work carried out at the ruins of Gallito Ciego by Phyllis Martin, a wall that had been covered by a later one was found with the remains of painting on it. The monument had been very badly damaged by looters and all that could be seen were traces of yellow paint with red spots; it is hard to say whether the wall was simply painted or bore designs. The wall that covered the painted one corresponded to the Chimú epoch. The painted one is earlier but its exact age is difficult to establish (Phyllis Martin, personal communication, February 1982).

DEPARTMENT OF LAMBAYEQUE

From the far north we have little information regarding Early Intermediate Period murals. A possible exception is Tello's very vague reference to the Huaca la Ventana. This monument is next to a large cemetery, which, according to Tello, is "almost ten thousand square meters" (1937). It is located on the right side of the Illimo branch of the Leche River, a bit less than half a kilometer from the confluence of the Túcume and eight kilometers east of the village of Illimo, department of Lambayeque. That, at least, is what Tello said in 1937; the reference points may have changed. Tello's excavations in the *huaca* revealed, in the fourth stratum, "fragments of adobes, plastered and painted with polychrome relief figures like arabesques" (Tello, 1937). It is not clear whether or not there were painted murals as well as painted reliefs. There is no further information on this point, and the chronological placement of these remains is also unclear, although they seem to be of the Early Intermediate Period or later epochs, since the fragments were found associated with "Pre-Chimú, Muchik, Marañón and Pre-Chancay styles in the lower part and black pottery of the Chimú type in the upper part" (Tello, 1937).

In 1975 at Pampa Grande in the Lambayeque Valley, Martha Anders, a member of the Royal Ontario Museum Lambayeque Project, discovered a painting in Unit 24 of Sector B (see Anders, 1979, figs. 3 and 17 for plans). This unit has an entry court bounded on the north and south by two rows of adjoining rooms. At the southeast corner of the entry court is a doorway leading into a hall through which one reaches a plaza located to the north. To the west of this plaza is a room, bearing on its east wall a painting that is incomplete at both ends, in part of the center, and on top (Anders, 1979, pp. 266–67). The wall had been painted white, and the mural was executed upon this ground. According to Anders, on the north end:

> All that remains is the drawing of a leg, of a deep pink color outlined in black, with a black circle on the ankle [fig. 71]. Above the foot at the left is a black triangle.
>
> At the south end is an anthropomorphic figure [fig. 72] with yellow legs (with black boots and a deep pink circle on the ankle) and fan-shaped plumage of varying colors (from left to right: deep pink, light blue, dark blue, yellow, dark blue, yellow, black, deep pink, light blue, dark blue, yellow, light blue) issuing from a circular red center. A black spike projects from the center of the plumage. Flanking this figure are two sets of two vertical, deep pink bands with light blue circles. These bands rest on light blue lenticular bases with wavy tops.
>
> To the right of the figure is a warrior [pl. 19]. His extremities and face are yellow, his hair black and eye white. He wears a red shirt with a blue collar, a short red skirt outlined in black; a blue bag hangs from his waist and he wears a nose ornament colored black and dark blue. Above his head are red, blue, and yellow elements that could be the remains of a headdress. In his right hand he holds a light blue club with a black head

Fig. 71.
Pampa Grande, Lambayeque, mural detail from north end of wall, showing human foot and ankle. End of Early Intermediate Period or beginning of Middle Horizon.

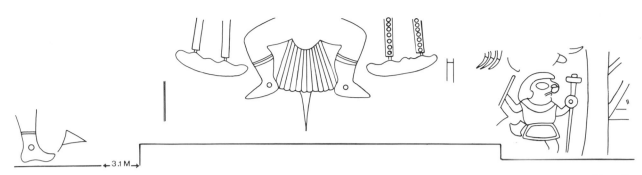

Fig. 72.
Pampa Grande, Lambayeque, mural in Unit 24.

and a circular, black and red shield. In his left hand he bears a black object. To his right is a red column with black and dark blue stripes. (Anders, 1979, p. 267, as amended by Anders, personal communication, 1983)[1]

The mural measures approximately 3 m long by 56 cm high and must originally have been a very large scene, since the wall upon which it is painted is about 10 m long and of unknown height.

While the description given above is in general accord with the illustrations, I disagree on some points. I do not think that the personage with the plumage is wearing boots, but rather body paint (Bonavia, 1959b, pp. 36–37), nor do I think that the element hanging from the warrior's waist is a bag, but rather a rattle, as noted earlier with regard to the Pañamarca plaza mural (fig. 36). Moreover, the few elements that remain above the small warrior do not seem to form part of his "headdress," as Anders suggests, but rather part of another personage who has been largely destroyed.

Stylistically the motifs of this painting are somewhat removed from classic Moche canons, although they are doubtless affiliated with that style. Above all, the small warrior on the right with a club and shield, and a rattle hanging on his back, is clearly a Moche "warrior." Not much can be said of the central figure. This personage with an apparently feathered tail is not, however, foreign to Moche mythology. The personage of the La Mayanga paintings, discussed below, also has a feathered tail, and there is an important personage with a plumed tail in a shamanic scene carved on a piece of bone from the British Museum, which Donnan has illustrated (1976, p. 114, fig. 102 upper left). There are, in fact, a number of mythological beings of this sort who are almost always anthropomorphic with a bird head and always warriors (Kutscher, 1954, pp. 33–44; Schmidt, 1929, p. 193, fig. 2 on p. 199). I think that we have here the same personage, although I do not know its meaning.

Anders, unfortunately, provides no information on the pictorial technique used, nor are the colors duly classified, but the polychromy corresponds to the Moche palette. On the slides I have seen there are no visible incisions outlining the motifs; the figures were painted directly onto the white ground color. Apparently the local tradition intervened to modify the Moche style.

We know from Anders's work that Unit 24 underwent several building phases. The entrance complex, the courtyard, and the enclosure seem to have been built at the same time; and the room with the mural belongs to this same phase (Anders, 1979, p. 266). The principal occupation at Pampa Grande corresponds to Moche Phase V (Anders, 1979, p. 246), although there is evidence of occupation at other times, including Moche IV. Anders decided to test Unit 24 because she thought it might be a variation on the storage pattern she had observed elsewhere on the site. "The excavation data suggest that it was an entry complex which would accommodate eight guards/supervisors seated on either side of the entry court to oversee traffic in and out of the unit" (Anders, personal communication, 1983).

The precise chronological placement of the painting is hard to determine. It does not have the classical ingredients of Huari influence as found, for example, in the third repainting of the Huaca de la Luna at Moche or in the La Mayanga painting discussed below. Indeed, at Pampa Grande the concept of scene, which disappears under the impact of Huari influence on the Moche tradition, is still maintained. I think that the Pampa Grande painting is earlier than that of La Mayanga and can be assigned to the end of Moche IV or the beginning of the first epoch (1A) of the Middle Horizon, that is, to Moche V.

But the mural that truly represents the Middle Horizon is on a monument I call the Huaca La Mayanga. It is located twenty-five kilometers northeast of the city of

Chiclayo on the lands of the former hacienda Batán Grande, about six kilometers northeast of the four great adobe structures known as the Batán Grande Group. The site is hard to reach.

There has been some confusion regarding the naming of the site, which I shall try to resolve. In the first published study of the mound it was called Huaca Facho (Donnan, 1972). Schaedel, however, mentions the paintings studied by James A. Ford "at the Huaca Pintada," evidently the same paintings published by Donnan, since we know that they are the only ones Ford studied (Schaedel, 1967a, p. 456). Schaedel refers to a personal communication from Ford, so we do not know the origin of the confusion, but in no way is this painted mound the Huaca Pintada, a well-known monument to which I shall refer below. The name "Huaca Facho" applied by Donnan to the painted structure is not correct either, however.

Jorge Rondón, who is very knowledgeable regarding the regional archaeology of Lambayeque, explained to me that local residents apply the name Facho to an entire complex of three or four *huacas* named for an old woman who lived in the place many years ago, probably in the last century (personal communication, 1973). To the northeast of this complex is another structure known as La Mayanga, also named for a farmer who lived in that area until recently. It is some three to four kilometers in a straight line from the Facho group to La Mayanga. The structure with the paintings studied by Ford and published by Donnan is La Mayanga.

The error apparently goes back to Ford, who initially thought that the structure was the Huaca Facho. Ford was informed of his error by local experts and Rondón says that he personally wrote a newspaper article in *La Industria* of Chiclayo in 1958 discussing the matter (personal communication, 1974). Ford died in 1968 without having published all his research. He may not have corrected his field notes so that Donnan, using them, carried on the error. Whatever the case, Schaedel was mistaken when he said that the location of Huaca Facho is unknown (1978, p. 28).

According to Donnan (1972), more than three decades ago looters uncovered polychrome paintings at La Mayanga. In 1958, when Ford was working in the area, he heard of the paintings, studied the remains, and made a tracing, which I saw at the time. When Ford died he left all this material to the American Museum of Natural History in New York and Donnan published part of it in 1972 with commentary. The work of Ford and Donnan is one of the few solid contributions on this theme.

With the invaluable aid of Jorge Rondón, I located the person who directed the looting operations at the time the paintings were uncovered. It was Augusto Bances, who became known for having dug the famous "Illimo knife" (also known as the "Lambayeque Tumi") out of a sand dune at Batán Grande. According to him, the polychrome murals of La Mayanga were found in 1941, when Oswaldo Aurich ordered a team of laborers under Bances's direction to search for treasure on what was then the hacienda Batán Grande. Apparently the paintings were found perfectly preserved and with very bright colors. The advanced age of the informant prevented our gathering any further information about the discovery.

The murals were located on the main wall of a courtyard that also had lateral walls that were badly damaged. The central sector of the main wall had been painted red, while the two ends were yellow, as was one of the lateral walls. The central section, which projected forward from the two ends, contained ten niches, and each end section had five. Donnan visited the site in 1969, accompanied by Joel Grossman, at which time they not only checked Ford's information but made additional observations (Donnan, personal communication, January 1983). He reported that "traces of a second row of niches positioned directly above those in the wing sections of the wall, suggest that there were originally at least thirty niches in the main wall" (1972, p. 87). These traces are no longer visible. Each niche is reported to measure 80 cm wide, 70 cm high, and 81 cm deep. The inside of the niches was painted a color contrasting with the façade, so the niches in the central part were yellow inside with the façade red and the side niches were a red tone inside in contrast to the yellow façade. The outside of the opening of each niche had a blue-black border.

On the back wall of each niche was a polychrome mural representing a winged figure in a running position, each bearing in its hand a gobletlike object (fig. 73). All these images were presented in profile and all faced the center of the wall. Apparently all the figures are derived from the typical Moche arms: club and shield. The head of the club is transformed into a human one, and the lower point generally represents a foot. The circular shield forms the body of the personage, who has been provided with a tail and wings as well as feathers projecting from the back of the conical helmet. The poor condition of the figures renders any comparison among them difficult, as it was even when Ford did his work (see fig. 74). There is, however, a significant difference in the two center niches, which Donnan numbered 10 and 11. Here two human feet and legs have been added to the club and shield, while in all the other figures there is only one foot and leg. Moreover, at least judging from niche 11, the two central motifs were also more elaborate in other ways; they had vertical stripes on the club handle and on the torso of the figure, and painted chevrons on the tail feathers. The other differences that can be seen among the figures on the basis of Ford's material appear to be accidental: the shape of a nose, treatment of a jaw and an eye, presence or absence of spots on the knees, ear ornaments, variation in the number of bands painted on the ankles, and differences in the rendering of the objects that the individuals are carrying.

The colors used on the figures follow the same red and yellow contrast seen between the façade and the inside of the niches. Thus the murals of the central portion of the wall are on a yellow ground and were painted mainly red with a little yellow, while in the five murals on either side of the central part, the painting is mainly yellow on a red ground. White and blue-black were the only other colors used. Small variations can be seen in the choice of colors in certain parts of the design. For example, even though the feathered tails are frequently painted red or yellow with the shorter feathers blue-black, some of the figures have the longer plumes painted blue-black and the shorter ones red or yellow.

The murals were executed freehand. The motifs were first drawn with light incisions, then the colors applied, and finally a line of blue-black added to outline the colored areas in the different parts of the design. Generally the red or yellow pigment was applied before the white and blue-black. In at least two designs the colored pigments were apparently superimposed several times, which suggests retouching after the mural was completed. Probably all the colors, those used in the murals as well as those covering the walls, were applied immediately after the walls were plastered with a layer of clay. This still damp base offered the artist a smooth surface and the possibility of greater adhesion of the pigments.

There are numerous incised motifs on the back and side walls of the niches as well as on the façade of the main and lateral walls (Donnan, 1972, pp. 90–91). These motifs represent a mixture of Moche and Huari elements, and Donnan notes that it is often difficult to tell if the incisions were made before or after the walls were painted. Pottery of both the Moche and Huari styles, as well as of mixtures of the two, has been found in the area (Donnan, 1972, p. 91).

While basically correct, there are some apparent errors in the description. All the niches are said to be almost cubical, and so they appear in Donnan's reconstruction drawing (1972, pp. 86–87). In the projecting central part of the main wall there were originally ten openings, of which only the first eight (counting from the left) are now visible. Only a portion of the ninth re-

Fig. 73.
La Mayanga, Lambayeque, artist's reconstitution of two of the winged personages.

4

5

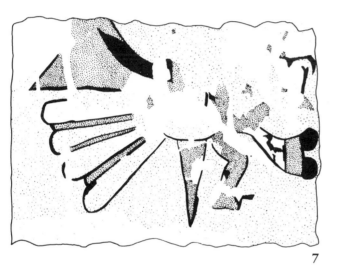

7

10

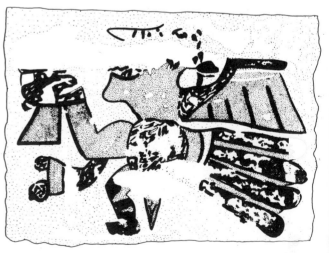

11

14

15

Fig. 74.
La Mayanga, drawings by Ambrosi based on original tracings of murals made by James A. Ford in 1958 and now in the American Museum of Natural History, New York. The drawings correspond to Donnan's niche numbers 4, 5, 15, 7, 10, 11, 14, and 17, as marked. Moche phase V, Middle Horizon Epoch 1.

17

mains, and the tenth is entirely gone, since all this part of the monument has been cut up by looters. The evidence is, however, very clear and shows that the three left-hand niches were alike and were different from the rest in having not an almost cubical shape but rather a longer parallelepiped shape with their tops at the same height as the others but their bases lower.

Regarding the paintings themselves, it is no longer possible to compare the reproductions to the originals, since only fragments remain. At the time of my visit the most complete was in what was the second niche from the right on the end of the wall (Donnan's niche 19), but even this one was not clear. The article, however, illustrates drawings of eight of the original twenty paintings (fig. 74). From the remains of niche 7, the second from the left on the central part of the wall, the drawing appears not to have been a tracing, since there are clear differences between its details and those of the original. The incised motifs are still largely preserved and the representations seem correct. The article does not mention, however, a series of incised elements located below the niches on the central section of the wall. Some of these are stepped and they always correspond exactly to one of the openings. They may have been exposed after Ford's work.

The colors of the La Mayanga pigments in Cailleux and Taylor's terms are: the red plaster of the wall façade, E-14 "light-red"; the red in the mural motifs, between H-24 and H-23 "intense red-brown"; black, between F-61 and F-90 "intense gray-brown" and "intense gray"; white, between B-81 and B-82 "light gray" and "pale yellow"; yellow, C-74 "pale yellow"; the yellow used as background, B-66 "yellow."

Donnan is quite right in saying that the La Mayanga murals are similar to those of Pañamarca and the Huaca de la Luna in pigment and technique of execution (1972, p. 91), in spite of the fact that the palette and its use vary from place to place. I would add that the conception and treatment of the themes differs among these three monuments. While the elements of the La Mayanga figures basically correspond to the Moche style (club, shield, anthropomorphization of inanimate objects, running winged figures, plumed headdress, conical helmet, eye form, tasseled fringes, knee spots, banded ankles, etc.), Donnan quite properly notes that, as far as we know, Moche murals always show scenes and never isolated personages, and they also have a broader polychromy. The fact that all known Moche murals have a white ground may suggest that this is a diagnostic trait that should not be ignored. To these points should be added the presence in the La Mayanga paintings of two characteristics foreign to the Moche artistic tradition, also noted by Donnan: a systematic color contrast and the concept of dividing the surface into squares in a way that is clearly influenced by textile design. Both are elements typical of the Huari style. On the other hand, the Huaca de la Luna mural discussed by Garrido, Moseley, and Mackey and Hastings also approaches this concept in the representation of isolated elements, the reduced number of colors, the treatment in squares, the subdivision of the surface by painting, and a background color other than white—all elements of the Huari artistic tradition.

The incised designs fall within the Moche tradition in some cases but, judging from Donnan's illustrations, could be later in others. Incised motifs also occurred at Pañamarca, but they no longer exist and were never described or studied. It is my impression that they were superimposed on the paintings and therefore later. It is worth noting that the same process of incising elements such as steps and even human faces is seen on decorated pottery of the Middle Horizon. To explain this phenomenon today would be difficult.

Donnan's suggestion regarding the personage depicted at La Mayanga and its possible distant relationship to the classic figures of the Monolithic Gateway at Tiahuanaco is very interesting. This personage is repeated in innumerable variants in several artistic expressions of the Middle Horizon. The similarity is found not only in the figure itself but in the general spirit reflected in the group: a series of personages, evidently foreign to the Moche tradition, in the act of running toward a central axis. This suggestion is reinforced by numerous observations related to the architecture, which I shall not pursue since they are outside the purview of this work. Nevertheless, in a later work Donnan identified this personage with one of the secondary personages of his "Presentation theme" (1976, p. 129). I do not, however, think that the two positions are mutually exclusive.

Donnan believes that this mural dates to Middle Horizon Epoch 1B, which would place it about A.D. 850. This position seems correct, so that the painting could be placed within the final decades of Moche V. Mackey and Hastings, with no substantiation, place this painting in Moche Phase IV or the beginnings of Phase V (1982, Table II, pp. 310–11). I absolutely reject the early placement.

Another important monument with mural paintings in the department of Lambayeque is called the Huaca Pintada. It is located beside the Panamerican Highway,

one kilometer north of Túcume and one kilometer south of Illimo (Horkheimer, 1965, p. 10) on a small sand hill. There are several adobe structures, and two paintings have been found. We have information about both paintings, but for only one is the information trustworthy. The second painting was reported by Carrión Cachot (1942) and will be discussed later. The first mural was reported by Orrego on the "front page of the Chiclayo newspaper" dated May 25, 1916 (Schaedel, 1978, p. 28). I have not been able to consult this source, but, according to Schaedel, there is a copy in the Hamburgisches Museum für Völkerkunde; a summary was published in 1927 (Orrego V., 1927). Both paintings are now gone; the first was already missing in 1924. Bennett provides no additional information, but reproduces the summary of Orrego's description from which the following particulars are taken (Bennett, 1939, p. 117).

The *huaca* is described as covering some 650 square meters, not counting fallen walls or disturbed soil. It comprised a single structure with various intercommunicating compartments enclosed by walls forming a quadrangle. The inner faces of the outside walls were adorned with a series of paintings in various colors, which, according to Orrego, symbolized daily life and, especially, warfare, "since a horizontal band about a meter wide in the middle part of these walls bore the aforementioned pictures, predominantly drawings of men in military garb, marching or engaged in a skirmish." The "warriors" wore a "turban" with two bunches of feathers, smaller ones at the forehead and longer ones attached to the rear; a cuirass; a garment wrapped around the waist with its ends hanging down; and anklets and bracelets. They also bore a shield in the left hand and a lance with a triangular head in the right. In some squares the lance rests on the shoulder and in others is held in a combative fashion (see original in Orrego V., or Bennett, 1939, p. 117).

Bennett, unaware of the earlier newspaper article, mistakenly states that Orrego's description should be taken with reservation, since he wrote it several years after visiting the site (1939, p. 117). While Kauffmann Doig contradicts himself on this matter, stating both that Orrego "described" the painting in 1916 and that he "visited" this *huaca* of Túcume in 1917 when it was in better condition, and that it was then that he described the paintings (Kauffmann Doig, 1964, pp. 62, 138; 1970, pp. 402, 630). The facts are that Orrego visited the site on May 20, 1916, and, according to his own words, published his report five days later, on May 25.

Brüning referred to this mural in the following terms:

About two kilometers north of Túcume right on the road from that town to Illimo is the "Huaca Pintada." This huaca . . . is renowned for a wall with fresco paintings in five colors that some huaqueros discovered when they went treasure hunting in Holy Week. . . .

The huaqueros . . . have destroyed the greater part of the paintings; the rain showers that have just fallen probably have increased the destruction. (Brüning, 1916, p. 199)

This and other paintings are also mentioned by García Rosell (1968), but his work contains so many errors and distortions that it is not worth discussing. Until 1978 the only known photograph of this mural was one published in the magazine *Variedades*; it is of such poor quality that no details are visible (Urteaga, 1917, p. 450). The only reference to the subject matter is in the caption: "Remains of a stretch of wall with large squares in which a series of Yungas warriors are seen."

Fortunately, in 1976, while investigating the documents left by Brüning to the Hamburgisches Museum für Völkerkunde, Richard Schaedel found black-and-white photographs of the painting, together with notes that specify, among other things, the colors (Schaedel, 1978; 1980; all references on the following pages are to 1978, since the other is just a literal translation of it). Shortly thereafter, Wolfgang Haberland of that museum found a partial color reproduction that Brüning had had made of the mural and that is dated September 1916 (pl. 20).

Schaedel characterizes the painting (fig. 75) as composed of "a central figure, eleven impaneled processional figures and assorted elements located above the level of the panels" (1978, p. 29). From each side the procession approaches a central figure, of which only fragments are preserved, including its right foot, which is clawed; bits of its costume; and a raised platform on which it stands. Other fragmentary elements are discernible on either side of this figure and below the platform, but they are not readily identifiable.

To the left of the central figure (when facing it) are six profile figures. The first four (fig. 75, 1–4; fig. 76) stand inside rectangular frames bordered with white paint outlined in black. The fifth figure is not framed on the right, while the sixth is different from the others in several ways (fig. 77): he is larger, carries no mace, and has no feathers trailing behind his headdress. "The tail-like appendage behind his body suggests the loop characteristically seen in Mochica art which was used by runners to attach ceremonial wings" (Schaedel, 1978, p. 33). Facing these six figures are five others with similar char-

acteristics. Schaedel comments that there is no photograph extending to the extreme right edge of the panel he designated 11, but that the right-hand figures are clearly framed in the same way as those on the left of the central figure. "Some parts of the frieze itself are poorly preserved: one figure (8) consists of little more than a pair of feet facing left and scant remains of borders. The two figures flanking the central figure correspond to each other, since both are somewhat larger than the other warriors and their arm depiction and costume differ from those of all the other figures" (Schaedel, 1978, p. 33).

Above panels 4 and 5 on the left and 9 on the right is a "ribbon-like" element, which contains bird and fish designs. Below the end of the left ribbon is the lower body and legs of a large anthropomorphic figure that boasts a "feathered" tail, while within the bend of that same ribbon can be seen the feet and lower edge of the garment of a much smaller figure. The corresponding portions of the right-hand ribbon are missing, so no comparison is possible. "One treatment which is the same for both ribbons, however, lies in the rows of painted 'bricks' of alternating colors which parallel the ribbon borders" (Schaedel, 1978, p. 33). There are other elements in the upper portion of the mural, some of which cannot be identified, but Schaedel has identified others as "bird heads, at least one feline head, two fish tails, *strombus* shell" (1978, p. 33). The two sides of the lower portion of the mural are not exact mirror images of one another, but there are numerous similarities in the figures, including the clubs borne by the figures, ear ornaments, necklaces, headdresses, and stepped designs on the tunics. ". . . Most of the decorative space-fillers used in the panels are found on both sides of the frieze, except for the darts in the second panel and the small weapons or mace-heads of the fourth" (Schaedel, 1978, p. 33).

The painted segment that Brüning left us (pl. 20) does not, in its entirety, represent a portion of the mural. While the panel to the left corresponds to Schaedel's panel 2 (designated B by Brüning), the background elements shown immediately to its right represent all four kinds that were used rather than those of a particular panel. Brüning's note, which can be seen to the right of this section, says, "4 different forms of the secondary decoration. Each field contains only *one* of these decorations" (emphasis in the original).

Schaedel estimated the panels, excluding the borders, to be 80 cm high and 130 cm long, using as a scale a person shown in front of the mural in a black-and-white photograph of the period. He calculated the horizontal

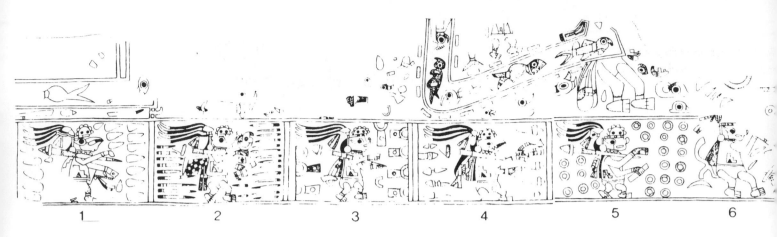

1   2   3   4   5   6

Fig. 75.
*Huaca Pintada, Lambayeque, great mural drawn for
Schaedel from photographs taken by Brüning in
1916. Middle Horizon.*

borders to be about 3 cm high and the verticals 5 cm wide. Brüning's measurements for the painted panel (pl. 20), including the borders, are 93 cm high by 155 cm wide, showing Schaedel's figures to be only about 6 percent too low. We can thus calculate the total length of the mural when found to have been about 17.75 m.

Brüning listed the colors used as black, white, yellow, red, and blue. He also coded them, but to what source has not yet been determined. Schaedel, who had not yet seen the painted reproduction, noted that the blacks and whites are very clear in the black-and-white photographs, but there are small areas of a very light shade that might be the blue mentioned by Brüning (figs. 76, 77; Schaedel, 1978, p. 34). Brüning indicated that the ground color was red and the legs of the personages yellow, and Schaedel based his color reconstruction on this description (Schaedel, 1978, p. 32). But in the reproduction made for Brüning, the ground color appears more brown than red. It is possible that the artist, one N. Moreno, as indicated at the foot of the painted copy, erred in his choice of colors, but it is also possible that the color was originally of a redder hue, having changed during the sixty-six years of storage. There is now no way to ascertain the truth.

Both Brüning and Orrego interpreted the scene as one of combat, but Brüning also suggested the possibility of a maritime theme, mentioning a balsa (raft or reed boat) as the possible explanation for "the curved, ribbon-like motif that seemed to be almost symmetrically draped over the bottom row of processional figures" (Schaedel,

1978, p. 35). Schaedel comments, however, that while arms are shown in the lower panels, they might represent hunting rather than war. He adds that the weapons are not clearly those of the hunt, and, even if they were, it is not clear what sort of game was sought, or whether on land, along the shore, or in the air (1978, p. 35). To support his suggestion he illustrates a ceramic representation with two armed individuals flanking a fish (1978, p. 34).

Some elements were interpreted by Schaedel as parts of clubs, though they cannot be positively identified, and he classified them under the general heading of "gear" (1978, p. 35). The personage in his panel 2 is carrying one of these elements, which appears to terminate in a bird head, thus complicating the identification; it may be a goblet. Schaedel also considers the rings to be a problematic element, suggesting that they might be either detachable spearpoint guards or clubheads. The upper, wavy bands containing fishes and forms like birds may be compared to Moche or Chimú drawings that can be either canals or boats; thus Schaedel thinks that the central personage could represent the god or goddess of the sea or moon (1978, pp. 34–37).

Fig. 76.
*Huaca Pintada, Lambayeque, 1916 photograph of mural
detail corresponding to personages 1–3 of fig. 75.*

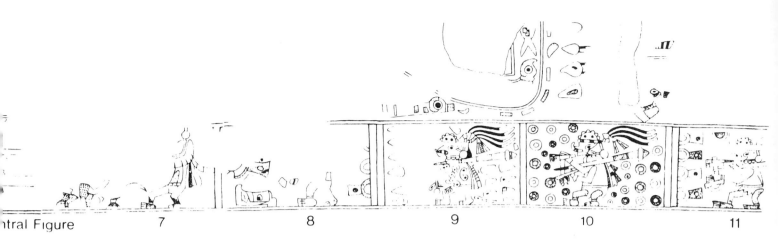

Fig. 77.
Huaca Pintada, 1916 photograph of mural detail including the central figure and numbers 5 and 6 of fig. 75.

I agree with Schaedel that the painting described by Brüning is the same one reported by Orrego, a view of which apparently even circulated on a postcard with an English text. But I do not see how, as Schaedel suggests, the mural can be related to the legend published by Augusto León Barandiarán, which I shall discuss in the following chapter. The reconstruction of the mural that Schaedel published seems correct, and his color recon-struction may well be quite close to reality. As far as the interpretation of the scene shown in the painting, I would not venture an opinion. There is no doubt that in the upper part of what remained of the mural there is a predominance of maritime elements, but I do not think we have enough evidence to associate them with a ma-rine deity. Moreover, on the lower part there is no scene; rather there are isolated, repetitive elements (even though

Mural Painting in Ancient Peru

the same personage is not repeated) of unknown meaning. While these personages bear clubs, they are not the typical "warriors" to which Moche sceneography has accustomed us. The concept is very different and it is difficult to specify their function.

Schaedel suggests that the details of this painting are of local derivation and thinks, on the basis of what little remains of the "central figure," that it can be connected with the personage found in Huaca del Oro (see chapter 5). He relates the side personages to Moche V and suggests two possible interpretations: either there was a parallel development during the last Moche phases (for which there is evidence in the area), or the scene represents an immediately post-Moche trend (1978, p. 35). But he concludes that the most logical chronological placement for the mural would be the first phase of the Middle Horizon (1978, p. 34). There is no doubt that the personages in the bottom panels bear a series of Mochicoid traits indicating a distant affiliation with Moche, but there is more in this painting that is not Moche than there is typical of Moche properly speaking. Again I repeat that the sceneographic idea so characteristic of Moche art is lost here, and we find instead the isolated personage typical of the Middle Horizon styles. On the other hand, the treatment of the hands and feet, as well as the chevrons that can be seen on the figures in panels 4, 5, and 9 and in details of the central figure, are typical of the southern styles associated with the Huari phenomenon, as are other details, and have nothing to do with either the Moche style or the local Lambayeque styles of the Early Intermediate Period. Likewise, the concept of the central figure upon whom lesser personages converge is an idea probably derived from Tiahuanaco. The red ground of the painting is also foreign to Moche. For all these reasons, I cannot agree with Schaedel's suggestion that the details are of local origin. The entire concept of the mural comes from the south. It is foreign to the Lambayeque area, and it is precisely the details, with roots in the Huari-related styles, that come from farthest away.

I see the posited relationship of the central figure to the Huaca del Oro personage as very forced. Only the bottom of the Huaca Pintada figure is preserved, while only the upper part of the Huaca del Oro figure is known; Florián's version of the feet (1951) has no evidential value whatsoever (see next chapter).

We know that Moche traditions were not extinguished under the sway of the Huari empire but rather mixed with the ideas of that empire. Moreover, during the northward expansion of the empire and even after its de-

cay, there persisted in the Lambayeque area not only the influence of this mixture of ideas but even power centers. While the mythical beings of the Moche religion are not very different from those of Huari religion, there are very important differences in the organization of religious concepts, as Menzel has pointed out (1977, p. 61). These similarities permitted a rapid syncretism between the northern religions and that of Huari and at the same time stimulated a new and vigorous flourishing of northern regional culture.

In Moche religion there is evidently a more complex differentiation of mythological concepts than we can see in Huari. In the latter the principal deities are isolated from the secondary ones and those of lesser importance. In the syncretism of the two religions the Moche divinities, who earlier appear associated with complex scenes, are isolated (Menzel, 1977, pp. 59–66). While we are not yet in a position to identify these deities, I think that the Huaca Pintada scene reflects these changes and clearly shows us the new religious version, the result of this syncretism of the Huari and Moche religious concepts forming a religious phenomenon typical of the Lambayeque area, which is also reflected in the La Mayanga paintings.

Stylistically, I see no way to relate this mural directly to the Moche style, not even to its late Phase V. Thus, I disagree with Schaedel's placement in the first epoch of the Middle Horizon. In my judgment, the Huaca Pintada painting is later than that of La Mayanga and can be assigned to Epoch 2A of the Middle Horizon or perhaps even 2B.

The second Huaca Pintada painting, which is mentioned by Carrión Cachot (1942), presents serious problems and, if the information we have is correct, is more closely tied to the Late Intermediate Period styles. I therefore prefer to deal with it in the following chapter.

Other Middle Horizon paintings have, however, been located in the department of Lambayeque, and many of them were still in a good state of preservation until 1972 (personal communication, Jorge Rondón, 1973). However, on my last visit to that region, in 1974, I observed that only insignificant details can now be seen of the paintings known at that time. Most of these sites have been looted by treasure hunters, and the walls that bear the murals are cut or perforated, almost always through the center of the paintings themselves.

I was told by Izumi Shimada that there is another monument with painted remains near La Mayanga (personal communication, 1980).

—5—
Late Expressions on the North Coast

After the fall of the Huari empire a renaissance began, leading the Andean societies to resume their ancient traditions and resulting in the rise of a series of local kingdoms, each with its own cultural characteristics. This is the birth of the Late Intermediate Period.

The spread of Huari had resulted in extensive movements in which many cultural patterns, up to that time confined to certain groups, became generalized. Thus, the idea of the city became universal and with it spread the idea of organization. Most interesting for this study are the coastal cities, which vary in size but hold many elements in common, providing a certain sense of uniformity. All of them were built with moldmade adobes, although *tapia* was also used. They also share a rectangular layout, the result of true planning, and a series of internal features: temples, courtyards, platform mounds, terraces. But the outstanding characteristic of all these cities is the frequency of the use of painted or flat relief decoration on walls. There was also no lack of minor rural centers and of military outposts strategically located to defend the intakes of the great irrigation canals.

THE MOCHE VALLEY

Remarkable examples typifying northern architecture of the period are two monuments located near each other in the vicinity of Chanchan (Moche Valley near the present route of the Panamerican Highway). They are the Huaca Tacaynamo and the Huaca del Dragón. The former was originally very heavily decorated but was almost totally destroyed by 1956 (Garrido, 1956b, p. 4). It apparently had relief decorations painted in many colors.

The work on the Huaca del Dragón, also called Cientopiés, is represented by one of the rare good reports (Schaedel, 1967a). This monument, which was probably a temple, was entirely decorated with clay low reliefs, which are still preserved but have been altered by a poorly conceived "restoration" in 1963. These reliefs were originally painted. Horkheimer mentions traces of reddish yellow on the clay walls (1944, p. 70),[1] and when Schaedel cleared the structures, he found the remains of white and yellow on the low reliefs on the better-preserved portions of the outer wall and on the base of the base wall of the principal platform (Schaedel, 1967a, pp. 402, 403). Although green and red were found on fallen fragments in some rooms, none was found *in situ* on the reliefs (Schaedel, 1967a, p. 405). Schaedel suggests that the terrace decorations were originally covered by a roof with a "frieze cornice" that was painted in red and green on a white ground (p. 422). He identifies the *huaca* as "the only pre-Chimu structure which is walled and has the stucco-type low relief friezes" (p. 452), a new architectural and decorative mode that was to influence the builders of Chanchan (pp. 452–53).

There is still little that can be said about the architectural details of Chanchan, although it seems absurd to say so about one of the most important cities of antiquity. There have been endless comments on how attractive it must have been because of the number of reliefs adorning its buildings, but almost nothing has been written of the painting that covered these decorations and must have made them still more striking. Unfortunately, of this aspect almost no evidence remains, save in some elements that may still be buried and would provide clues to the original colors.

In 1877 Squier observed that there was much decoration in relief and in color, and that "the interior walls of some of these outstanding buildings had been painted with vivid colors, among them a delicate purple" (Squier, 1877, p. 143). Some pages later he added that traces of color could be seen in some probable tombs of the city (1877, p. 149). He speaks in general terms of red and yellow (p. 150) without specifying the colors for each section, adding that "The First Palace" of the Rivero and Tschudi sector was painted (p. 154). Later authors provide no further information on the subject. Bennett simply refers to "traces of painted walls" (1946, p. 140), while Schaedel states that there was no preserved polychromy in the Chimú city, but in some cases the reliefs were painted in white or yellow (1967a, p. 453). We also know that there used to be some fretwork painted ochreyellow in the Ciudadela Martínez Compañón, but it disappeared around 1940 (Garrido, 1956b, p. 3). Some reliefs newly found in 1975 were painted (Robert Feldman, personal communication, 1975).

While we know that the tradition of mural painting continued in the Late Intermediate Period, at least on the north coast, in most cases we have no details (Ravines, 1980, pp. 110, 247–48). Recent finds have not yet been completely published.

LAMBAYEQUE

In 1957 Schaedel published, with no additional information, a black-and-white photograph of a polychrome painting found in Lambayeque (Schaedel, 1957, fig. 7). At that time the mural no longer existed and there were contradictory rumors about it. In 1958 I spoke to Oscar Lostaunau, one of the people who saw the painting and who, moreover, gave me his field notes and some photographs of the find. At the same time I encountered other photographs (including one in color) taken by Hans Horkheimer, Jorge Rondón, and Abraham Guillén. On the basis of all this material, I have managed to reconstruct some of the characteristics of this painting.

Túcume

The mural was located in the northeast sector of the archaeological complex of Túcume, or El Purgatorio, on the upper part of a building that was probably sacred in nature. It was uncovered by looters November 10, 1953, and examined five days later by Hans Dietrich Disselhoff, Oscar Lostaunau, and Oscar Fernández de Córdoba. The paintings adorned a doorway that had been closed by an adobe wall (fig. 78). The exterior, with the decoration, was also sealed by another wall. The exposed part was only a fragment of a much longer wall (pl. 21, fig. 78). The doorway was distinguished by two jamblike clay pilasters, also decorated. This section of the decorated wall was approximately 2.8 m long, but its true height cannot be calculated, since its base was buried in rubble and a considerable part of the top was cut at the time of the discovery. In fact, very little remained of the mural, much of which was destroyed by some pointed instrument, whose traces can be clearly seen in some photographs (pl. 21).

The section of wall to the left of the doorway was not flat but rather contained three horizontal rows of small niches in a checkerboard pattern. Above this portion was a barely projecting cornice bearing a broad, horizontal band, black in the center and bordered at top and bottom in white. A series of schematically represented diving birds was painted on the black, but only three of them remain (fig. 79). Individual differences aside, these birds are very similar. They have a very regular triangular tail; the wings were drawn with curved lines as was the head, which is circular with a pointed beak. On the cornice the birds are alternately white and red. In the center of each body is a diamond, white on a red ground, and red if the ground is white. In one case the diamond

has a black center while in another the outer part is outlined in black. The eyes are circular and different in each of the three cornice examples: in one case red with a black center, in another white with a black center, and in the last black with a red center. The beak contains a triangular element, which, in the only preserved case on the cornice, is white.

In the main part of the niche checkerboard only the facade was decorated, while the interiors were simply painted with the ground color. There is not a single complete square, so a total reconstruction is impossible. The ground color was red and each square of the façade bore a representation of a diving bird similar in form, treatment, and individual variation to those already described but slightly smaller. The birds here alternate in black and white. The white birds have a red central diamond outlined in black with the same combination used for eyes and the triangular shape forming the beak. The black birds have a red central diamond outlined in white and the same treatment for the beak and eyes (pl. 21). The bottom of the niched section is separated from the rest of the wall by two broad bands, the upper white, the lower black.

The left-hand pilaster, that is, the one adjoining the wall just described, had the best preserved paintings. It

Fig. 78.
*Túcume, Lambayeque, unique photograph showing paintings
adorning a doorway that was closed with an adobe wall
during a later occupation. Late Intermediate Period.*

Fig. 79.
*Túcume, detail of wall portion of mural showing
stylized diving birds.*

was entirely decorated and the motifs were very similar to those described but larger. A broad vertical black panel occupied the center, bordered on each side by a narrow white stripe ending at the edge of the pilaster. On the black panel was a vertically oriented series of diving birds varying in detail from one another. The birds alternate red and white in this case. The red birds have a black central diamond and eyes formed of three concentric circles in one of two color combinations: from the center out, either red, black, and white, or white, black, and red. In one case the beak is marked by a white triangular shape with a black center, while in the other it is black with a white center. The two white birds are the same, their central diamonds of red with a black center, the circular eyes red with a black center and the beak the same combination as the eyes.

Almost nothing is preserved of the outer finish of the right-hand pilaster, barely a small lower section showing the remains of a bird motif similar to those described (fig. 78), suggesting that it was decorated like the left-hand one. From the shape of the birds, I suspect that they represent the Peruvian booby, or *piquero* (*Sula variegata*).

colors), it was so applied that a very suggestive and truly lovely effect was achieved. Lostaunau collected samples of the red and white colors so that they have been identified; in Cailleux and Taylor's terminology, they correspond to a light red-brown, C-14, and white, A-81.

In the absence of other evidence, it is impossible to determine the precise epoch to which this painting belongs. I am inclined to relate it stylistically to the Chimú style. Such placement would fit with other information we have regarding the Túcume area. There are at least two other cases in which diving birds of the same shape and similar treatment have been found. The first is a petroglyph, which it has not been possible to date, in the locality of Yonán (Cerro Shansis), Jequetepeque Valley, department of Cajamarca. The other, in the Lima Valley, is the Huaca La Palma (in the Maranga archaeological zone). The *huaca* has clay flat reliefs outlining diamond-shaped areas in each of which was a diving bird. The similarity of this decoration to the Túcume figures is striking, and the construction of this monument should correspond to the same time period. The La Palma wall was well preserved until 1964. I have also seen a Chimú vase exhibited in 1977 in the Museum of the Smithso-

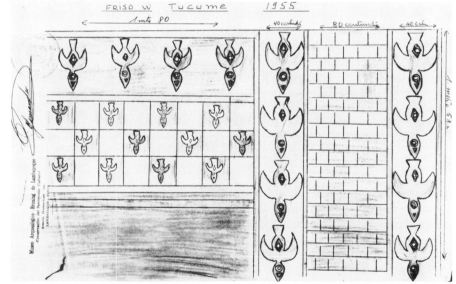

Fig. 80.
Túcume, highly inaccurate sketch of mural, on file in the Museo Arqueológico Brüning, Lambayeque.

Regarding technique, the wall seems to have been finely plastered and painted and then the bird motifs sketched by incision before the areas were filled in with color. It is clear that each motif was made freehand, given the considerable difference among them. Apparently the artist gave free rein to his or her creative impulses when painting the details, without hewing to fixed norms. In spite of the limited palette (only three

nian Institution in Washington, which bore a representation in high relief of a Peruvian booby bearing a marked similarity to the Túcume representations.

There is some information, including a drawing (fig. 80), of this mural in the Museo Brüning in Lambayeque, but it contains notable errors. For example, a yellow color is noted that was absent in the original; the right-hand pilaster is shown as if it had been found intact, which it was not; and the dimensions are totally inaccurate. There were more paintings in the Túcume complex; in 1958 I saw traces of an almost totally obliterated mural there, on the Huaca Grande.

Huaca Pintada

According to Carrión Cachot (1942), there was another painting in the Huaca Pintada of Illimo, but, as we shall see, there is some doubt about this. She suggests that the second Huaca Pintada painting was found near the end of the 1930s. She published a drawing (fig. 81) but notes that "it has not been possible, largely because of weathering, to obtain an exact copy of the figures of this fresco" (Carrión Cachot, 1942, p. 584). This mural must have been of considerable size; according to Eduardo de Peralta, Carrión Cachot's informant and the discoverer of the painting, the principal figure measured 2.80 m high. Carrión Cachot mentions that the Museo Nacional de Antropología y Arqueología, Lima, acquired a copy of a reduced "and somewhat reconstructed" drawing of the work in question (1942, p. 584). While I was working in that museum I tried unsuccessfully to locate that copy, and none of the personnel who had worked there in Carrión Cachot's time could provide information about it.

> . . . the principal figure is situated between other secondary ones and is luxuriously bedecked. The deity is easy to identify, since she wears the same garb, jewels, and recognized attributes. The accompanying figures are humanized birds, two of which have a mantle with star designs. They must have formed part of a more complete scene. . . . in this picture there is nothing foreign to true Chimú art. It should be noted that several colors were used in this fresco—which are not indicated here because of the brief reference made to it—which permit a better understanding of the figures represented. A pair of birds similar to those in this painting adorn a gold ear plug. . . . (Carrión Cachot, 1942, p. 584)

In Schaedel's study of the first Huaca Pintada mural, discussed in the last chapter, he deals incidentally with the Carrión Cachot painting (Schaedel, 1978, p. 29). He suggests that the drawing she presents might have been copied from the central personage of the mural that Orrego published in 1916. This suggestion, however, contradicts Carrión's statement that the painting was discovered "a short while ago" (1942, p. 584). While her work was published in 1942, she presented it to the International Congress of Americanists in 1939, so she

must have been referring to a time near that year, considerably removed from 1916, when Orrego first saw the other Huaca Pintada paintings.

As Schaedel observes (1978, p. 29), when Bennett investigated the same *huaca* around 1937, he saw no trace of paintings (Bennett, 1939, p. 117), which caused Schaedel to speculate that perhaps some other painting was discovered after Bennett's work. I think, as will be seen, that this alleged mural, in the version given by Carrión Cachot, never existed. But in fact there is no way to ascertain the truth; nothing remained of this mural in 1965, so that direct observation is impossible. Carrión Cachot's description is so poor as to be essentially valueless; I take it simply as a reference.

Stored in the Museo Nacional de Antropología y Arqueología, Lima, I found three samples of pigment that bore the sole identification "Illimo." It may be conjectured that they come from the monument in question and belong to the mural to which Carrión meant to refer. In that case, the colors according to Cailleux and Taylor would have been at least a light red, D-26; a dark gray, H-10; and a light gray, B-10.

Carrión Cachot relates the scene to the "lunar deity" associated with sacrifice, with whom her study dealt. For more detail on the subject, I direct the reader to the source. Referring to her figure 17 (fig. 81), the author wrote: "The drawing was obviously made simply by sight and by a person untrained in this kind of work, thus occasioning certain omissions that may be noted in it" (Carrión Cachot, 1942, p. 584). I would argue the contrary; the elements of the motif are coherent and demonstrate a knowledge of the source. If there is anything in doubt, it is whether this motif was really executed on a wall. I rather doubt it and think, given its detail, that it was copied from some ceramic or metal object, or pyroengraved gourd. It is possible that, in this sense, Carrión was deceived. Thus Schaedel's suggestion that her illustration might be an "imaginative reconstruction" (1978, p. 29) does not strike me as likely. Rather it is a copy of a motif, I repeat, almost surely never painted on a wall. Nor do I see where Schaedel finds the analogy between the "clawed or webbed foot" of the central figure of the first Huaca Pintada painting (fig. 75) and the personage illustrated by Carrión Cachot (fig. 81), since I find them totally different (Schaedel, 1978, p. 29).

Carrión Cachot considers the motif to be Chimú, and to support her thesis relates it to analogous motifs represented on a gold ear ornament, illustrated by Antze in 1930, which she reproduces in her figure 18 (Carrión

Fig. 81.
*Drawing that Carrión Cachot published in 1942, attributing
it to the second painting of the Huaca Pintada, Lambayeque,
which may have been discovered about 1930.*

Cachot, 1942, p. 586). But her entire proposal is stylistically untenable. The analogies are correct, but not so the chronological position assigned to them. The motif of her figure 18 is clearly related to the Middle Horizon styles of the central and north coast; moreover, it is strongly reminiscent of some themes common on painted textiles from the central coast, which are generally associated with the pottery called Three-color Geometric. The most characteristic elements on the ear ornament are: the treatment of the feet, the tassels hanging from the waists of both personages and one headdress, the serpentiform head associated with the headdress of the right-hand figure, and the chevrons forming the hair or headdress of the left-hand figure, who is upside down. Some of these elements are clearly represented in Carrión Cachot's figure 16, although in more geometric form, since they come from a Pachacámac tapestry, where they are unquestionably of Middle Horizon date.

On the other hand, the mouth treatment of the principal figure of the mural is clearly copied from an old Moche pattern (compare Hocquenghem and Lyon, 1981, fig. 3; Donnan, 1976, fig. 112). In my opinion, then, the motif of fig. 81, whether or not it was part of a mural painting, is stylistically an epigonal of the Middle Horizon, one of those elements transitional to the Lambayeque style, which is confused with the Chimú style, to which it is clearly related. The exact stylistic and temporal relationships of the Lambayeque style have not yet been properly defined.

Rondón maintains that there is a mix-up and that Orrego and Carrión Cachot are referring to the same painting, which was completely destroyed by the rains in 1952 (personal communication, 1973). He adds that it showed "human figures with little expression that were painted red." This description agrees with nothing so far described and raises the question of whether there may have been yet a third mural that is otherwise unknown.

As a further note, although it has no possible direct relationship to the preceding material, Augusto León Barandiarán recorded a legend from the mouth of Mrs. Nicolasa Gonzales, which deals with the Huaca Pintada of Illimo and is quoted by Kosok (León Barandiarán, 1938, pp. 69–71; Kosok, 1965, pp. 176–77). While its value for studies such as the present one may be questionable, since, as the North American author warns, there is no way to verify these legends that reach us after more than four centuries, I think it worth repeating:

> The Huaca Pintada, which is about one kilometer south of the village of Illimo, was long ago a shrine or religious temple dedicated to the worship of the Moon, rivers, rain, iguanas and spiders. It was built entirely of *adobón*[2] with no decoration or painting either inside or out. Before the government of the Inca Pachacútec, when the conquest of the Yungas by the Incas had not yet taken place, the priest, called Anto Tunga, who directed the activities of that shrine, dreamt that the Sun drew near him burning the shrine entirely and leaving stamped upon his face the appearance and color of that star as though to remind him that he was obliged to render it the homage of his worship. But the old priest, rejecting the warning, continued to offer his sacrifices and libations, his vows and prayers to the Moon, the waters and the animals, scorning the premonitory dream. But when, at dawn, he awoke and made his preparations, cooking the maize for the sacred *chicha* [fermented drink usually based on maize] with which he propitiated his gods, he found the shrine colored entirely red outside, and the inside of the walls decorated in three colors: the red of the Sun, the blue of the Sky, and the yellow of gold. And he felt on his face that blazing fire of the sun that had seemed to burn him the night before, and he fell dead, but bearing on his face, as a sign of the power of the star, a golden mask. And the Huaca Pintada of Illimo was decorated by the Sun himself and the golden mask found in the Huaca at the beginning of this century was that of Anto Tunga, punished in this way by the star because of his refusal to adore it, because he did not wish to establish the new religion of the Incas in the Yunga towns, and as a certain warning of the coming conquest of the victors from Cuzco.

Huaca del Oro

Another mural that must have been of great importance and interest, also discovered in the department of Lambayeque, was described and published by Mario Florián (1951). It is unfortunate that his language is essentially literary and not as precise as necessary in these cases. He approached the problem from the artistic standpoint and, lacking training, could not separate reality from fantasy, so that his writing, while undeniably useful as the only evidence we have, leaves great gaps and many unanswered questions. Florián maintains that he discovered this painting, which is not true (1951, p. 2). It was found in 1948 by Richard Schaedel, who, in the course of an archaeological survey of the zone, even took some photographs. Later Mario Florián, then an inspector for the Patronato Nacional de Arqueología, cleaned off the wall and published his observations in 1951 (Kosok, 1965, pp. 163, 165).

The painting was found in a very large monument known as the Huaca del Oro, located close to and on the right side of the Leche River (Kosok, 1965, p. 165). Only the top part of the motif was visible when Schaedel found the painting, the other half covered by rubble (fig. 82). Florián explains that when he carried out his work, only a few details could be discerned (basically the eyes, nose, and mouth) of a figure whose general outlines were barely visible. It was located on the back of the wall forming the eastern façade of the monument, which faced a great plaza and was covered by fallen adobes and sand. He had to excavate to see the figure, which remained incomplete since several parts, especially the top of the head, had been destroyed by weathering. The wall upon which the painting was found must have measured 3–4 m high. While the only figure remaining was the "anthropomorphic and idealized supreme Deity," as Florián calls it, apparently the entire eastern façade of the Huaca del Oro was originally decorated with paintings of which there were still vestiges in 1950.

The measurements of the figure were 1.85 m high with a maximum width of 1.32 m (for further detail I refer the reader to Florián's article). Florián suggests that it must have been larger, since surely the personage must have been wearing some sort of "diadem or miter," so that it might have measured as much as 2.5 m in height. Florián's article contains two illustrations of the figure, one on the cover and the other on page 9. They do not agree entirely, and I have assumed that the one in the text should be the more exact. Therefore, all succeeding references are to that figure, which I have reproduced here as fig. 83.

According to Florián, the head of the figure was truncated, the "face was relatively hemispherical," and the forehead, ears, and half of the left eye could not be seen. The eyes are circular, indicated by three very regular concentric areas. The toothless mouth is half open, with an elongated form "slightly narrower in the center and widening at the ends" (Florián, 1951, p. 7). He attri-

Fig. 82.
*Huaca del Oro, Lambayeque, top portion of mural as discovered
by Schaedel in 1948. While within the Chimú tradition,
it probably dates to the end of the Middle Horizon.*

Fig. 83.
Huaca del Oro, Florián's drawing of the mural, of no value as documentation.

the base angles of the first and second 1 solitary feather and 4 longer ornamental ones from the third or last. Painted white with a blue border, the earrings display 3 small, elliptical, gold beads, one set in the center of each stylized tail. (Florián, 1951, p. 7)

Of none of this is there evidence in Florián's drawing; there is only a single loose element in the upper right part, which does not correspond to the description.

The personage is dressed in a sort of *uncu* or tunic, which reaches to the bottom of the trunk. From the drawing the middle of this garment is decorated with a series of circular elements and the borders with geometric elements. There appears to be a series of feathers hanging from the bottom of the *uncu* like a fringe. On each side of the tunic is a pendent tassel, and behind the personage hangs a broad, pendent element, which may have been correctly identified as a *huara*, or breechcloth, but might be a continuation of the tunic (Florián, 1951, p. 8). The figure lacks upper arms; "they may have been hidden—doubled up inside the wide sleeves of the *unku* or, perhaps, stretched upward at the sides of the head to hold the tiara, but erased by the effects of rain-borne mud on the wall" (Florián, 1951, p. 10). The legs are represented apart and slightly bent, the feet in profile with the toes pointing outward. In the drawing all these elements are represented with quite even, broad lines exaggerating the muscular curvature. From Florián's fantastic description it is hard to imagine how the feet were really represented; I prefer to quote him directly.

> The form of the feet and ankles is like metallic anklets—rectangles with white and red bands touched with dark blue—where 2 large round golden beads of yellow with blue-white center are accompanied—in a horizontal line and to the sides, by other smaller golden beads of irregular shape and with the same coloration as the large ones. These anklets exhibit at their ends at the edge of the open space, somewhat curved, colorful feathers set one above the other, painted white with a blue outline and with spaces—between feather and feather—clearly red; a bunch of feathers suggesting the form of a plume or better the feathered tarsi of a raptorial bird. (Unless these ornamental signs represent the curved claws of a feline—jaguar or puma—which would be explained by an Andean artistic ancestry.) [The personage is standing on a] *base, support or pedestal. . . .* (Florián, 1951, p. 11)

The colors used in the painting were "old-rose, red, Indian-red, white, dark blue, natural sienna and king-yellow on a red ground" (Florián, 1951, p. 6). Kosok mentions only red, yellow, and blue-black (1965, p. 165). The execution of the painting, according to Florián,

butes to it "an air of similarity to a feline mouth," but the drawing reveals a geometric regularity at odds with that description. The nose also is described as "a small, white, irregular space," while the drawing shows a regular, geometric inverted step shape. From the lower edge of the eyes "descend the curves of two tear lines" (Florián, 1951, p. 7), which are nowhere visible on the figure. In a display of fantasy, Florián associates them with the falcon symbols described by Yakovleff (1932). A broad band bordering the lower part of the face is interpreted as a chinstrap, possibly attached to some headgear, but, judging from the drawing, it could be part of the garment worn by the personage. This white band is divided into four parts by transverse stripes. Of the "diadem or miter" that the author assumes the personage to have worn, there is no evidence whatsoever. He continues:

> From the hidden ears there hang, brushing the sleeve area, two somewhat ornithomorphic earrings: three motifs of geometrically stylized open bird tails which broaden progressively toward their end; pendent from

demonstrates ability and technical knowledge. His interpretation of the motif is not worth mentioning, being largely fantasy. His comparison with the "Illimo knife" is very forced.

When I consulted Richard Schaedel about the mural, he thought that Florián's drawing contained "some variations in the form of the arms and the shirt" (personal communication, May 1974).

In the 1948 photograph (fig. 82) only the top half of the figure, part of the face, and part of the *uncu* are visible. The upper part of the face was destroyed and there was no evidence of a "diadem or miter." The proportions of the face are slightly different in the drawing from those of the original. The nose is nonexistent in the photograph and the eyes, while circular, are totally different in both size and composition; they are represented by two concentric circles, the inner painted a solid dark color and the outer ring white. In Florián's illustration, in contrast, they appear composed of three elements. There are no traces that can be interpreted as "tear lines," and the mouth, apparently correct in general form, seems too symmetrical. The part Florián calls a chinstrap and I consider to be the upper border of the *uncu* looks solid white in the photograph, with no division into segments. I suspect that the white paint scaled off in some places, leading to Florián's faulty interpretation. The "ear ornaments" seem to be part of the *uncu* decoration, like the other circular elements that adorn it. Their representation is exactly like that of the personage's eyes, that is, white with a dark inner circle, and not as Florián saw them. Nor are they as regular as they appear in Florián's reproduction. I surmise that the lower part of the drawing is an imaginative reconstruction by the author. Florián also greatly exaggerated the cracks in the wall bearing the mural.

In April 1974, I visited and examined the Huaca del Oro. Using Florián's description and directions from Jorge Rondón, it was very easy to locate the wall that had originally held the painting. Florián's location is correct, but absolutely nothing remains of the motif. Only on the lower part, almost at floor level and covered by fallen materials, I found a small section with the remains of painting that must have belonged to the outlines of the lost mural. Little could be observed at the site. I verified that the colored substances were applied on a fine plaster finish, which was first covered with a red ground color. The tones identified were: red-brown, E-32 to F-32; white, A-81; and bright brown, E-68. I also noted that there were still almost imperceptible traces of paintings on the top part of the *huaca*.

As I have mentioned, there are not only serious contradictions and inexactitudes between Florián's text and his drawing but also elements described in the text that do not show in the drawing. Using what few sources there are on this topic, I think some valid conclusions can be reached. For this purpose it is important to compare the Huaca Pintada figure published by Carrión Cachot (fig. 81) to the Huaca del Oro motif drawn by Florián nine years later (fig. 83). Examining both with care, it will be seen that while the Huaca Pintada drawing has secondary flanking figures with no counterpart in the Huaca del Oro drawing, the central personage of the first not only greatly resembles the second in general conception but is identical to it in many details.

Florián suggested that the Huaca del Oro personage must have had a "diadem or miter," although there was no evidence for it. Why, or as a function of what, did he reach this conclusion? I do not know, but the figure illustrated by Carrión Cachot does wear a headdress. Florián's description of the mouth of his personage does not relate to the form in which it is represented in his drawing but is identical to the mouth shown in the Carrión Cachot article. His description of the nose disagrees with his drawing but relates rather well to the form represented in fig. 81. Florián describes two "ear ornaments" that do not exist in his drawing, but his text corresponds well to the two pendants on the personage of the Huaca Pintada. Florián also compares his personage to the one on the "Illimo knife" with no further commentary; it is surely significant that that artifact is not only illustrated by Carrión but is basic to her entire argument regarding the lunar deity of the Chimú. Kosok made a seldom-read statement regarding his figure 42, a reproduction of Florián's drawing: "A similar frieze was found 20 years ago in the Huaca Pintada, near Túcume, but has been destroyed" (Kosok, 1965, p. 165). He doubtless refers to the mural published by Carrión Cachot. Although Kosok's work was published in 1965, his observations and field notes were made in 1948 and 1949 at the time that Schaedel found the Huaca del Oro mural and shortly after Carrión Cachot had reported on the presumed murals of the Huaca Pintada. Kosok may have mentioned this similarity to Florián, who later used it.

Given the disagreements between Florián's text and illustrations, we cannot tell which most closely fits the truth. In my opinion, he saw the painting, took either no notes or very few, depending on his memory to describe it, and finally used as an aid the figure published years earlier by Rebeca Carrión Cachot, with whom, for professional reasons, Florián was in close contact. The illustration is clearly a drawing, like the one of the Huaca Pintada figure, and not a tracing, so that it does not provide concrete evidence.

It is hard to decide when this mural was painted. Kauffman Doig considers it Chimú (1964, p. 62; 1970, p. 402), while Florián, in chronologically unintelligible language, assigns it to "a *Coastal-Andean Artistic Period* influenced by the aesthetic norms of Tiahuanaco: a *Muchic (or Chimú) Tiahuanacoid Artistic Period*" (1951, p. 13). From its relationship to the Huaca Pintada motif and from the illustrations, I am inclined to place it in the last phases of the Middle Horizon within the Chimú artistic tradition but with concepts taken from the secular Huari style.

Kauffmann Doig has also illustrated Florián's drawing and, as early as 1964, stated that "approximately 10 years ago" it was already gone (1964, p. 62; 1970, fig. 682). Thus we may infer that the painting vanished shortly after Florián's publication. In this case the mural was destroyed by natural forces, not by man, but the various questions I have raised must remain unanswered.

The paintings of the Huaca Colorada, which Florián refers to, should also be mentioned. He notes the presence of "fragments of mural friezes—sculptural and incised" (1951, p. 4). The monument still exists and is located not far north of the Huaca del Oro. It is also known as the Huaca del Horno, from the remains of burnt adobe that are to be seen there. At present there are no signs of the reported paintings.

Huaca Corte

In 1980, again in the area of Batán Grande, the Princeton University archaeological project made a discovery of great interest at the Huaca Corte. I refer to the remains of a valuable mural, which is not only revealing from the stylistic standpoint but can also be properly integrated into a carefully controlled and excavated archaeological context.

According to Izumi Shimada, director of the Batan Grande—La Leche Project, there are at least two major construction phases associated with Classic Lambayeque ceramics at the principal pyramid at Huaca Corte (1981, p. 43).

> The original pyramid was built on a foundation of adobe chambers filled with loose rubble and refuse. A major north-south wall with polychrome murals ran the full length of the pyramid (about 40 meters) and probably acted as a backdrop for activities. At a later date this wall was removed, its fragments used as fill for later construction which increased the height and length of the mound, and another backdrop wall was built. The few preserved mural designs . . . seem to be parts of elaborate headdresses or clothing. . . . (Shimada, 1981, p. 43)

It was not on the pyramid, however, but on another wall that the most impressive paintings were preserved. "Several mural panels, clearly of Classic Lambayeque style in six colors identical to those in the principal pyramid, were exposed" (Shimada, 1981, p. 44).

> The murals from Huaca Corte are all copied from a major north-south running adobe wall which had been cut in several places by huaqueros with the result that much of the murals have already been destroyed. I believe this wall enclosed the burial precinct and three principal mounds arranged in a U-form. The wall still stands about 1 to 1½ meters in some places. However, all the murals recorded occurred close to floor level within a meter above the floor. (Izumi Shimada, personal communication, 1981)

Thus, there was apparently a large mural, which, because of looting activity, we know only partially. There are some stepped motifs (pl. 22, fig. 84) together with other designs that are also geometric, although not clearly defined (pl. 22, figs. 84, 85). These elements probably bordered both the top and bottom of the mural. Among the motifs are very stylized human heads (figs. 84, 85). In one sector the remains of a representation of a standing human personage were found (fig. 86), with only the lower part of the body, from the knees down, preserved. It appears to have bare feet, which are turned out so that the heels are together. While details of the left foot are not visible, the right is complete, and clearly discernible is the fact that the artist, whether through carelessness or by intention, painted six toes rather than five. A band at the ankles might indicate body painting.

One detail that distinguishes this mural from others in the same area, as well as from those of other time periods, is the carelessness with which it was executed. In the first place it seems that the artist did not plan each motif for the space it was to fill but simply started to paint, adjusting the motifs to the area remaining as the work progressed. In the second place, there is no uniformity of line; it is narrow in some cases and thick in others. Finally, no attention was paid to the surface finish. The mural does not appear to be the work of a professional. The lines are irregular, the outline unsteady;

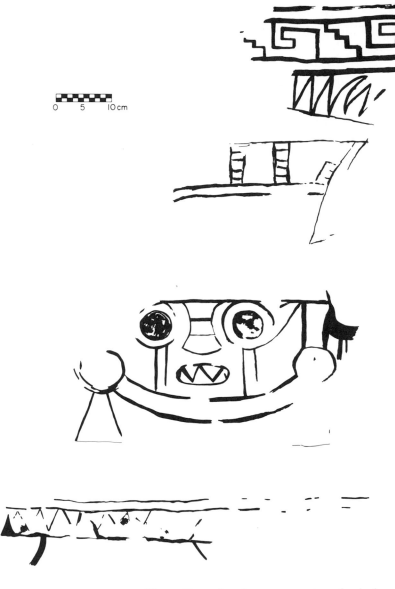

Fig. 84.
Huaca Corte, Lambayeque, portion of polychrome mural showing head with elaborate headdress and border elements. End of Middle Horizon 4.

there is no symmetry or purity. All this diminishes the painting and is, moreover, remarkable, since normally the anonymous prehispanic artist who executed the mural decorations was a skilled artisan with a sure and elegant line.

The colors employed in all the murals were light green, black, white, ochre, red, and maroon. Since the study is still in progress, the pigments have not yet been analyzed (Izumi Shimada, personal communication, 1981).

Shimada informed me that their

careful architectural survey of Huaca Corte indicated that the wall and murals are contemporaneous with the final phase of occupation at the principal pyramid of Huaca Corte. This pyramid was burned and the charcoal provided a carbon-14 date of 985 ± 65 (Beta-1802). This date is in perfect agreement with other carbon-14 dates of the Classic Lambayeque sites in Batan Grande. Our recent ceramic analysis, however, indicates the distinctive Classic Lambayeque style had emerged by 850 A.D., if not earlier. The style is clearly distinct from Chimu and indigenous to the Batan Grande area, although it has its roots in Moche, Huari and Pachacamac

Fig. 85.
*Huaca Corte, portion of mural with head similar
to that in fig. 84.*

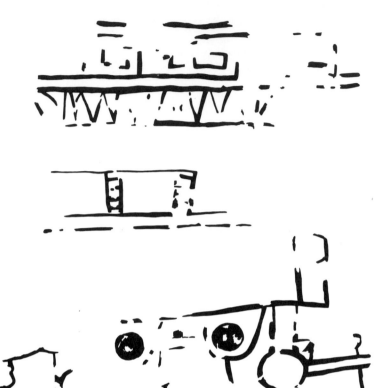

Fig. 86.
*Huaca Corte, portion of mural portraying feet and legs
of human figure.*

styles. Influence from Pachacamac appears to have been more important than anticipated. (Personal communication, 1981)

Thus, Shimada considers the Huaca Corte complex to have been a "religious and elite burial center," which functioned between about A.D. 850 and 1050 (Shimada, 1981, p. 43).

A stylistic analysis of the motifs of this painting would doubtless reveal that the stepped elements are copied from or influenced by the Moche culture. Shimada's identification of the human faces with the funerary masks of the Classic Lambayeque style is clearly correct (1981, p. 44, caption p. 42), and they are further related to the pottery representations of the so-called *huaco rey* (king vase?) common in the Lambayeque area (Zevallos Quiñones, 1971). The "winged eye" is an archaism deriving from at least the late phases of Moche or perhaps earlier, since we find it on the "great priestess" of Pañamarca (figs. 41, 43) and on the mural of the third repainting phase at the Huaca de la Luna at Moche (fig. 68). Its relationship to Moche is evident in the Huaca Pintada mural (Schaedel, 1978, p. 32). This element diffused with the Middle Horizon Huari expansion. On the other hand, the treatment of the feet of the standing personage at Huaca Corte (fig. 86) is typical of southern Middle Horizon manifestations from the earliest epochs of that period. All these are elements foreign to the Lambayeque area that combined with local traditions to form the Lambayeque style.

As noted above, Shimada considers the findings of the Batan Grande—La Leche Project to establish the essential independence of the Classic Lambayeque style from the Chimú style to the south. "The rapid evolution of the Classic Lambayeque style—with its characteristic 'comma' shaped eyes and pointed ears—during Middle Horizon times, seems closely related to the expansion of agriculture in the Lambayeque Valley Complex, as well as the initiation of large-scale mining and metallurgical activities in the Leche Valley" (Shimada, 1981, p. 44). I am in general agreement with Shimada's position and the need to reassess the problem of the cultural sequence and its content in the Lambayeque area. The commonly accepted idea of seeking direct connections between the Chimú and Lambayeque styles should be abandoned. This point has already been noted several times by students of the Peruvian past. Now is neither the time nor the place to enter into a long discursion; suffice it to recall that Seler (1893) was probably the first to point in this direction and that Larco Hoyle very clearly set apart

the "Lambayeque Culture" when he established his chronology of the north coast (1948). It is also a position espoused by local scholars, one I have often heard defended by Jorge Rondón both formally and informally, and when Jorge Zevallos Quiñones undertook to define the "pottery of the Lambayeque culture," he wrote: "not only do its general shapes belong to *original* patterns, different from those used by other regional cultures, but so does the spirit of their decoration . . ." (1971, p. 15; emphasis added). Moreover, the chronological chart in the same work coincides in general with the data that have resulted from Shimada's research.

In my opinion the Huaca Corte painting is later than those of the Huaca Pintada and the Huaca del Oro, and dates to the end of Middle Horizon 4. It is the only known example of mural painting that can be directly connected to the Lambayeque style, except for the Huaca Pintada painting reported by Carrión Cachot, if it really exists. The other murals are one way or another related to Chimú art, the purest example being the Túcume paintings. All of them form part of the Moche tradition and show the continuity of a style that began in the Early Horizon.

Chornancap

One of the most remarkable documents of mural art, in both its state of preservation and its thematic richness, was discovered in the lower Lambayeque Valley in 1981 by Christopher Donnan. Donnan has most generously provided me his notes, drawings, and photographs for inclusion in this book. The following description and discussion is based entirely on Donnan's materials (ms.).

I have purposely placed these paintings at the end of this chapter because I consider them to represent a problem *sui generis*. They represent the only case so far that is entirely separate stylistically from those with which I have dealt so far.

The paintings are located in the Chornancap complex between the Panamerican Highway and the Pacific Ocean, approximately one kilometer from the famous Huaca Chotuna. This complex comprises a great platform mound surrounded by various structures that are now covered by sand (fig. 87). The paintings were found in the area immediately north of the principal monument, an area of structures including rooms, corridors, and courtyards that were covered by a deep accumulation of sand. The evidence of structural superposition reflects a long period of occupation. The paintings were

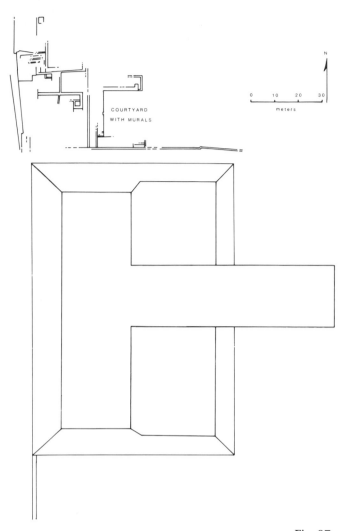

COURTYARD
WITH MURALS

Fig. 87.
*Chornancap, Lambayeque, site plan showing relationship
of murals to the* huaca.

placed on one of the early buildings, although not the earliest.

The murals adorned the inner walls of a large open courtyard (fig. 88). The eastern side of this space has been destroyed by erosion, but the north, west, and part of the southern sides remain. In the center of the west wall is a sort of broad vertical channel of unknown function, which divides the wall into two sections. The murals were not painted on the entire wall, but only within a sunken horizontal panel, approximately 45 cm high, near the top. The panel is 2.65 m above the floor of the courtyard and runs the entire length of the preserved walls, broken only on the west wall by the aforemen-

tioned vertical channel. The top of the wall was probably finished in a small cornice, and the rest of the wall was painted white. The sunken panel has been preserved only on the western and southern walls, since the top of the north wall has been destroyed; but there were presumably murals there too.

Six colors were used in painting the murals: red, yellow, dark green, light green, black, and white. Analysis has shown them all to be mineral pigments.

To execute these paintings, red ground paint was first applied to the vertical face and lower horizontal surface of the sunken panel, while the upper horizontal surface was painted yellow; the motifs were then applied to the vertical face. No incised lines were found, but if the artist had used charcoal to outline the motifs before painting them, its traces could have been lost.

In the execution of the painting the artist first applied yellow directly to the red surface. The next color was white, usually painted directly onto the red base without overlapping the yellow. Then the two shades of green were added. They are fugitive and have spalled off in many areas; only slight residues remain of the dark green. The greens were generally painted over areas already colored either yellow or white, although in some cases they were applied directly to the red ground. The light and dark green were used in different parts of the design, for example, light green for feet and dark green for the lower part of the tunic (pl. 23). Some triangular elements probably representing tassels, like those in front and in back of personage 36 (pl. 24), have both shades of green in parallel stripes. Black was applied last and in a thicker coat than the other colors and often shows traces of brush strokes. It may have been prepared thicker to cover the colors over which it was painted. Black was used to provide detail and to outline the green, yellow, and white areas. This sequence applies to the whole mural and, together with the stylistic unity, suggests that the entire painting was made at one time.

Considering the entire scene, we find that there is a difference between the objects and activities painted on the south wall (fig. 89) and those on the west (figs. 90, 91). On the south wall, the only personage with human characteristics is no. 5, who is only partly visible; the rest are anthropomorphic birds (pl. 25). Personages 1 and 3 carry indefinable objects in their hands, and apparently so does personage 4, although its upper part is worn; at its feet is a jar. Human personage no. 5 seems to be represented fullface and gives the impression of holding something, which may well be plants, in each hand. Donnan suggests (ms.) that figure no. 6 may have

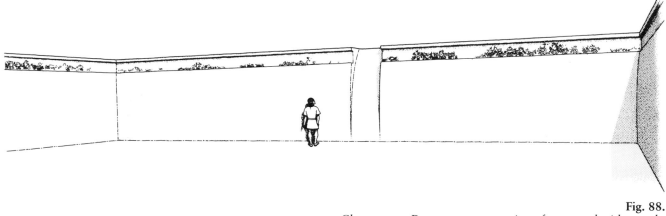

Fig. 88.
Chornancap, Donnan reconstruction of courtyard with murals.

been similar to no. 5. It is difficult to interpret the series of oblong elements to the right of personage 7. Donnan thinks it may be part of the representation of a plant, with a central staff or trunk and similar oblong objects to the left of personage 8 (fig. 92).

The mural on the west wall seems to represent a different theme: a series of personages associated with trophy heads. With a single exception, all are standing, and in most cases their feet point toward the center channel. Personages 15, 18, and 22 are facing away from the central division, personage 25 is in frontal position with his feet pointed outward (fig. 93), and personage 27 seems to be lying down but with his head fullface (fig. 94). Donnan considers all figures in the west wall scene to be human except no. 26, which has a tail, and the bird in front of personage 31. I think, however, that except for the bird between personages 30 and 31 (pl. 26), all the figures are anthropomorphic, but among them are two categories. Some are human, like 34, 38 (pl. 27), and 41 (fig. 95), and perhaps 27; the rest have human bodies

but animal faces. This distinction is ambiguous in many personages on both sides of the channel, since they are very weathered or incomplete (Donnan, ms.).

The majority of the personages carry or are next to a trophy head. However, there are some who are distinctive. Thus, no. 29 (pl. 23) carries two elements that could be darts, 37 (pl. 24) has, in his (apparently right) hand what could be a club, and 40 (pl. 27) and 43 hold something difficult to define, which Donnan thinks could be a whip or sling. There are some objects in the hands of other personages (e.g., no. 38 in pl. 27) that cannot be identified.

No clearly associated material has been found to permit chronological placement of the mural. Donnan thinks that it is difficult to assign it either stylistically or chronologically. He believes, nevertheless, that there are some elements suggesting that the mural belongs to the Early Chimú style, dating to between A.D. 750 and 900. The first such element he mentions is the animal head that hangs back over the shoulders of many figures and

Fig. 89.
Chornancap, mural from south wall, including figures 1–8. End of Middle Horizon.

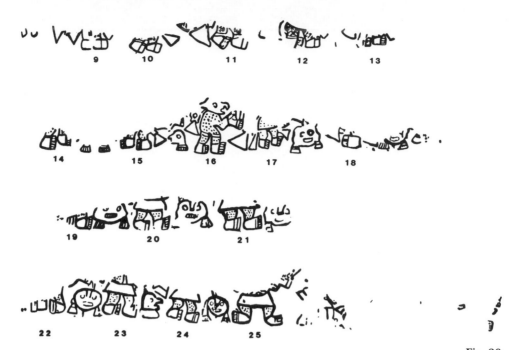

Fig. 90.
*Chornancap, mural from west wall to left of cleft,
including figures 9–25. End of Middle Horizon.*

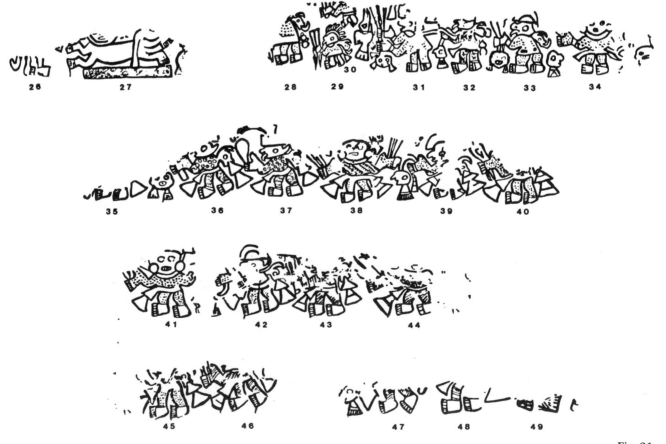

Fig. 91.
*Chornancap, mural from west wall to the right of cleft,
including figures 26–49. End of Middle Horizon.*

▲ Fig. 92.
Chornancap, detail of mural from south wall showing
"plant" between personages 7 and 8 and part of
personage 8. Middle Horizon 4?

▼ Fig. 93.
Chornancap, detail of mural from left side of west wall,
showing personage 25. Middle Horizon 4?

Fig. 94.
*Chornancap, detail of mural on right side of west wall,
showing personage 27. Middle Horizon 4?*

has a tongue that curves upward and ears pointed forward (e.g., pls. 26, 28). This representation appears frequently in Lambayeque pottery decoration and is often seen on the right and left sides of the well-known "king vases" of that culture, except that in such cases this motif always has the characteristic "winged" or "comma-shaped" eye, which does not occur at all in this mural. Donnan also notes "remarkable similarities between the Chornancap murals and certain Pacatnamu textiles" from the Jequetepeque Valley, including one that represents figures he sees as resembling nos. 1 and 5 of the Chornancap south wall mural (pl. 25; Donnan, 1984, p. 36).

The purpose of the Chornancap mural remains an enigma to Donnan. He considers that the scene on the south wall, with birds and possible plants, might relate to agriculturally connected religious phenomena. The scene on the other wall, which is associated with trophy heads, an element also appearing on some Pacatnamú textiles, seems to represent a procession, and the two-part division marked by the channel suggests that the architectural aspect was fundamentally important (Donnan, ms.).

One very important point noted by Donnan is that the mural was purposely covered at some time following its use. In fact, another wall was built in front of the one bearing the mural, and the intervening space filled with rubble, apparently broken adobes, so placed that the paintings were not damaged (Donnan, ms.).

I have no argument with Donnan's description; this is clearly one of the rare cases in which a good study has been made of a mural painting. The points where I dis-

Fig. 95.
*Chornancap, detail from right side of mural on west wall,
including personage 41 and part of 40.
Middle Horizon 4?*

agree are his statement that "it is difficult to assign either stylistic or chronological attribution to the mural," and his subsequent identification of it as Early Chimú. (The term Early Chimú has been applied to various manifestations of Andean archaeology. Donnan and Mackey give it a very specific typological meaning [Donnan and Mackey, 1978, pp. 215–89], for which I direct the reader to that source. I shall discuss this point later, indicating my disagreement with their position.) As I have said more than once, the criteria traditionally employed to establish chronologies based on ceramic traits are not entirely applicable to mural art. Nevertheless, there are stylistic criteria that may be used, although without absolute certainty, to provide an approximation, and I believe a close one, to correct chronological placement. The greatest difficulty lies in the fact not only that we

have few examples of mural art, but that even these are incomplete, so that in many cases, like Chornancap, we are faced with unique examples to which no direct comparison is possible.

We have seen that the late manifestations of north coast mural art present essentially two well-defined tendencies: the Huaca Corte paintings, which relate to the Lambayeque style, and those of Túcume and the Huaca del Oro, which fall within the Moche tradition and are related rather to the Chimú style. Now I do not consider the Chornancap mural to fall within either of these two tendencies. Rather it represents a distinct manifestation, so far the northernmost, which is related to the last of the Middle Horizon styles.

In the first place, there is nothing in the Chornancap paintings that can be defined as Mochicoid. They are entirely outside the canons of the Moche tradition. In fact, not only is the treatment of the figures foreign to the Moche style, but one of the classic rules of that style is violated, namely the play of different figure sizes to differentiate hierarchies and provide a sense of perspective. Moreover, the Moche artistic tradition is more detailed and the execution of the figures more agile, with more movement within a given context.

In the second place, there is an emphasis on the trophy head motif at Chornancap. While not entirely foreign to the Moche style, this is not at all one of its common motifs, but rather exceptional. Trophy heads appear associated almost exclusively with that deity I have called the "Sacrificing God." Moreover, from the technical point of view, incisions were not used to outline the motifs, a usage so far found in all murals painted by Moche artists. Moreover, the Moche palette is more colorful, brighter, not dull like the Chornancap mural, and does not use so much green.

Donnan (ms.) places great emphasis on the aforementioned animal head, and uses it as an important element in trying to relate the Chornancap mural to the Chimú and Lambayeque styles. Undeniably this element appears in Chimú art (both textile and ceramic) and is very common in the Lambayeque style, where it is a basic component of both "king vases" and the metal recipients upon which the "king vases" were based and from which they were copied. Donnan is also correct in his discussion of the eye treatment: Chornancap eyes are round, while in the Chimú and Lambayeque styles, eyes are usually "winged." But it must be remembered that the "winged eye" is historically earlier, already occurring in Moche.

In my opinion, the simple fact that an element appears in a given style is not enough to establish a relationship. The history of the element must be sought and its antecedents analyzed. The animal head is an element whose history has evidently not been traced, but it appears to have originated in the south, perhaps during the first epochs of the Middle Horizon, and then spread to the north in modified form at the same time that other southern influences appear in the various local styles as a result of the spread of the Huari empire. Donnan's suggested relationship between the Chornancap mural and some Pacatnamú textiles rests in part on a scarflike element, terminating in these animal heads, around the neck of some personages on the textiles. But it is important to recognize that the same element occurs on late textiles from the central coast that are not exactly Chimú in style, even though they date to the Late Intermediate

Period. The history of this animal head as a terminal on tassels or "scarves" should certainly be traced, but so should its occurrence in other contexts, for example, as ear ornaments on a Late Intermediate Period textile from Pachacámac illustrated by Schmidt (1929, Tafel XVII). I also think there are earlier variants of this element, possibly including the head with a forked tongue that terminates the belt of the "great priestess" of Pañamarca (figs. 41, 42, 43).

With regard to the trophy head, an important element in the Chornancap mural, while it may not be totally foreign to the northern tradition, it is not typical either. As Proulx noted (1971), all indications are that the custom of taking trophy heads, which I believe to have originated in the tropical rain forest, is reflected in the early styles of the south coast. It is first found in the final phases of the Ocucaje style and is typical of the Nasca style. It is almost surely through the great Nasca influence on Huari that the trophy head became an important element in that religious system. The trophy head is, in fact, a frequent element in the Huari styles (e.g., Schmidt, 1929, Tafel VI). With Huari expansion the representation of trophy heads spread throughout the central Andean region without losing its close relationship to religious phenomena. In the Late Intermediate Period, at least on the central coast, the trophy head frequently appears in the hand of a personage who carries a staff in the other (Schmidt, 1929, p. 476, fig. 1), indicating the importance of the personage in the theogony of the time. Thus we see a clear influence of Middle Horizon religious ideas in the execution of the Chornancap mural. The idea of a group of humans in a procession bearing trophy heads goes back to Nasca and occurs frequently on the south and central coast. Such a scene is found on a textile from Ancón that could well date to the end of the Middle Horizon or early epochs of the Late Intermediate Period (Schmidt, 1929, p. 503). It shows a series of personages, each dragging another by the hair with one hand and holding a trophy head in the other. Here also one of the personages bears a staff in one hand, as did the one mentioned above. The scene on this Ancón weaving is obviously not the same as the one in the Chornancap mural, but it may have been inspired by the same idea.

Donnan (ms.) suggests that the Chornancap motifs may have been copied from textiles. I do not share this opinion, since I do not see the presence of shared form in the personages of the Lambayeque paintings. There is nowhere the rectilinear and angular treatment characteristic of plectomorphic forms, as Semper called them, which unnecessarily copied the limitations of warp and weft to which the weaver is subject. In mural art this textile loan is very rare, but clearly visible in the first phase of the painting found at the Huaca de la Luna (figs. 62, 63). Thus, if there was any loan in the Chornancap case, it must have been in the opposite direction, from mural to textile.

I consider the Chornancap painting to be closely related to what Larco Hoyle called Huari Norteño B (1948, pp. 40–42). I believe Menzel is correct in placing the origin of this epigone of Huari, which has been mistakenly called Santa, in the Huarmey Valley. The treatment of the Chornancap hands and feet, as well as the animal head, is typical of various Middle Horizon styles. But there is something in the mural that is foreign to the Huari style: the dots and little circles with which the bodies of the personages are filled. And this feature is typical of Huari Norteño B (e.g., Amano, 1961, fig. 13; PESCA Perú, 1981, fig. 184). Unfortunately, Menzel did not describe these late styles in her seminal study of the Huari problem (1964), and we do not yet have any detailed study or even a good catalog illustrating this very late Middle Horizon manifestation. But I have had the opportunity to see many ceramic vessels of this style, especially from Huarmey, and I find a startling similarity to the Chornancap mural not only in the treatment of the motifs but also in the general coloration, with dark, rather dull tones predominating. There are even some similarities between personage no. 16 of the Chornancap mural (fig. 96) and the one on a typical Huari Norteño B vessel published by Larco Hoyle (1948, p. 41 far right). This same personage seems to be represented on a painted cloth found at Pachacámac (Schmidt, 1929, p. 508, fig. 3), which dates to the end of the Middle Horizon.

Moreover, Larco Hoyle himself remarked that one of the most characteristic motifs of this northern mode of Huari "is that of an individual with open arms . . ."

Fig. 96.
Chornancap, detail from left side of mural on west wall, including personage 16 and parts of 15 and 17. Middle Horizon 4?

(1948, p. 42), which recalls personages 34, 38, and 41 at Chornancap. As I noted earlier, Larco Hoyle astutely separated Huari Norteño B from what he called the Lambayeque style. In this regard it is worth noting that the Lambayeque style, in at least one of its phases, shows a clear persistence of Moche influence (Zevallos Quiñones, 1971, unnumbered illustration of "Tipo A"), which is not found in specimens of the Huari Norteño B style. And, as I have already commented, Moche influence is totally absent in the Chornancap mural. Here I must clarify one point to avoid confusion. It can be noted that what Donnan and Mackey call Early Chimu (1978, pp. 215–89 and especially pls. 12, 13) is quite close to what Larco Hoyle called "Huari-Lambayeque" (1948, pp. 45–47), but they include some press-molded elements that are apparently contemporary but not mentioned by Larco Hoyle. The chronological placement of these late Middle Horizon styles has not been defined. It is very possible that for a time the style called Huari-Lambayeque by Larco Hoyle and Early Chimu by Donnan and Mackey coexisted with Larco Hoyle's Huari Norteño B; that is, they may be placed in Middle Horizon Epoch 4, as suggested by Patricia Lyon (personal communication, 1983), with whom I have discussed this matter and with whom I agree. But they are different stylistically and originate in different areas: while Huari Norteño B almost surely arose on the north-central coast (the Huarmey area), Huari-Lambayeque is northern, as its very name implies. This matter requires a much more detailed discussion than is possible here, but it is evident that my position differs from Donnan's.

If I am correct in relating this fine example of mural painting from Lambayeque to the Huari Norteño B style, it would then date to the end of Middle Horizon 4. This placement is very interesting, since it suggests the simultaneous proliferation on the north coast of multiple religious manifestations at the time of the transition from the Middle Horizon to the Late Intermediate Period. Perhaps we find here a struggle among priesthoods seeking supremacy through the imposition of new patterns, many of them foreign to the zone, with roots probably far to the south, in the birth of the Huari phenomenon and even earlier. It is clear that there is urgent need for a study of this material to separate and understand these convergent traditions.

I shall not venture to interpret the meaning of the Chornancap paintings. The theme represented on the south wall may be different from that on the west wall, as Donnan suggests. His impression that the former may be related to agricultural activities while the second seems rather to represent some procession related to the trophy-head cult may be correct. As Donnan himself states, however, the true message of these scenes continues to be an enigma.

—6—
Late Manifestations on the Central Coast

On the central coast the remains of murals dating to the period between the fall of the Huari empire and the Inca conquest are not widely reported. While such paintings clearly existed, they seem to have been largely covered or destroyed by later construction—Inca, colonial, and modern—and by the expansion of irrigated fields into what were formerly built-up areas.

THE LURÍN VALLEY

In the lower part of the Lurín Valley is the urban complex of Pachacámac, which housed an oracle, one of the most important if not the most important on the coast (fig. 97). It is also one of the most important archaeological sites in Peru, with a continuous occupation of ap-

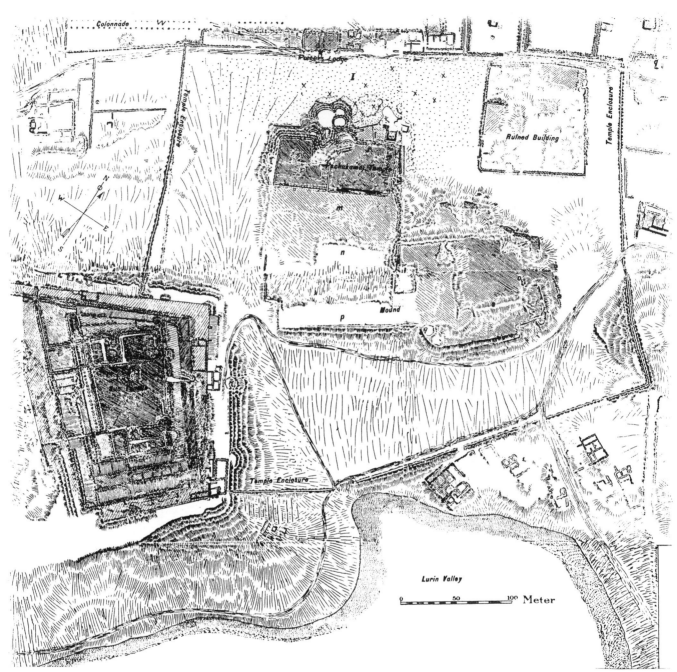

Fig. 97.
Pachacámac, detail of southern section of the site including the Temple of Pachacámac (upper center) and the Temple of the Sun (lower left). The painted terraces are on the northwestern face of the Temple of Pachacámac.

proximately fifteen hundred years.

Pachacámac must have been truly impressive in all its color and attracted the attention of the first Spaniards to see it. Miguel de Estete, chronicler of Hernando Pizarro in 1533, expressed obvious admiration when he spoke of "a fine house, well painted," within which was the image of the god Pachacámac, who was worshipped there (Jérez, 1938, p. 85). Later, when he passed through the site in 1547, Cieza de León reported that the Temple of Pachacámac "had many doors which, together with the walls, were painted with figures of wild animals" (Cieza de León, *Crónica*, cap. LXXII; 1922, p. 239). Some of these paintings were still visible in the first half of the seventeenth century, since Cobo, referring to the Temple of the Sun,[1] says:

> In these buildings there were many rooms, chambers and cells, which were like chapels in which the idols were placed and the priests and minister lived. Thus the walls of these quarters, as well as those of the terraces and of the other buildings embraced by this great structure, were plastered with earth and paint of several colors, with many curious designs to their taste, although crude to ours, and various figures of animals, poorly formed as was everything these Indians painted. . . .
>
> Although many doorways full of varied paintings can be seen in the façades and outer walls of this great temple, to climb up to it there was only one, with a long stairway of dry-laid fieldstone with such low risers that, although it was very long, it was mounted effortlessly. This entrance fell on the landward side, that is, to the east, and the stairway made ten or twelve turns with their landings and highly painted doorways at each turn. (Cobo, *Historia*, lib. 13, cap. XVII; 1956, tomo 92, pp. 187–88)

While the comments of these chroniclers indicate admiration, they are vague and general. And as time passed the coloring was lost and the structures gradually covered.

By the nineteenth century, when Squier visited Pachacámac (probably 1863), little remained of the paintings, since when he mentions the Temple of the Sun, he says: "The walls of each terrace . . . were . . . at one time painted red, as there are still many spots of red paint to be seen" (1877, p. 68). Then, regarding the temple platform, he observes in more detail: "The rectangular work has been greatly injured by excavations, but was originally stuccoed and painted; the walls, after all the destructive agencies that have been employed to effect their ruin, still bearing traces of the figures of trees and men" (1877, p. 68).

Charles Wiener, who visited the site somewhat later, provides still more detail:

> At Pachacamac the walls were covered with an even layer of clay. On the walls so prepared there was red and yellow paint. The base and some unrecognizable parts of the paintings still exist in many places. Thus, the façade of the temple of the Sun oriented toward the necropolis has preserved a layer of a most beautiful red. On this wall the painting is also more complex. On the pisé floor is a layer of yellow clay covered by a layer of red clay. The layers of color are about 1.5 cm. thick; they are very hard, brilliant and polished as though enameled. (Wiener, 1880, p. 495)

By that time the paintings to which Squier referred were apparently no longer visible, since Wiener does not refer to them. Nor does Middendorf, who must have visited the site at about the same time, but with regard to painting mentions only "great walls painted in red and yellow, colors that are still preserved" on the top part of the Temple of Pachacámac (Middendorf, 1973, p. 83).

It is a great pity that work has been concentrated in a single sector of Pachacámac, while the rest remains covered by sand, partly destroyed forever, and now spoiled by poorly conceived reconstructions. The re-creation of all its splendor must be left to our imaginations, since the only scientific data we have are those provided by Uhle (1903), an article by Muelle and Wells (1939), and a partial tracing of the paintings, now very old and faded, deposited in the Museo Nacional de Antropología y Arqueología in Lima.

In the course of his pioneer labors at the site in 1896, Max Uhle sought to identify the "fine house, well painted" referred to by the chronicler Estete, and recognized it in the terracing of the Temple of Pachacámac (fig. 98; Uhle, 1903, pp. 11, 13). The work of Uhle and later investigators like Villar Córdova (1935, pp. 215–21) and Muelle and Wells (1939) confirmed that the Temple of the Sun was painted red, while the Temple of Pachacámac was adorned with murals representing animals and plants, which were studied by Muelle and Wells. Uhle did, however, report traces of murals on the "Temple Plateau" of the Temple of the Sun, although they were so badly damaged he could not make out the designs. "At the point where presumably the main entrance was laid may be seen the remains of a chamber-like cavity, five feet deep . . . , the inner walls of which still bear traces of frescoing. This is the only instance of a mural painting in the entire building; it shows a pattern in yellow, ochre and green upon a red ground" (Uhle, 1903, p. 79). Muelle called attention to the fact that

Fig. 98.
*Temple of Pachacámac, Lurín Valley, old photograph of terracing
including in the foreground some of the paintings studied
in 1938. The site was occupied from at least the
Middle Horizon through the Late Horizon.*

light blue was used for the walls of the structure he called the Hall of the Columns of the Temple of Pachacámac as well as for its columns, a color used only in that temple (Muelle and Wells, 1939, p. 266).

Although Uhle found traces of murals during his stratigraphic excavations of the terraces and substructures of the Temple of Pachacámac, he says little about these decorations in his 1903 monograph. It is also very difficult to establish on the basis of his report the association of these paintings with the more recently excavated remains.

> During the progress of excavations in the direction of the stone wall *b*, a fragment of masonry, *p*, fell and unexpectedly disclosed a section of wall which was covered with frescoing. The design was faint and barely traceable in its general outlines; it showed human figures in yellow, white or a greenish tint with black contours painted on a background of red. The further uncovering of the wall, as far as it was still in tolerable preservation, exposed to view eight human figures, arranged as if walking in a procession, some of them connected by a line, as by a rope; there was also some oval

others of figures "somewhat resembling birds in the conventional style of the textile designs of the coastland" (fig. 101; Uhle, 1903, p. 21), and others that "show distinctly the form of fishes, probably sharks" (fig. 102; Uhle, 1903, p. 21).

Uhle provides no new information in later publications. In 1910 he simply notes: "The figured frieze I found at the Temple of Pachacamac also reminds me now of Ica, since the same figures occur on vessels from that region" (Uhle, 1910a, p. 366; 1910b, p. 345). In 1935 he repeats in general terms the concepts emitted previously:

> A further reminder of Protochimu at the Temple of Pachacamac is the painting of the original façade of the Temple [fig. 99], newly exposed in the course of the excavations by the collapse of a covering wall; originally rather unintelligible, it may now be related to the stylistic influence of the Protochimu culture. The main part represented a sort of procession with a bundle in the center that may have been carried by the people joined to it in front and in back. Even though the special nature of the Protochimu style is not fully realized, it is

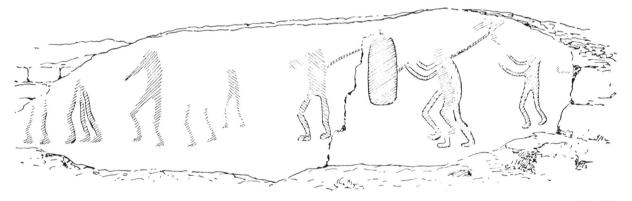

Fig. 99.
Temple of Pachacámac, mural exposed by Uhle in 1896.
Late Horizon.

object indicated [see fig. 99]. This mural painting, in point of style, has no relation to any other find made at Pachacamac, nor to any object of Peruvian antiquity, except perhaps, to the designs upon some of the most important of the Chimu vases from the region of Chimbote, Trujillo, etc. (Uhle, 1903, p. 20)

He further mentions "some well preserved frescoing in bluish green, red and yellow" (p. 20) and presents a drawing of a figure that cannot be identified (fig. 100),

called to mind as much by the overall idea of the scene as by the way the people are represented. (Uhle, 1935, p. 40)

Today we find that Uhle's pronouncements on the possible relationship between the motifs of these paintings and those on "Chimu vases" or in the Protochimú style were incorrect.

In preparation for the twenty-seventh International Congress of Americanists, some monuments in the Lima

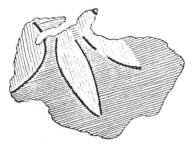

Fig. 100.
Temple of Pachacámac, mural fragment found by Uhle on terrace wall. Late Horizon.

 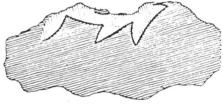

Fig. 101.
Temple of Pachacámac, mural fragment found by Uhle on different part of same wall as fig. 100. Late Horizon.

 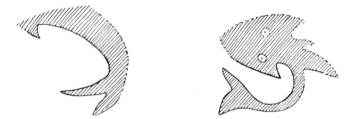

Fig. 102.
Temple of Pachacámac, mural painting found by Uhle on a different terrace wall. Late Horizon.

region, including Pachacámac, were cleaned in 1938 and a number of walls uncovered that "had been buried since the first years of the conquest" (Muelle and Wells, 1939, p. 265). The Pachacámac paintings were found by Alberto Giesecke and José Ricardo Respaldiza, and Muelle

and Wells took advantage of the opportunity to study them. Judging from the motifs and Uhle's plans, these paintings must have been very near those he studied.

Muelle and Wells comment that "the complex must have been attractive, not so much for the skill in the

Mural Painting in Ancient Peru

Fig. 103.
*Temple of Pachacámac, Muelle's Section B of terracing,
clearly showing remains of the paintings seen in 1938.
Late Horizon.*

drawings, of which there was none, or for the richness of the polychromy, which also cannot be commended, but rather for the sprinkled distribution of the few colors in the decorator's repertoire" (1939, p. 266). Two tones of ochre were used predominantly, pink and a pale yellow, and they were used the same way on the entire set of terrace faces: alternating, in broad vertical bands within which the motifs were painted in one color while the other served as ground (fig. 103). On the highest and most central parts, a light blue-green was used on a

smaller scale.[2] Muelle suggests that color selection was subject more to the availability of colors than to any other factor, a deduction based on the pigment analysis (to which I shall refer later), which showed local natural earths:

> Therefore red and yellow predominated; nevertheless it can be noted that white, equally abundant in nature, does not appear, at least not in sufficient quantity to be taken into account, while the light blue, which is not so easy to obtain, was used to paint entire walls in the chamber on the uppermost platform of the terracing, called [the Hall] "of the Columns" since a row of four circular bases with plain shafts painted the same color was recently found there. Moreover, we found light blue so freely applied only in the Temple of Pachacámac, signal of an esteem comparable only to that given it in textiles of the style called "Epigonal" or "South-Andean" and the intention of the grays of proto-Nasca pottery; this color constitutes the basis of what have been called *moon tones*. Red, on the other hand, was the predilection of the Temple of the Sun.
> Doubtless a greater variety was sought, and if they had obtained it they would have used it on the stairways of the Temple of Pachacámac. Some small surfaces show that there was a dark green and a brilliant yellow. They also undoubtedly sought bright or primary colors; gray and brown, which they could have achieved by mixing, did not interest them. In terms of demand, red occupied first place in the Peruvian cultures as in others. Red, which played such an important role among the Incas, was not slighted in the Temple of Pachacámac either. (Muelle and Wells, 1939, pp. 266–67)

Further details on the painting techniques used at the Temple of Pachacámac are discussed in chapter 8.

The motifs are of unequal size and placed without symmetry or planning. The paintings were renewed with certain frequency by either patching the flaked or damaged parts or totally erasing the paintings with a thin layer of clay upon which were applied similar or totally different motifs from those that had been there before. Muelle counted up to sixteen superimposed layers of paint in the western angle of the entrance to the top platform of the terracing at the Temple of Pachacámac (Muelle and Wells, 1939, p. 277). It is worth noting here that Uhle had also commented on the existence of mul-

Fig. 104.
Temple of Pachacámac, detail of painting from top terrace face of Section B.

tiple layers of paint at this site on the Temple of the Sun (Uhle, 1903, p. 80).

Muelle and Wells's study is unfortunately incomplete in that it includes no description of the motifs comprising the Pachacámac paintings. The following brief description is based on their illustrations, although the fact that they were reproduced at a very small scale may have resulted in some errors or involuntary misinterpretation. Muelle and Wells's figure 5 illustrates Section A of the northwestern terracing, where the following colors are reported: ochre-rose, 5 E 11; Naples yellow, 9 H 2; light blue, 28 E 1.[3] On each of the nine terraces shown in the illustration is a row of fishes all facing left, except one, in the bottom row, which is positioned vertically with the head up. Although the motifs were already worn when discovered, they are clearly schematic and give the impression that the artist wished to record the different known species, since the differences in form are very clear. In some places the fish motif alternates with figures of plants, apparently maize, always very stylized. In this series of fish the motifs are repeated one behind the other the length of each of the terraces, always in a single line; the same is true of the plants.

Section B of the terracing (figs. 103–105) with Wall C at the top is shown in Muelle and Wells's figure 6. Here the predominant theme is again fish, with bird and human forms in lesser numbers. Given the small size of the drawing and the total lack of comment in the text, it is impossible to know if all the elements illustrated are on the same layer of paint or not, in view of the possibility of superposition, repairs, and successive retouching. All the fish are very stylized, some geometricized in a clear copy of textile motifs (fig. 105), others based on curved lines (fig. 104). In this sector the motifs are not always in a single line; there are places where up to three fish appear placed one above the other vertically. Almost all of the fish face left, and the composition is not symmetrical but rather grouped. The only sort of bird that can be clearly seen is very stylized and, as in the case of the fish, is copied from textile designs (fig. 105). Outlining is the same as in Section A. There are only a few plant representations (fig. 104), which also appear to be maize, and a very schematic human figure appears in two places. The artist simply outlined the form, and in each case the head, but not the body, has been destroyed. All indications are that these personages were walking or running, also toward the left; their hands are in front of their bodies and, in each case, there is a fish near the hands, possibly indicating that the men are in the act of catching the fish (fig. 103).

Muelle and Wells's figure 7 shows the decoration of the bench on Wall C and a detail of the wall (fig. 106);[4] judging from the drawing, there were several superimposed layers of paint. On the first layer of paint on the bench is a series of plants, some of which I cannot identify while others are very well-depicted maize (pl. 29, fig. 106). On the second layer is a scene of which few motifs remain. The first layer of the wall paint (pl. 30, fig. 106) includes a half-moon shape, possibly the tail of a fish. The only part that can be clearly seen is the major figure, which represents a very interesting human personage. Part of the head is missing and the figure is depicted only in outline, with rather broad strokes. The figure is facing left and carrying in each hand a leaf-shaped object, possibly representing a shield. What little can be seen of the second layer of paint, at the extreme right of the mural, cannot be identified with certainty and could be the remains of either a human shape or a plant.

Figure 8 corresponds to Area D of "small altars" at the entrance to the Hall of the Columns. Here Muelle counted sixteen paint layers; the one in the drawing (fig. 107) is the fifteenth layer, counting from the original surface. The author indicates that the sixteenth was ochre-red with an indefinable decoration; the fourteenth was also red with motifs very similar to those of the fifteenth layer but done in Naples yellow; the eleventh to eighth all had an ochre-red ground; the seventh was ochre-red with indefinable figures (probably plants) painted in light blue with black outlines. The sixth through first layers had red grounds, and the first was decorated with small, light blue circles with yellow dots (potatoes). The drawing (fig. 107) is very clear and the design painted on what remained of the fifteenth layer represents eight diving birds drawn schematically with curved lines. They have long beaks, heads indicated by circles, and arched wings; the tails are not visible, having been cut or otherwise lost. In a few places some traces are visible that are hard to identify and may well be motifs belonging to one of the underlying layers.

Muelle and Wells's figure 9 includes three figures from the thirteenth layer of the same area as figure 8, painted in green on a yellow ground (fig. 108). Figure 108a depicts a stylized human facing right; fig. 108b is a schematic bird with a very large beak (a pelican?) standing on a semicircular object; fig. 108c contains some schematic elements that are probably plants but not readily identifiable.

Their figure 10 (fig. 109) seems to represent the only mural fragment that does not come from the northwest

Fig. 105.
Temple of Pachacámac, detail of painting next to that in fig. 104, a marine scene with a conspicuous bird (pelican?) catching a fish.

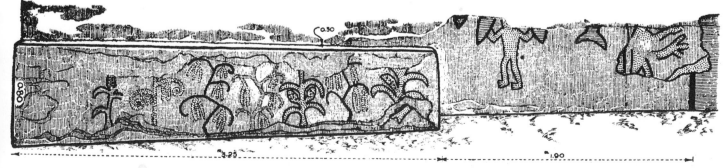

Fig. 106.
Temple of Pachacámac, decoration from Muelle's wall C with plant representations (including maize) in the foreground and some very worn human figures in the background. Late Horizon.

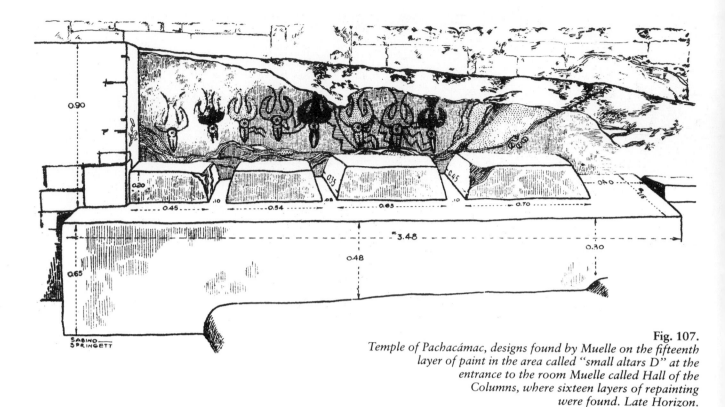

Fig. 107.
Temple of Pachacámac, designs found by Muelle on the fifteenth layer of paint in the area called "small altars D" at the entrance to the room Muelle called Hall of the Columns, where sixteen layers of repainting were found. Late Horizon.

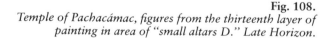

Fig. 108.
Temple of Pachacámac, figures from the thirteenth layer of painting in area of "small altars D." Late Horizon.

side of the Temple of Pachacámac. It was found in Section E, above and behind (southeast) the terraces containing the other murals. The figures are all plants, probably maize, and were painted in red and yellow with black outlines on a light blue ground. It is a great pity that the authors did not publish a detailed description of the complex.

Since we know that the Temple of Pachacámac was in use in 1533, when Hernando Pizarro reached the site, we can deduce that at least the last paintings belong to Inca times. Nevertheless, the motifs are in the stylistic tradition of the Late Intermediate Period and adhere most closely, as Uhle suggested, to the canons of the styles of that period. In fact, the geometricized figures are just like those on Ica and Chancay-style textiles, and the same can be said of the bird shown in the sixth figure

Fig. 109.
Temple of Pachacámac, plant representations, probably maize, from Muelle's Section E, considerably removed from Section B. Late Horizon.

on the eighth terrace from the bottom (figs. 103, 105). The human figures are uninformative from the stylistic standpoint; I personally relate them only to the personage I found at Huadca or Huatica, which I shall describe in the following chapter and which I suspect is Inca. In that scene there are also some fish that are very similar to those of Pachacámac. There is, however, a truly startling similarity between the diving birds in fig. 107 and those at Túcume (El Purgatorio, Lambayeque) discussed in the preceding chapter (pl. 21). I consider them so similar that were the motifs presented alone, out of context, they could be confused. The differences are in detail—the curvature of the wings, for example. I think there is no doubt regarding the Chimú relationship of the Túcume motifs.

We know nothing of the significance of the scenes rep-resented at Pachacámac except for some comments from Garcilaso. He expounds the pre-Inca origins of Pachacámac, attributing its construction to the "ancestors" of "King Cuismancu." "In the temple the [coastal people] placed their idols, which were figures of fishes, among which they also had the figure of the female fox" (Garcilaso de la Vega, lib. 6, cap. XXX; 1945, tomo II, p. 68). This statement suggests a close relationship between the paintings and the cult to the sea as well as an explanation of the predominant fish motif.

THE RÍMAC VALLEY

Examples of decorated structures from this period abound in the Rímac Valley. In the present urban area of

Fig. 110.
*Remains of painting that adorned an edifice of the San Juan
archaeological complex in the middle Rímac Valley.
Late Horizon.*

Lima, east of the archaeological complex of Maranga, is a group of five large structures that are now being destroyed. They originally formed an aggregate delimited by high merloned walls, and are called the Huacas de Mateo Salado or Huacas de Ascona. The mound called the Palacio del Curaca contained red and yellow painted walls (Villar Córdova, 1942, pp. 248, 252–53). Furthermore, in the course of some work in 1962, I saw a small flat relief panel representing two birds joined at the beak on a background painted with white lines (Bonavia, 1962; Bonavia, Matos, and Caycho, 1963). The type of decoration and its treatment recall Chimú specimens or late textile motifs from Ica and Chincha. And there were other important monuments around Lima. Between Bellavista and Maranga was a series of "citadels" discovered about 1870 and preserved until the 1940s. Tello notes: "The temples located inside and outside of the citadels had walls adorned with arabesques, or they were plastered and elegantly painted" (1936). In the Maranga area, now totally absorbed by the city of Lima, rises a great mound known as Huaca Concha, where

even today many plastered walls painted yellow can be seen in the sector cut by Avenida Venezuela and by the construction of the Naval Hospital (see chap. 7, fig. 115). The precise temporal placement of these monuments is not certain, but we would not be far off the mark to assign them to the interval between the Middle and Late Horizons. Another painting in Lima that almost certainly belongs to this period is the second painting at the site of Huadca (see fig. 118). I shall postpone its discussion until the next chapter, however, when I consider the first mural at that site, which is later.

In the lower part of the Rímac Valley are two monuments that bore paintings. Their chronological placement is uncertain, but from what we know of the ruins and the kind of buildings on which the paintings were found, they are doubtless late and could well belong to the Late Intermediate Period or the Late Horizon. I know them only from photographs, since the paintings no longer exist.

The first of these paintings was on a wall beside a doorway of the San Juan complex, located on the left

Fig. 111.
*Top of a destroyed wall from an anonymous archaeological complex
near Ñaña, Rímac Valley, displaying remains of scroll motifs
and other unidentifiable figures. Late Horizon.*

side of the Rímac River. It was a horizontal series of stylized motifs representing birds, painted in white on a darker ground (fig. 110). I do not know the exact colors, nor is the exact shape of the birds known, since what little remained of the painting when the photograph was taken was already damaged. The motif recalls the sort of birds common on Chancay and Chimú style textile designs. The photographs were taken many years ago by Rogger Ravines.

In the second case the remains of paintings were found on a large fragment of a fallen wall in an unnamed archaeological complex in the locality of Ñaña on the right side of the Rímac River. The photographs were taken by some German citizens and given to Hans Horkheimer around 1960. He in turn, knowing of my interest in the material, gave them to me (fig. 111). The portion of the fallen wall corresponds to the top of a wall that bore a broad band of a dark color (unspecified, since the photos are in black and white), upon which the motif, representing a series of spirals very similar to those used in Moche art to terminate motifs or represent ocean waves, was painted in white. Below this band were apparently large figures in black, but they are so faint they cannot be identified.

THE CASMA VALLEY

Finally, in this account of the later mural art of the central Andes, it is worth recounting Mejía Xesspe's comments on the "great waka of Moxeke" in the Casma Valley (Mejía Xesspe, 1956, p. 327), a monument not to be confused with the "Waka de las Llamas" of the same valley (Tello, 1956, p. 303; Mejía Xesspe, 1956, p. 327). Mejía reported that when he was in Casma with Tello in 1937, they came to know a local resident, Don Miguel San Román, at that time more than sixty years old. He told them that in 1890 Dr. José Mariano Macedo commissioned a Polish engineer, N. Perkovich, and Armando Macedo Mas to excavate in some archaeological sites searching for treasure. One of these sites was the Huaca Grande of Moxeke, where "they found some walls painted with figures of the sun, moon and other stars, vestiges of which are still preserved" (Mejía Xesspe, 1956, p. 327). When I asked Mejía Xesspe about this matter in 1973, he remembered no particular details except that the monument upon which the paintings were found must have dated to the Late Intermediate Period or the Late Horizon.

Murals in
the Inca Empire

Inca expansion ushered in the Late Horizon, which was the second great South American imperial experience; one that was ended by the European conquest. The Incas began, perhaps for the first time, a true urban policy for the purpose of locating the population near agricultural lands in order to achieve maximum crop yield. Imperial architects were occupied in the immense labor of building the many political and administrative centers that were created by the state. Nevertheless, the Incas cannot be called great city builders.

Inca architecture is one of clear and concrete ideas demonstrating great knowledge and incredible technique. The buildings were of stone and adobe, and there were many types of structures: adobe and *tapia*, simple stone masonry, cut stone blocks, great megalithic polygonal architecture, as well as a modified polygonal style and one of squared blocks with rounded faces and sunken joints. The perfect union of these stones without the use of mortar is famous, almost proverbial. Domestic architecture was very simple, of fieldstone or adobe, with one room with a single entrance serving an extended family. There are many examples of both isolated structures and complexes embellished with painting, and some are in quite good condition, perhaps because they belonged to the last era of independent Andean culture.

Buildings were decorated with mural paintings in the Late Horizon just as in the preceding periods, as demonstrated by the words of Father Bernabé Cobo, one of the most observant chroniclers of the seventeenth century, who wrote: "they were not accustomed to whitewash [the houses] as we do, although the principal ones of the chiefs commonly had the walls painted in several colors and figures, all rough and graceless" (Cobo, *Historia*, lib. 14, cap. III; 1956, tomo 92, p. 242). A number of these paintings must still have been visible in the past century, since Rivero and Tschudi comment: "In some ancient edifices the remains of abstract, or architectonic, paintings are still recognizable; and from all appearances, the Peruvians did not know how to paint palace walls in any other way, the art of design among them remaining in its earliest infancy" (Rivero and Tschudi, cap. IX; 1851, p. 230). These authors conclude quite correctly, "The old historians leave us in the dark regarding Peruvian painting . . ." (p. 230), although the comment could be extended to include modern historians as well. For example, in a recent study dealing exclusively with all aspects of Inca architecture including the aesthetic, mural decoration is ignored, save in a very general comment (Gasparini and Margolies, 1977, p. 132; 1980, p. 126). The authors further state that in Inca architecture "the formal decorative and ornamental repertoire is minimal" and that "no 'time was wasted'" in making any sort of geometric, phytomorphic, zoomorphic, or anthropomorphic ornamentation (1977, pp. 330–31; 1980, p. 320).

As we shall see, this opinion is incorrect. Rowe once alluded to this point in the following terms:

> The Inca decorated wooden cups, pottery, and probably the walls of their houses with geometric patterns and life designs which were often informative and always charming. Motives are most often plants and flowers, next insects, then men, and last animals, especially llamas and pumas. Battle and hunting scenes are common, and women are usually shown with flowers. The figures are conventionally reduced to an idealized, somewhat geometric shape, filled in with simple areas of flat color. (1946, p. 287)

He concluded: "Wall paintings and decorative hangings prevented monotony and added a touch of color without destroying the structural lines of the wall" (p. 288).

Bennett was still more specific when he wrote of Inca architecture: "Some adobe or stone walls were covered with a clay plaster which was painted in various colors. Definite wall-painting designs have not been found in the Highland sites, but on the Coast good frescoes are preserved" (1946, p. 146). The accuracy of this statement is demonstrated not only by surviving examples but also by ceramic representations that, although not as numerous as those from other cultures, are preserved from Inca times. A handsome model of an Inca *cancha* is illustrated by Gasparini and Margolies (1977, figs. 188–90; 1980, fig. 171).[1]

Not only building walls were painted but also the walls lining the famous Inca roads, as we know from the observations of one of the first Spaniards to travel the coast of Peru. Of the roads, he says: ". . . in the places with frequent settlements, there are stretches two and three and four leagues more or less, planted on either side with trees which meet overhead and shade the travelers; and where these are lacking, walls are built on either side, and on them paintings of monsters and fish and other animals, so that looking at them the travelers pass the time . . ." (Noticia del Perú, 1938, p. 244).[2]

In spite of being the most recent of their kind, few of these artistic examples have survived to our times more or less complete. Their loss probably results from several factors: weathering acting directly on the paintings that had not been covered like earlier ones, the iconoclastic fury of colonial clerics, the vandalism of treasure hunters, etc. But I venture to suggest that these paintings have disappeared especially because they were the object of systematic destruction in the sixteenth century by order of the Spanish authorities. To support this viewpoint I offer a portion of the instructions issued by Viceroy Francisco de Toledo in connection with his great General Inspection, which was carried out between 1570 and 1575.

> Item, because of the ancient custom the Indians have of painting idols and figures of demons and animals to which they have been accustomed to offer worship on their stools, seats, cups, staffs, walls and buildings, mantles, tunics, spades, and on almost anything they need, it seems that they somehow preserve their ancient idolatry, you will see to it, on entering each tax district, that from this time on no craftsman will carve or paint said figures, under [pain of] severe penalties, which you will carry out on their persons and goods should the contrary occur. And the paintings and figures that they may have on their houses and buildings, and on the other implements that may be removed reasonably and without much harm and you will order them to place

crosses and other insignia of Christians on their houses and buildings. (Toledo, 1924, p. 171)

It was doubtless feared that there might be a resurgence of such ancestral religious ideas as might still persist. Apparently in this context the paintings played an important role, much more important than has been realized. In this Toledan order we find yet one more crime of *lesa cultura* to add to the many others wrought by the Spanish conquest.

THE PISCO VALLEY

Surely the finest example of the many painted Inca structures on the Peruvian coast is Tambo Colorado in the province of Pisco, department of Ica.[3] Walls and trapezoidal niches with multicolor decoration in red, yellow, and white (Cailleux and Taylor's F-28, C-63 and A-81) can still be seen, as well as the remains of reliefs. There is, unfortunately, no archaeological study of the monument and, as noted by Ynez Haase (1958), for example, there are very few references to it in sixteenth-, seventeenth-, and eighteenth-century sources. Adolphe F. Bandelier took notes on the site, but they have never been published. And while Max Uhle spent a month and a half studying it in 1901, as well as photographing it and making plans, his plans have been lost, although the photographs and a description are in the files of the Robert H. Lowie Museum of Anthropology at the University of California, Berkeley. Fortunately, Haase published fragments of a letter from Uhle to Mrs. Phoebe Apperson Hearst, dated September 24, 1901, and summarized other portions, all containing valuable information:[4]

Uhle spent one and a half months (from August 23 to October 11 of 1901) investigating the intermediate valley of Pisco. The greater part of this time was dedicated to photographing and measuring Tambo Colorado. He finished his work in September and on the 24th wrote a thirty-two page report to Mrs. Hearst from the Hacienda Pallasca.

The letter sparkles throughout with Uhle's vivid imagination. Not satisfied simply to provide accurate architectural information, he wanted to breathe life into these ancient structures, to revive the greatness that had surely been theirs, desires in no way contravening his keen sense of observation. But the loss of his plans, combined with his inadequate command of the language of his adopted country, render difficult a complete understanding of his letter. For example, [on the subject of painting, he wrote]:

"Painting was applied as manner of decoration in two ways, as painting of the inner of the niches—and as painting of the walls. No patterns of painting are met with in all the building ([referring to the] palace on the north side). On the other hand, it is to be said that [there was no room without its painting] or at least white washing. Nearly all rooms—with few exceptions—show various colors of painting . . ." [f. 61v]. He found that the greater part of the walls had many coats of paint, sometimes separated by thin layers of unpigmented clay. In general, the colors were white, yellow and red. Sometimes, he said, the yellow had an orange cast, and in others olive. There was a "lead-colored" room, but this hue occurred in only one case. Except for the south façade of the north palace, which was painted entirely red, and many of the "inferior" rooms, which were whitewashed, paint was applied in "horizontal stripes, setting one color above the other, nearly without exception in this way that the wider lower part is uniform, and the remaining colors applied as if they were wide border stripes (up to about 1 meter in width) above [fig. 112]" [f. 67].

The painting of the niches revealed daring but sensitive color combinations. Square niches were painted in one or two colors, those that were taller than wide were only one color, while the double jamb niches [see fig. 112] showed the greatest variety. (Haase, 1958, pp. 1, 2–3)

There are two other aspects of the Tambo Colorado ruins that are little known and very interesting. One is ornamental brickwork, the other, low-relief decoration. In spite of the very few remains, one can gain a general impression of the original elegance. Uhle discussed, described, and sketched these elements in his letter. The ornamental brickwork occurred in three forms. The first, "in the shape of pinnacles, falling off at one side in three steps . . ." (Uhle, ms., f. 54), that is, a series of three-stepped step blocks, which might face either left or right but always the same direction on any given wall, placed on top of the walls. Uhle referred to these pinnacles and to the following decorative form as "ornamental crests." The second design could be described as a negative step pyramid. That is, the wall was cut away from the top so that each side of the cutout had four steps. The third form of ornamental brickwork Uhle reports for Tambo Colorado is not considered among the "ornamental crests." It consists of two patterns of open work that occur on balustrades and enclosure walls. He notes: "Both patterns correspond in some way to patterns used in the textile art of the Kechua civilisation. Both may have been produced by leaning every two bricks of adobes against each other" (ms., f. 61).

Uhle thought the ornamental crests symbolized rank,

Fig. 112.
*Tambo Colorado, Pisco Valley, detail of one of the
trapezoidal, double jamb niches at this
important Inca palace. Late Horizon.*

and notes especially that the pinnacles doubtless marked a high rank, like that of chief, since he had observed that "on a great deal of the other prominent scepter-like symbols quite the same ornament often is repeated, while on common objects it never occurs" (ms., f. 55v). Here he refers specifically to what we now consider to be a ceremonial digging board, which was later illustrated by Menzel (1977, fig. 9 and cover).

Of all the ornamental crests, Uhle considered the decoration in low relief to mark the highest rank. It was found on the remains of the northern wall of "a tower-like building at the south-western corner of the palaces. The southern front-wall is incomplete at the top. According to many parallelisms it is to be supposed, that it showed originally more or less the same finish, as the northern corresponding wall of the same tower" (ms., f. 56v). The relief ornament was repeated six times (see Kroeber, 1944, pl. 20 bottom; Ishida and others, 1960, p. 228, fig. 4). The design is a sort of three-step pyramid, from the top of which issue two elements curving in opposite directions, like plumes. There is a sunken equilateral triangle in the base of each motif, and the steps of the pyramid do not form right angles, but rather slant slightly outward to join the step below, or the base line, at about a 60° angle. Uhle suggests a similarity of the motif to a "plumed helmet," and further conjectures:

> The locality, on which this figure was represented, in order to make it visible from far like the sign-board of a merchant, the manner in which it has been applied by setting an especial small wall, which served to no other purpose but to bear these signs, upon the architectural walls of the tower [served to signal] the people looking at the palace from the outside about the determination of the building with the respect to the [rank] and position of its residents. (Uhle, ms., f. 57)

Uhle did not, however, find any painting other than that described above.

THE CHINCHA VALLEY

Painting was common in the Chincha Valley, and the majority of Inca structures there have "colored plaster" (Bennett, 1946, p. 137; Wallace, 1971, pp. 32, 35). The monument known today as the Huaca de la Centinela, a name it has borne only since 1820 (Alva Maúrtua, n.d.), must have been a magnificent example of decorated architecture of the Inca epoch. I recall many years ago having seen walls there painted red and yellow, and until

some twenty-five years ago part of the motifs could still be distinguished if one knew where to look for them. I checked them personally, even taking some photographs, and Wallace corroborated the presence of such painting in the course of his work in 1957 (Wallace, 1971, p. 5).

This monument has several superimposed building phases belonging to different epochs, the last of which is Inca. It was apparently during the last phase that a series of structures was built around the "temple" (Uhle, 1924, p. 75). In one of these, located immediately to the south of the *huaca*, Middendorf reported: "In two rooms paintings are still seen that covered the lower part of the walls and consist of white, red and blue lines" (1973, p. 107). The most complete information, however, is given by Uhle. There were murals in one of the small rooms of the section he called "the palace."

> Its southern part is elevated and shows wall painting on three sides. The painting, which is of pure Incaic character in every sense, forms a strip continued from the first wall, over the second, to the third, and is similar to the designs frequently met with on Inca vessels of the amphora or aryballos type. The colors are red, black and green (the latter nearly faded away) on white. The pattern [fig. 113] consists of rhomboid figures cut in triangles as well as the spaces left between them. Each triangle of a pair shows the same color, either red or green, while the confining triangles are of opposite color. Within each triangle a maeander-like hook is spaced out in white, in such a way that the hooks of the confining triangles are turned in opposite directions. (Uhle, 1924, pp. 77–78)[5]

Uhle conjectured that this room might be the dwelling of some priest, of "the Inca himself," or of some high-ranking lady.

In 1958, John H. Rowe paid a brief visit to the site of La Centinela and photographed the remains of what was apparently the room described by Uhle (pl. 31). He studied the remaining portions of the mural decoration and attempted to draw a reconstruction of the design then visible (fig. 114). There were traces that might have represented some sort of design in the triangular spaces of the design reconstructed as white, but they were so faint that it was impossible to ascertain their form (Rowe, personal communication, 1984). Unfortunately, Uhle's description was not available to Rowe at the time he made these observations. It seems clear, however, that the undecipherable traces that Rowe reconstructed as white triangles correspond to Uhle's green triangles with a "meander-like hook" in white, which are comparable

Fig. 113.
Huaca de la Centinela, Chincha Valley, photographic detail taken in 1958 of a badly damaged mural on west wall of Inca structure, described by Uhle. Inca style, Late Horizon.

■ Black

▨ Red

□ White

0 1 2 3 4 5   10cm

Fig. 114.
*Huaca de la Centinela, reconstruction drawing of mural
on walls of Inca structure as seen by John H. Rowe
in 1958. Inca style, Late Horizon.*

to the red triangles reconstructed by Rowe. All traces of the green seem to have disappeared by 1958, leaving only the ghost of a white meander on the remaining white ground color (see fig. 113).

THE CAÑETE VALLEY

In his description of the Cañete Valley, which he calls Guarco, Cieza de León mentions the construction not only of a new Cuzco but also of a fortress to mark the conquest of the valley. He calls it "the most charming and handsome fortress of the kingdom of Peru . . ." and mentions that it was "heavily adorned with paintings" (Cieza de León, *Crónica*, cap. LXXIII; 1922, p. 244). We do not know if he referred to murals or simply painted walls, but his clear admiration leads me to sus-

pect murals. At any rate the datum is interesting. This fortress was apparently still in good condition about 1560, since Garcilaso says: "When I passed by there the year sixty, it still showed what it had been, the more to wound those who looked upon it" (Garcilaso de la Vega, lib. 6, cap. XXIX; 1945, p. 67). Cieza de León did not indicate the precise location of the fortress but, thanks to the investigations of Larrabure y Unanue (1935, pp. 323–58), we know that it was located on Cerro Azul, northwest of the Cañete Valley, even though only vestiges remained by the year the author was there, and he does not so much as mention the paintings Cieza spoke of. It should be kept in mind that the 1935 article was originally written in 1874 and reprinted in 1893. When I visited the site in 1979, I could see that Cieza's description is correct. Moreover, while the monument is almost entirely destroyed, in the remains of some typical Inca

Murals in the Inca Empire _____ 157

niches, there were still traces of white and yellow paint.

Larrabure y Unanue also left us an excellent description of Incahuasi in Lunahuaná. He mentions "vast corridors and terraces . . . whose walls, well plastered with fine clay, were decorated with paintings of which there are barely traces" (1935, p. 428). Again we do not know whether there had been murals or simply painted walls.

THE LURÍN VALLEY

The Lurín Valley is one of the zones where Late Horizon rural settlements might best be studied. Many, especially those in the lower part of the valley which are still well preserved, must have been profusely decorated, not only with color, which was limited to red and yellow, but also with flat relief. The most characteristic of these sites are Campo de las Flores, Tambo Inga, and Potrero de Santa Lucía (Bonavia, 1965a). Campo de las Flores is composed of various sectors, and when I worked there in 1960 no paintings were visible. Earlier, however, in the part I called Sector II (Area A), Juan Ossio and Rogger Ravines had seen a very poorly preserved wall with quite clear remains of polychrome decoration. Thanks to Ossio's slides, taken at the time, something can be said about these paintings.

The wall was not very high and was damaged at both top and bottom. On the highest part there were unidentifiable motifs in white on a red ground. Immediately below them there was a very faded yellow ground color. On the bottom portion there were motifs painted in yellow on a red ground that was applied directly to the plaster. Three of these motifs are visible in the slides, a larger central one and two smaller ones. The two left-hand ones were painted in yellow, the one on the right in white; they seem to represent plants. The central stem appears to have a thick outline and several rectilinear branches on both sides but issuing symmetrically from the same point on the stem. On the tip of one of the right-hand branches of the central figure can be seen the remains of an amorphous large white form. Ravines and Ossio suggested that the figures were stylized representations of maize plants. They do not appear so to me, however, since the branching elements are very long and straight. Moreover, the white element on the central figure resembles a flower more than it does an ear of corn. It is worth asking whether the modern name of the complex, Field of the Flowers, might not be a direct result of these supposed flowers, which must originally have been more brightly colored, adorning this wall and perhaps others. The ruins are of the Inca epoch, so we can assume the paintings are of the same date.

In the course of archaeological research in the Lurín Valley in 1958 (Bonavia, 1965a), I had several opportunities to visit the ruins of Huaycán,[6] today being rapidly destroyed. I had learned of a ruined wall with the remains of murals there, but was never able to locate it. In the lower part of this same valley, of course, is the complex of Pachacámac, which was discussed in the preceding chapter.

THE RÍMAC VALLEY

That there was a considerable occupation in the Rímac (Lima) Valley from very early prehispanic times until the arrival of the Spaniards is well known, even though most of the remains of these settlements have now disappeared under urban sprawl. Garcilaso, referring to the Rímac Valley, explains that the name came from "an idol which was there in the form of a man, which spoke and answered what it was questioned" (Garcilaso de la Vega, lib. 6, cap. XXX; 1945, p. 68); *rimac* means "speaker" in Quechua. "They had the idol in a sumptuous temple, although not so much so as that of Pachacámac, whither the lords of Peru used to go and to send their ambassadors to consult about those things that were of importance to them" (Garcilaso de la Vega, lib. 6, cap. XXX; 1945, p. 68). He adds that the Spanish historians confused the temple of Rímac with that of Pachacámac, but that "the speaking idol was in Rímac and not at Pachacámac" (lib. 6, cap. XXX; 1945, p. 68). Although the Rímac oracle was originally locally venerated, the Incas maintained its worship after their conquest of the valley.

The identification of the temple of the oracle of Rímac has been the subject of considerable speculation in more recent times. Squier places it near the "small village of Magdalena" (1877, p. 83) and, quoting an unidentified "native author," says it was called Rimac-Tam-pu, although Squier clearly distinguishes it from "modern Limatambo," which was on the road to Chorrillos (p. 86). Again according to the "native author," who in turn cites Pinelo, the temple contained an idol: ". . . *Rimac*, 'he who speaks.' . . . who responded to the consultations according to the character of the offering made by the people. [The attendants of the oracle] painted in this temple, as hieroglyphics, the answers most favoring their ideas. And, to make mysterious these paintings, which are to be seen on the walls of this structure, they covered them with other walls . . ." (Squier, 1877, pp. 84–85).

Mural Painting in Ancient Peru

Middendorf locates this oracle in the "huaca del Estanque" (1973, pp. 66–67), which today is known as Maranga or Tres Palos (see fig. 115). In so doing, he contradicts statements by Calancha and Odriozola that he himself quotes. These others indicate that the temple was "near the hacienda of the Dominicans which was called *Rimac-tampu* in antiquity and is now, through mispronunciation, known as Limatambo" (Odriozola cited by Middendorf, 1973, p. 67).

Toribio Mejía Xesspe suggested that this structure might be the one that used to be in the place now occupied by the Gran Unidad Escolar Melitón Carbajal, near the Lima Expressway. The monument was known as Limatambo and dated to the Late Horizon (personal communication, 1973).

María Rostworowski de Diez Canseco has also attempted to clarify the matter. She erred, however, in citing Squier, since she states that "following Calancha he located the temple of the Lima oracle in Maranga" (Rostworowski de Diez Canseco, 1978, p. 69). While it is true that Squier believed the oracle to have been located in the area of Maranga, that is not what Calancha said. According to that seventeenth-century writer, "the Huaca of this idol is the one that today is on the lands that we Spaniards call Lima Tanbo and the Indians Rimac Tanpu" (1638, lib. I, p. 236). Rostworowski accepts this statement later in her book by referring to Limatambo "as stated by Calancha" (1978, p. 70), thus contradicting herself. The interesting point is that Rostworowski does not believe that the temple was in either Maranga or Limatambo. On the basis of seventeenth-century documents by Cristóbal de Albornoz and a study by Vargas Ugarte, she reaches the conclusion that this "guaca of the Indians of Lima" called "Rimac," was located right in the center of the city of Lima, behind what used to be the Hospital of Santa Ana (Rostworowski de Diez Canseco, 1978, pp. 70–72). At that location there was a "huaca destroyed by the ecclesiastical authorities because it was an important native shrine," according to Eguiguren, whom Rostworowski cites (1978, p. 72). It should be noted, moreover, that Cristóbal de Albornoz, referring to this *huaca*, says: "Rimac, guaca of the Indians of Lima . . . where the City of Los Reyes [Lima] is settled, it was a round stone. It is on a flat place where Geronimo de Silva has an orchard" (Duviols, 1968, p. 34). Thus, it would appear that Garcilaso, who mentions an idol "in the form of a man" and Albornoz, with his "round stone," were not referring to the same thing.

In spite of this confusion, which renders a definitive location of the oracle impossible, it can be argued that the author who came closest to the truth was Middendorf. When Squier refers to the ruins "including a temple of the famous oracle-deity Rimac" (1877, p. 84), he says that they were "between Lima and the sea," near the small village of Magdalena (p. 83). However, Squier also illustrates a wall, captioned "huaca near Limatambo" (p. 87)—a wall that could be part of the Huaca La Palma, which was in a good state of preservation until 1962 and which I saw. Both the "small village of Magdalena" and the Huaca La Palma are in the area of Maranga, an area far from the zone today known as Limatambo. And it is in the latter that the monument noted by Mejía Xesspe was located, surely the "modern Limatambo" mentioned by Squier. Now, when Middendorf suggested the possibility that the famous oracle might have been in the Huaca del Estanque, he also mentioned the decorations that existed in a room of the Huaca La Palma (1973, pp. 58–59), which might coincide with the decorated wall illustrated by Squier.

While certain details lead me to think that the oracle was in the area indicated by Middendorf, I think it may not have been situated in the Huaca del Estanque. In the first place, there has never been any mention of paintings in this monument, and the temple of the oracle is said to have been painted. Second, Squier cites Calancha as saying that the walls of the oracle "were painted with figures of Indians and animals" (1877, p. 85). It so happens that in 1962, at the site of Huadca, I discovered the remains of a painting that I shall describe and illustrate below. I also found in the archives a photograph taken in 1940 of another painting that should correspond to the same monument. Both paintings represent humans and animals and could be the "figures of Indians and animals" that Calancha mentioned. They could be the last remains of the famed oracle, and if so, its location would have been within the perimeter of the ancient "citadel" of Huadca (fig. 115). Since these remains are close to the Huaca del Estanque, if my interpretation is correct, then Middendorf was not far from the truth.

The Maranga Group is one of the most impressive and important complexes remaining in the Lima Valley. Within the complex, and enclosed by walls, is the famous "citadel" of Huadca, whose origins must go back at least to the Early Intermediate Period with successive reoccupations. Today only a few walls remain (fig. 115). In 1962, the Metropolitan Deliberating Council for Historical and Artistic Monuments and Archaeological Sites of Lima placed me in charge of mapping the archaeological remains still surviving within the urban area

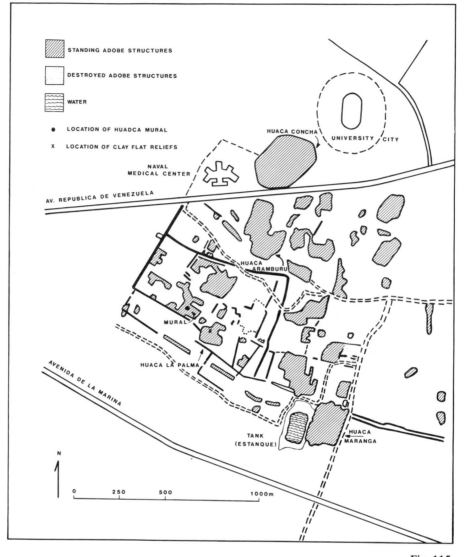

Fig. 115.
*Maranga Archaeological Group, Lima, locating the mural
found at Huadca in 1962. The plan reflects the
condition of the Group in that year.*

(Bonavia, Matos, and Caycho, 1963). In the course of this work, within the perimeter of Huadca, very near what is today the Parque de las Leyendas, I found in the month of November the remnants of a fine mural, which was destroyed in December of the same year.[7] Aside from the earlier edition of this book (Bonavia, 1974), the only published documentation of this mural was in a newspaper note (Bonavia, 1962).

The wall on which the painting was executed was built of *adobón*[8] made of clay mixed with gravel, and was 1.14 m wide. On the basis of the traces remaining at the time of the study, the wall was probably 13 m long and formed part of a room that must have been quadrangular (13 × 12 m). Onto the *adobón* wall was applied a plaster, carefully made of very fine clay, free of impurities. The wall on which the painting was found (fig. 116) was oriented northwest-southeast, and very clear traces remained of the mound, probably artificial, upon which the building was originally located; the top of this mound was 3.13 m above the cultivated zone.

Fig. 116.
Huadca, Lima, general view of painted wall. Late Horizon.

When we reached the site we found recent offerings of coca.

What remained of the painting on the wall had the following measurements: maximum height, 161 cm; maximum width at the top, 25 cm; at the center, 87 cm; at the bottom, 129 cm. There were two superimposed layers of painting, and the mural appeared on the lower one. When I first reached the site, all that was visible was the top one, which had been almost entirely destroyed by natural phenomena and human activity. It was entirely covered with dust and the surface had been scratched, displaying the marks of some pointed instrument. In some places the top layer had fallen, permitting glimpses of another underneath. The first layer was very pale red, clearly faded from a much more intense shade. There were traces suggesting that there had been some sort of decoration on this outer layer that could no longer be distinguished. Close examination revealed that the top-most layer of painting had not been applied directly to the second one, but rather onto a very thin layer of extremely fine plaster free of impurities. It is impossible to know if the pigments were mixed with this fine layer of plaster or were painted on top after it was applied.

When we arrived, only traces of painted figures with very faint black elements were visible on the right center of the wall. It was possible to recognize a fish motif drawn with the head facing up and slightly inclined to the left. To the left of the fish were lines from another indeterminate figure. Nothing could be seen of the rest of the mural. Analyzing this detail, I realized that the figure of the fish was actually on a layer of plaster underneath the one covering the rest of the wall. The black motif had been exposed accidentally when a piece of the overlying plaster had fallen. It had doubtless been of a much more intense color, which was lost through weathering.

Behind the painted wall was an irrigation canal that

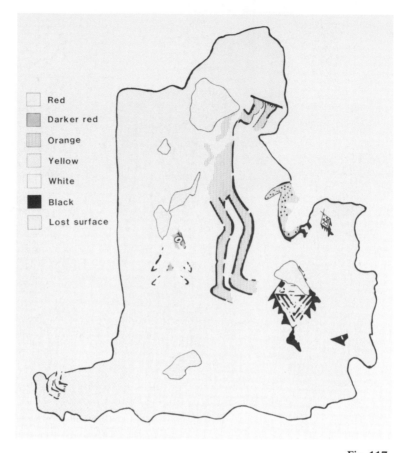

Red

Darker red

Orange

Yellow

White

Black

Lost surface

Fig. 117.
*Huadca, drawing reduced from tracing showing portion of
the mural visible at the time of discovery. Late Horizon.*

watered the vineyard planted on the mound and surrounding area. The entire wall had become soaked through capillary action and might fall at any moment. Moreover, the painting was already falling off from the effects of the water, sun, and accumulated salts. It was these factors that impelled me to remove the top layer of plaster in order to bring to light the doomed painting underneath. We gently scraped the first layer of painting and plaster, which detached very easily, and the new mural began to appear.

It must have been composed of several panels with alternating ground colors upon which the figures were painted. We found evidence of at least two such panels, one with a red ground, the other yellow (fig. 117, pl. 32). The painting studied here had a red ground and occupied practically all the remaining part of the wall. The bottom of the painting had been completely destroyed by salts and humidity. On the lower left were the remains of the panel with a yellow ground. The vertical division

between these two sections was very clear, very regular, and marked only by the color change. I noticed that the red panel was painted first and then the yellow, since the yellow covered the red at the juncture. The yellow ground color was more resistant than the red and appeared to have been applied more densely. Much of the red was lost when the overlying plaster was removed, leaving a very faded shade, while the small sector of yellow maintained a well-preserved surface. Unfortunately, the color samples gathered for analysis were lost when they were taken to a European laboratory for analysis; when I returned to collect more, nothing was left.

The motifs of the newly exposed mural were executed in an intense black with a thick line averaging some 6 mm. The other colors were used to fill in the figures. The layer of paint was very thin, perhaps 0.5 mm. The outlines seemed sure, though of uneven width, and were made with a brush. The artist had a steady hand, since the paint filling in the outlined areas nowhere covered the black line. There was no evidence of the use of any pattern or template. The process followed was apparently first to paint the prepared wall with the ground color; the motifs were then outlined in black; and, finally, the figures filled in with the different colors.

Only a small fragment remained of the panel with a yellow ground color on the lower left (figs. 116, 117). It contained only two human feet, both turned to the right and shown in profile so that one appeared above the other. They were outlined in black, with five toes, and were part of a representation of a complete individual. The drawing was stylized and obviously freehand, since the two feet were different. The area occupied was about 9 × 10.5 cm.

On the red panel the first motif, left of center, was a fish (pl. 33, fig. 117), only partly visible because of damage, whose figure was very different from the other fish in the scene. Its head faced up and was probably triangular with two lateral central fins, probably also triangular. We cannot tell if it had a mouth. The tail was a triangular appendage. A bare indication of the right eye can be seen in a white circular shape with a solid black center. The entire motif was outlined with a black double line, the intervening space filled with white, and the innermost area of the fish preserved the red ground color. The double line outlining the figure had a constant width except for the two central fins, which were much broader. Total size of the figure could not be estimated, but its maximum width was 16 cm.

The central figure was a very stylized human originally about 88 cm high and with a maximum width of 13 cm (pl. 32, fig. 117). Only two very long, thin legs and part of the lean, elongated trunk remained. The arms had vanished, leaving only the hands, which seemed to be holding an object represented by a somewhat slanted thicker black line. Precisely where the individual's head should have been, the plaster had fallen from the wall, removing all evidence. The person was represented in profile, probably nude, facing right and apparently walking. Only traces of toes could be seen on the right foot; on the left everything had been destroyed. Any fingers had been erased and damage to the trunk area removed any possible detail. The figure was painted freehand with a uniform black outline. The entire area within these lines, that is, the silhouette, was filled in with an orange color, of which clear evidence remained on both legs, though it had disappeared almost totally on the rest of the figure. The color we found almost certainly was not the original hue, which must have been affected by being covered by the later plaster.

On the lower right, at the level of the feet, another stylized fish was drawn with straight lines in a vertical position with the head up (pl. 34, fig. 117). The body was based on a rhombus divided into two triangular parts. The upper one, where the mouth should have been, could not be reconstructed since it was almost entirely destroyed, perhaps by a blow from a pick that caused part of the plaster and the wall itself to fall. Inside the lower triangle were three others, sharing as a common base the line dividing the rhombus in two. Triangular fins were appended to the outline, four on the left and probably four more on the right, although only two were still visible. To indicate the tail there was another triangle, whose vertex touched the lowest point of the rhombus. The entire design was executed in regular black lines of even thickness, except the lateral fins and tail, which were solid black; no other color was used in this figure. It measured approximately 35 cm high by 23 cm wide at the extreme points. To its right there were black traces probably representing another figure already lost.

In the center of the far right edge of the mural remains was a fragment of another figure (pl. 32, fig. 117); a strange being effectively impossible to identify. It had a long, possibly narrow, body with an elongated perpendicular prominence joined to its top on the left, and two small inverted V-shaped appendages, one above the other, on the lower right. The figure was outlined with a fairly regular black line, perhaps a little thicker than in the other figures, showing clear evidence of the use of a brush. The two V-shaped appendages were thicker. The silhouette thus formed was filled with the same orange color used to paint the human figure, and on that a series of quite uniform dots was placed at regular intervals. Approximate measurements of this figure were 10 cm high by 4.5 cm maximum width.

Farther right and again on the edge of the fallen portion was another figure, the smallest in the mural. It was the only complete one, but was very faint since it had probably been exposed to weathering longer than the rest. It was this motif that I saw when the wall was exposed and that made me suspect the existence of the mural that we found under the plaster. It also represented a very stylized fish with the head up and slightly inclined to the left (fig. 117). The body was also rhomboid with a V-shaped mouth formed by the extension of the top two lines beyond their point of juncture. One line was added inside the figure, bisecting the top angle. Small triangles were appended to the two lower sides to represent the fins, three on the left side and probably three on the right, although the third has disappeared. The triangular tail was drawn from the lowest point of the rhomboid. Inscribed inside the lower half of the rhombus was a triangle, and in the upper half, two circles, each with a central point, like eyes. From each circle issued a line, the two converging in a triangle inscribed in the lower half of the rhomboidal figure. Perhaps because of its small size, the motif was drawn with thin black lines and rather finely; only its fins and tail were solid color, and only black was used. In spite of being a freehand rendering, the skill of the artist is apparent. The maximum measurements were 10 cm high by 4.5 cm wide.

From the remains of the mural it can be deduced that it was part of a scene in which at least two individuals were walking. One of them was possibly represented playing a musical instrument, perhaps a *quena* or vertical flute. They were surrounded by representations of fishes and another unidentified being, perhaps a pelican or some other animal, marine or terrestrial. The two right-hand fish were doubtless modeled on textile designs and are especially reminiscent of the motifs from Chancay gauzes. The treatment of the personage evokes the figures found on the stairway of the Temple of Pachacámac discussed in the preceding chapter. The coincidence of the association of human figures with fish both here and at Pachacámac is also important. Precise dating is difficult for lack of associations, and the style is not identifiable with any other known. Judging by the type of *adobón* used to build the painted wall, and by the similarity of the mural to the Pachacámac paintings, I am inclined to believe that it belongs to Inca times, logically a local development with distant evocations of some earlier styles deriving from the Middle Horizon styles in the Lima Valley.

In 1973 I found in the files of Abraham Guillén a photograph taken in 1940 of a painting at the same citadel of Huatica Marca or Huadca (fig. 118). From the notes, it must have been in exactly the same place we found the mural just described. The following possibilities exist regarding this painting: it may have been on some vanished structure, or it was part of the chamber whose remains I studied. In the latter case, it may have adorned another wall of that room, as a continuation of the same scene, or it may have decorated the same wall without necessarily being contemporary with the painting just described. After analyzing the style of both, I lean toward the last possibility. In the mural described above, the personage was drawn in profile and with curved lines, while the human figures in fig. 118 are fullface and treated in more or less rectilinear fashion. On the other hand, the way the fish are shown in the first mural, while schematic, made use of curved lines, while in the second the schematicization was carried to the extreme of a totally geometric treatment.

The same technical procedures seem to have been used as in the one just described. Unfortunately, we have only a black-and-white photograph, and no notes were taken of the colors. However, the ground color is visibly darker than the shade used to paint the figures, which were outlined with firmly drawn dark lines. The wall was in poor condition when it was photographed and only a fragment of the painting remained. In it are four personages, two complete and two only partly visible, and the almost complete figure of a fish. The human figures are placed at different heights, a treatment that gives the impression of two planes in spite of the lack of perspective. All the humans are fullface, with arms open and raised to the level of the head, legs slightly flexed, and toes pointing out. Only its left arm and leg remain of the first figure on the left. The next personage seems complete. He wore a large quadrangular headdress and two round ear plugs. Most details of the hands and feet were omitted; on one foot only three toes are shown and on the other, four. There is no indication on the body of either clothing or body painting.

The third individual is somewhat larger in size and has the same characteristics, except that the headdress has been destroyed at the level of the forehead. Only the lower right portion of its body remains of the last figure on the right, which seems to have been treated like the others. Below these figures and slightly to the right is the representation of a fish, painted the same size as the personages and symbolized in a very stylized fashion. The mouth is V-shaped and each side of the body is indicated by three points formed by the vertices of triangles; the tail is trapezoidal. On the top portion are two eyes, indicated by dotted circles, while in the rest of the body are four nested inverted triangles.

The general treatment of the motifs corresponds to that of Late Intermediate Period central coast styles, particularly Chancay Black-on-White. There are also certain echoes of the derived Middle Horizon styles of the

Fig. 118.
Huadca, Lima, 1940 photograph of a mural probably related to the one shown in fig. 116; it was neither studied nor described. Late Intermediate Period.

same area. Chronological placement of this painting would be tentatively set between A.D. 1100 and 1400.

Somewhat farther north, at Chorrillos in the Lima Valley, there was until 1965 a notable urban complex known as Armatambo. In the last years it has been systematically destroyed, with the consent of the authorities. The sparse archaeological information regarding the site contains no reference to paintings. However, Monsignor Pedro Villar Córdova, a man dedicated to the study of the archaeology of Lima, recalled having seen murals on the Huaca Mayor de Armatambo in 1959 (personal communication, 1963). I searched for them fruitlessly, finding not a trace. There may be clues in the historical record, however. Raúl Porras Barrenechea refers to this Inca complex as "the most important of all, the town of Surco or Armatambo, on the slopes of the Morro Solar, where Hernando Pizarro rested before reaching Pachácamac. This was the foremost urban center of the Lima region . . ." (1954, p. 13). And if we turn once more to that rich source of information, Father Bernabé Cobo, we find in his *Fundación de Lima*, 1639, that he refers to the town of Surco, evidently Armatambo, explaining that "this last town was the greatest of all and was set on the eastern flank of the Morro Solar, where its ruins now remain, and it appears to have had a very large population; the houses of the chief may be seen, with the walls painted with various figures, a very sumptuous *guaca* or temple and many other buildings still standing lacking only their roofs . . ." (Cobo, *Fundación*, lib. 1, cap. VII; 1956, tomo 92, p. 301).

THE FORTALEZA VALLEY

Near Paramonga on the Panamerican Highway are the imposing remains of a great prehispanic complex that has been much discussed ever since the time of the Spanish conquest. It is known as the Fortaleza (Fortress) of Paramonga, and its construction has been attributed to the Chimú (figs. 119, 120). The Paramonga complex is in the department of Lima, province of Chancay, district of Pativilca. It must have been another monument

Fig. 119.
Paramonga, Fortaleza Valley, aerial view of the "fortress."

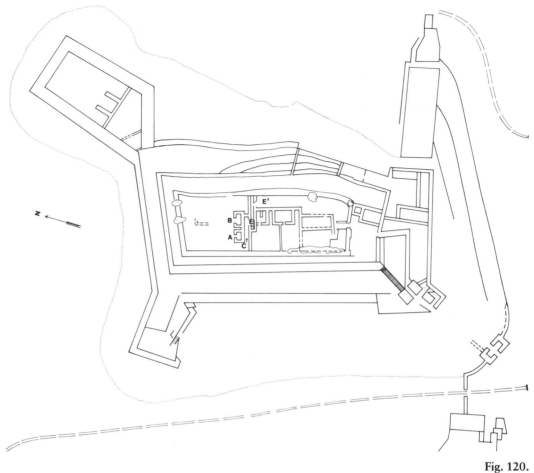

Fig. 120.
Paramonga, plan of "fortress"; murals were found in room E (see arrow and thickened wall line). No scale was provided in original plan.

impressive for its size, beauty, and coloring, as it is yet today, even though now damaged and lacking much of its wall finish. While considered to be one of the best-preserved ruins on the Peruvian coast, the complex has been little studied and described, and most of what has been said of it is simply repetition, adulteration, or exaggeration of the same few firsthand sources.

Paramonga was among the first native monuments seen and described by the Europeans. Miguel de Estete was there on January 27, 1533, and in spite of the fact that his travel notes are generally laconic, he provides a glimpse of his surprise at the sight of Paramonga: "Another day, Saturday, I went to a large town called Parpunga, which is next to the sea [and] in which there is a fortified house with five ramparts or parapets, elabo-

rately painted both inside and out with its doorways very well worked in the Spanish fashion, with two tigers at the principal doorway" (Jérez, 1938, p. 83).

Fifteen years later, when Pedro de Cieza de León passed by the same place, he found the buildings still in relatively good condition. More expressive than Estete, he has left us a vivid image:

> One thing that must be seen in this valley is an elegant and well-planned fortress in the manner of those who built it; and it is surely noteworthy to see where they carried water in canals to irrigate the highest part of it. The rooms and halls were very fine and have painted on the walls many wild animals and birds, everything enclosed by strong walls and well fashioned; now it is all in a state of ruin, and undermined in many places from

Mural Painting in Ancient Peru

searching for gold and silver in burials. At this time this fortress serves only as witness to what it was. (Cieza de León, *Crónica*, cap. LXX; 1922, p. 236)

Garcilaso de la Vega's version must be secondhand, since we know that he could not have been in Paramonga. He asserts that the monument was built by the Incas after the defeat of the Chimú.

Particularly in the Parmunca Valley the Prince [Inca Yupanqui] ordered that a fortress be built in memory and as a trophy of his victory over the Chimu King . . . and because the war was begun in that valley he ordered that the fortress be made there. They made it strong and admirable in the building and very elegant in paintings and other royal curiosities. But the foreigners respected neither the one nor the other to prevent them from demolishing it; some pieces remained that survived the ignorance of those who brought it down, to show how great it was. (Garcilaso de la Vega, lib. 6, cap. XXXIII; 1945, tomo II, p. 78)

His final comment suggests that one of his sources may have been Cieza; the site was still occupied at the time of Estete's visit.

Most important for the present study and, of course, what most attracted the attention of chroniclers and travelers, were the decorations that adorned this edifice, especially its painted walls. Raimondi's notebooks contain interesting information from his visit to the "Fortress of the Incas," as he calls it (1942, p. 166). But there were apparently no longer really striking painted elements, since otherwise the Italian scientist, noted for his observational powers, would have described them. He mentions only the rooms on the third terrace (fig. 120), saying: "Several walls of these rooms are sort of plastered and painted red with iron oxide. The entrance doorway leading from the first to the second terrace is also painted in small squares representing bricks, with different designs" (1942, p. 167). He then discusses the defenses of the structure. Once inside the outer wall, one must pass between two "small forts" to get inside the fortress; then there is a second doorway, also "defended on both sides, and a true doorway appears, which now lacks a threshold, but its sides are well built and painted red with varied designs" (p. 167).

Although E. George Squier mentions Paramonga, he clearly did not know it and had not visited the site. His reference to "the uncouth colored representations of birds and beasts" is credited to Proctor (Squier, 1877, p. 102).

The work of Charles Wiener, in contrast, is important. Not only are his impressions fresh, direct, and spontaneous, but he also carried out some excavations in the structures, uncovering some of the paintings for the first time. His information is not in the body of his text, but rather in a footnote and easily overlooked:

Many of the walls of Pativilca are covered with a sort of red and pink checkerboard, perfectly preserved. On the wall of an alley (gallery between two palaces), covered by adobes and which I caused to be uncovered, a complete and very well preserved fresco was found. The wall is 7.20 m. long by 1.80 m. high. Up to the height of 90 cm. it is covered with a checkerboard which terminates in a red border. The checkerboard is 48 squares long and 8 high. The top of the wall is crowned by a checkerboard of only 2 squares one above the other.
Between the two checkerboards, on ochre yellow, are two groups of three red animals, their heads turned toward the center; two *llamas* and four *huanacos* [fig. 121]. The painter has used these animals as a decorative element, I should say almost like an arabesque; he has exaggerated the curve of the neck and the parabola of the spine and has managed to produce with considerable taste what the modern artist calls a caprice. On the opposite wall, on a red ground, are some yellow polyps. (Wiener, 1880, p. 495)

While it is not clear in this note that the paintings are from the site of Paramonga, since the author mentions only Pativilca, the figure he illustrates on page 494 (my fig. 121) shows the painting mentioned in the note with a caption reading: "Fresco from the top platform of Paramonga, red silhouettes on yellow ground." Beuchat, in his *Manuel d'archéologie américaine* (1912), reproduces Wiener's illustration in his fig. 241, p. 689, but erroneously assigns it to Chanchan.

Middendorf, who visited the site on August 29 and 30, 1886, left us a valuable statement. He had read the chroniclers' statements (though he errs in citing Garcilaso), and so was aware of the paintings. While he photographed, measured, and made a sketch plan of the monument, he neither mentions nor illustrates paintings (Middendorf, 1973, p. 205). He does say, however, that all the outer walls of the fortress were painted an ochre color and that the interior of the rooms was painted yellow (1973, p. 200).

We also have a rather suspect report from Larrabure y Unanue (1935, p. 216). He says that "the walls of the rooms are carefully plastered and decorated with distempered paintings representing wild animals and various allegories alluding to the Inca victory," but gives us no basis for this statement. His mention of "allegories alluding to the Inca victory" implies the existence of scenes containing personages, or something of the sort, but no one else refers to any such thing. Larrabure y

Fig. 121.
"Fortress" of Paramonga, drawing of paintings exposed by Wiener. The checkerboard existed, but the animal representations are almost certainly distorted and strongly influenced by the aesthetic values of the French traveler. Late Horizon.

Unanue may have seen paintings that were already badly damaged and then disappeared, but the reference to "wild animals," copied from Cieza de León, does not fit any other information that we have on the Paramonga decorations and leads me to suspect that his statement is based largely on imagination.

Louis Langlois is the first scientist to examine Paramonga with some care and detail, and he provides the most exact description of the complex (Langlois, 1938). His short monograph is so far the only complete study that we have on this monument and, considering the time in which it was written, is of high quality. He describes the coloring of the Annex in some detail:

> . . . the plaster still covering broad walls is bright or pale red or yellow, or simply light gray. This plaster is made of a very smooth, polished layer of clay covered by a pigmented clay. I have tried to discern any rhythm or sense in the use of these different colors, for example, if they corresponded to a particular orientation or a certain position within the rooms. Red is generally not found on surfaces with southern exposures, but this rule is not absolute. Moreover, some wall faces seem to have been painted in two registers, one red, the other yellow. (Langlois, 1938, p. 290)

Referring to rooms A and B (fig. 120) located on the north end of the top level of the "Fortress," he says, "They are well built and covered on the outside with a beautiful ochre-yellow plaster and on the inside with pale yellow, almost gray, plaster" (1938, p. 41). Of special interest is his description of Room E:

> The doorway of passage C provides access to a very long narrow room (7.50 × 1.50 m.) which is unique in having preserved a part of its mural painting, unfortunately destined to disappear in the near future if not protected. The ground of this painting is a handsome clay plaster. The lower part, to a height of about 1 meter, is covered by a frieze formed of alternating red and white squares 0.19 m. on a side. Above it stretches a panel with a lovely bright ochre-yellow ground. On this ground, wavy red lines may represent serpents or the remains of fantastic animals that the old chroniclers saw. Above this register the frieze of squares run again, similar to the one below. Both the south and west walls bear the same decoration. The north wall is painted entirely red and vestiges of paintings can be seen but in such poor condition that I have been unable to grasp their meaning. (Langlois, 1938, p. 42)

I believe that the remains of paintings that Langlois describes are the same as those uncovered by Wiener (fig. 121), since the reports concur. Both speak of a passageway, and the measurements coincide, as do, in general, the motifs. The chroniclers must have seen another section, since we know that this one was covered by a wall when Wiener arrived. Langlois also mentions motifs in the form of squares on the exterior and the top platform. In some cases the squares alternated red and white, in others red and yellow (1938, pp. 45, 290).

We have several other reports of visits to the site shortly after Langlois's publication. Bennett adds nothing, stating that when he was there, there were no visible decorations, and repeating Squier, who, as I noted, is the least qualified to write on the matter (Bennett, 1939, p. 14). Pedro Rojas Ponce informed me that he was in the "Fortress" about 1940 and saw at that time painted walls in good condition. One of them, on the top part of the monument, bore a checkerboard motif and, in the open squares, figures of llamas and deer in solid color (personal communication, 1973). This information is interesting in its similarity to Wiener's; perhaps the animals the French author called "huanacos" are those that Rojas Ponce saw as deer.

Tello provides a brief but interesting description (1939a). It is clear that he did not make a lengthy examination of the ruins either, since we know that there were still remains of paintings at that time and he never mentions them. He is doubtless repeating the chroniclers when he states that "all the rooms and the walls of passageways leading to them were plastered and adorned with polychrome frescos," and "the principal entry to the temple . . . was adorned with the figure of two jaguars when the temple was visited and sacked by Hernando Pizarro on his first journey from Cajamarca to Pachacamac." It is worth noting that Paramonga was not "sacked by Hernando Pizarro," at least not according to any document that I know of. Tello seems to have simply expanded the accounts of Garcilaso and Cieza without checking his facts.

Giesecke also visited the ruins about the same time and saw the checkerboard motif but mentions no other decorations (1939, p. 118). Moreover, about thirty years ago I saw very clear remains of a red and white checkered design on a wall of the top platform (fig. 122 and wall indicated by arrow in room E, fig. 120), which should be the checkerboard painting seen by both Langlois and Wiener. On a recent visit to the site (July 1983), I found that all the red squares, as well as parts of the wall, had been maliciously chipped out. Some of the white squares still remain, thus creating a false impression of low relief that could lead to future errors. Kauffmann Doig has published a photograph of the same panel taken in 1962 (1978, p. 479, fig. 4, erroneously called fig. 5 in the accompanying text; he published the same photo in 1970, fig. 657, but without a date), which shows by comparison how much the paint had deteriorated by the time of my photograph in fig. 122.

Some of the paintings must have been destroyed between Estete's visit and Cieza's arrival, since it is hard to imagine that such an observant man as Cieza would not have seen and described the "two tigers" (I assume some sort of feline) at the main entrance mentioned by Estete. There is also no other mention of the "polyps" referred to so briefly by Wiener.

While this is hardly the place to discuss the question in detail, it is worth noting that the function assigned to the site all this time has been based simply on appearance, with no functional analysis whatsoever. Thus Tschudi (1847, p. 154), Middendorf (1973, p. 199), Rowe (1946, p. 279), and Gasparini and Margolies (1977, p. 302; 1980, p. 289) consider it a fortress, although the last named also note that it may have been "used by the Incas as a temple." The first to suggest that it was a temple was Tello (1939a). In Kroeber's synthesis of Peruvian archaeology in 1942, he lauds Tello's originality but does not himself take a position on the question (1944, pp. 46–47). Lanning, on the other hand, accepts Tello's suggestion without further comment (1967, p. 153).

Personally, I have grave doubts that the site was truly a fortress. This concept, which the Spaniards attributed to the most impressive structure at Paramonga (which is not an isolated monument but a complex), evidently derives from their own cultural conditioning, which prevented their understanding cultural patterns as different as those of ancient Peru. In fact, analyzing the Paramonga monument on the basis of the canons of sixteenth- to eighteenth-century European military architecture, a striking similarity is revealed to the bastions, which almost always had a pentagonal configuration, projecting from the juncture of two curtain walls and composed of two faces meeting at an angle, two flanks that joined them to the walls of the main structure, and a gorge for entry. In such a defensive system, bastions were always the principal construction, salients toward the open land so that both their faces and flanks fell under covering fire. Spanish soldiers were accustomed to, or at least had a very clear understanding of, this system and could not grasp the fact that this kind of defensive system had no function without artillery.

There is no doubt whatsoever that the shape of Paramonga was influenced by the natural formation upon which it was built. It is possible that the structure served administrative as well as religious functions, but it seems to me that Tello was basically correct in his suggestion.

There is no problem in dating the paintings. They are Inca in both style and composition and are located on structures belonging to Inca times. In 1959, together

Fig. 122.
"Fortress" of Paramonga, 1967 photograph of remains of checkerboard design on the wall of room E, as indicated by arrow in fig. 120. Late Horizon.

with Ernesto Tabío, I personally found fragments of imperial Inca-style pottery in clear association with the structures. While the urban complex of Paramonga could well have originated with the Chimú or earlier, the monument was entirely remodeled by the Incas, and the structures we admire today are of Inca origin, as Unanue so astutely observed in the early nineteenth century (Tschudi, 1847, p. 154). In the last century Rivero and

Tschudi attributed the ruins to this epoch (1851, p. 269), as did Middendorf (1973, p. 199). We cannot tell, however, whether these attributions were based on their personal observations or simply on Garcilaso's words.

The so-called Cerro de la Horca, which is considered to form part of the Paramonga complex, was also studied by Langlois (1938). I visited it in 1975 with Eduardo Jahnsen and observed the remains of red paint on one wall. We also recovered from the ground an adobe of typical Inca manufacture bearing traces of yellow paint on a red ground, which seem to have formed geometric motifs. Thus there may have been paintings at this site, too.

TUMBES

The last description from the coast comes from the northern extreme of modern Peru. When the Spaniards reached Tumbes, they were greatly impressed by the coloring of the temples and palaces (Vega, n.d., p. 25), as indicated by the statements of two of the men who arrived there in 1532. Juan Ruiz de Arce provides a description of one of the palaces in Tumbes, which he refers to as a town of about a thousand houses. "In this town there was a fortified house, made by the most attractive art ever seen . . . it had many apartments with many paintings. . . . The Indians said that he who made that house was called gutima Ay una cava [Guaynacapac] who, they said, was lord of all that land and he ordered the building of that house . . ." (Ruiz de Arce, 1933, p. 358). An unknown author says of one of the temples: "The temple of the sun in which they worshipped was something to see, because they had a large building and all of it, inside and out, painted with large paintings and rich colors, because there are such in that land" (Noticia del Perú, 1938, pp. 212–13).[9] Even in 1535, when Alonso Enríquez de Guzmán arrived in "the great city of Túnbez," he said, "there is a great house of the lord of the land, the walls fashioned of adobes like bricks and painted and varnished with many very fine colors [so] that I never saw a more beautiful thing" (1960, p. 147).

SOUTH HIGHLANDS

Again we have very little evidence from the highlands. What there is, however, demonstrates that the use of color in architecture was as widespread there as on the coast. Climatic conditions prevailing in the highlands doubtless produced very rapid destruction of such decoration.

On the Island of Titicaca, in Lake Titicaca, is the Palace of the Inca. Squier tells us that its walls were stuccoed and painted yellow, "while the inner parts and mouldings of the door-ways and niches were of different shades of red" (1877, p. 345). Of the Palace of the Virgins of the Sun on the Island of Coati in the same lake,

he says: "The exterior was painted yellow, with the exception of the niches and the undersides of the graduations of the cornice, which were red" (1877, p. 362).

Squier also left us a good description and a most interesting illustration of a *chullpa*, or burial tower, near Palca in the area bordered by the departments of Tacna and Puno and the Bolivian border (fig. 123). This building is square in section, and

> The surface had been roughcast with clay, and over this was a layer of finer and more tenacious clay or stucco, presenting a smooth and even surface. . . .
> The stuccoed surface of the chulpa had been painted in white and red, as shown in the engraving [fig. 123], where the shaded parts represent the red, and the light parts the white, of the original. The opening was towards the east, on a level with the platform, and was about eighteen inches wide and high. But every other face of the chulpa had a painted opening, which led me to think that the real one had once been closed and also painted over, so that the fronts corresponded in appearance. (Squier, 1877, pp. 243–44)

Fig. 123.
Chullpa *at Pallca as drawn by Squier in 1864. Late Horizon(?).*

Emilio Mendizábal told me about and showed me a photograph of another *chullpa*, also square in section, located near Macusani on the road to the foothill tropical forest in the department of Puno. This structure, like all *chullpas* in that region, had a rectangular doorway and a roof of overlapping stone slabs with projecting eaves. It was built entirely of stone, and its walls were covered with clay plaster that was painted red. In spite of poor preservation, the remains of painting were still visible on much of the wall. Mendizábal did not remember if the other walls were also painted. This structure corresponds, typologically, to Inca times. Rogger Ravines recalls having seen similar *chullpas* in the same region and noted that sometimes the painted areas were divided into sectors, so in some places the walls were divided in two and in others into four parts (personal communication, 1973). It would presumably have also been possible to paint one wall one color and another a different one.

Ravines also recalled that the same thing is found in Ancash, a statement confirmed by Pedro Rojas Ponce, who commented when he saw Mendizábal's photograph from Macusani on the great similarity to *chullpas* he had seen in the department of Ancash. The same phenomenon appears to have occurred farther north, since we hear of a series of *chullpa*-like structures in the area of Chota, in the department of Cajamarca, probably dating to the Late Intermediate Period, the interiors of which were painted pink (Daniel Morales Chocano, personal communication, 1976).

On the road between Cuzco and Sicuani, on the right side of the Vilcanota River, in Rajchi in the district of San Pedro de Cacha, stand the remains of the Temple of Viracocha (see Gasparini and Margolies, 1977, pp. 243–62; 1980, pp. 234–54). There is a design in red plaster on the lower portions of the central wall, which are of typical Inca stonework. The plaster does not cover the stone portion entirely, however, but was applied in the form of an inverted step pyramid, with the base at the top edge of the stonework and terminating at floor level in a small square (Rogger Ravines, personal communication, 1976). This design can barely be discerned in photographs in Moorehead (1979, fig. 35) and Gasparini and Margolies (1977, fig. 260; 1980, figs. 231, 238). It is the same design as the one cut into the tops of adobe walls at Tambo Colorado, mentioned on p. 153.

In spite of the fact that Cuzco, as capital of the Inca empire, was the center of special interest for the European conquerors, we do not really have many details regarding its architecture. While we have no archaeological information regarding the use of painted decoration in Cuzco, it has been possible to find some documentation in the chronicles.

The buildings were of stone, which was exploited for its beauty. Nevertheless, the use of color was not entirely neglected, as revealed by the comment of Pedro Sancho de la Hoz, Pizarro's secretary, referring to the structures on the plaza in Cuzco: "they are the finest of the city in painting and adornment, and [are] of stone; and the finest of them is the house of Guainacaba, the old leader, and its doorway is of white and rose marble and of other colors" (Sancho de la Hoz, cap. XVII; 1550, tomo III, f. 413). On the basis of this comment Prescott wrote: "The walls were sometimes stained or painted with gaudy tints" (1942, p. 314). And Squier concluded, regarding the question of color in the Cuzco buildings, that the more important ones "clearly, were neither stuccoed nor painted. The residences of the people, built of rough stones laid in clay, were probably stuccoed and painted yellow and red . . ." (1877, p. 453). This opinion is supported by Rowe, doubtless the foremost authority on prehispanic Cuzco today, who states: "The walls originally were covered by a uniform coat of mud plaster which might be painted" (1946, p. 227).

Much has been written of the Qoricancha in Cuzco, commonly called the Temple of the Sun, but I shall cite only Cieza de León and Garcilaso de la Vega. Cieza's reference to painting is brief. After describing other adornments in the temple, he simply states: "On other walls other greater things were sculpted and painted" (Cieza de León, *Señorío*, cap. XXVII; 1967, p. 94). Garcilaso is more specific. Speaking of the shrine of the Rainbow in the Qoricancha, he says: "This hall was entirely sheathed in gold. On the gold sheets on one of its walls the rainbow was painted very naturally, with all its vibrant colors" (Garcilaso de la Vega, lib. 3, cap. XXII; 1945, tomo I, p. 175). Although this adornment was not a true mural painting, it is worth mentioning because it is so close in concept.

Even had there been painted walls on buildings in the high tropical rain forest, they would have been destroyed by climatic conditions. Nevertheless, Manuel Chávez Ballón recalls having seen the remains of red, orange, and white on walls at Machu Picchu (personal communication, 1980). I was also told by Edmundo Guillén that the main building at Vilcabamba, also in the department of Cuzco, still bears the remains of plaster with traces of red and yellow (personal communication, 1978).

Near the Apurímac River, on or near the Inca highway from Cuzco to Quito, stood the structure housing the oracle of Apurímac. Pedro Pizarro, who saw it, notes that it was "highly colored" but provides no further details about the building, just its contents (Pizarro, 1944, p. 73). Cobo simply summarizes and embroiders on Pizarro's statements (Cobo, *Historia*, lib. 13, cap. XX; 1956, tomo 92, p. 199).

THE NORTH HIGHLANDS

Francisco de Jérez has left us an especially informative description of Atahualpa's residence in Cajamarca:

> The abode of Atabalipa which was in the midst of his encampment is the best that has been seen among the Indians, although small; made in four rooms, set around a courtyard, and in [the courtyard] a tank to which water so hot that the hand cannot touch it comes through a pipe. This water issues boiling from a nearby mountain. Cold water comes through another pipe and they are joined on the way and come mixed, through a single pipe, to the tank; and when [the people] wish only one to come they [close] the other. The tank is large, made of stone; outside the house, in one part of the enclosure is another tank, not as well made as this one; it has stone stairs by which they descend to wash themselves.
>
> The chamber where Atabalipa passed the day is a hall overlooking an orchard, and next [to it] is a chamber where he slept, with a window on the courtyard and tank, and the hall likewise opens onto the courtyard; the walls are painted with a bright red resin, better than red ochre, which is very striking, and the wood upon which lies the roofing of the house, is dyed the same color; another facing room has four domes, round like bells, all four incorporated in one; this [room] is plastered, white as snow. The other two [rooms] are service quarters. In front of this abode passes a river. (Jérez, 1938, pp. 66–67)

Finally, from southern Ecuador we have a comment from Cieza de León regarding Tumebamba, one of the principal Inca seats in this conquered territory. "The fronts of many structures were elegant and highly painted," he tells us (Cieza de León, *Crónica*, cap. XLIV; 1922, p. 155).

With that comment we come to an end of the evidence regarding mural painting in the Late Horizon.

—8—
Materials and Techniques

Because they have been much neglected, technical aspects are especially difficult to discuss. Moreover, many statements on this subject are merely speculative or hypothetical, or the result of superficial observations. A certain amount can be gleaned, however, from all that has been written. At least two basic facts emerge: (1) The techniques used to execute prehispanic murals were relatively simple and unsophisticated; (2) they did not vary greatly through time.

There is evidence that in the Early Horizon the wall finish was hardened by fire and, in some cases, so were the modeled reliefs (Tello, 1960, p. 32), but there is no evidence that this technique was used in the case of paintings. At Puncurí the walls were first plastered and then incised and painted, but we have no details on the procedure (Tello, 1970, p. 77). An identical technique was used on the two Lima-style murals found in the Chillón and Chancay valleys (Stumer, 1954; Ravines, ms.). The walls were first plastered and then washed with a ground color upon which the decorative motifs were then drawn.

In the case of Moche paintings a single technique was used on the monuments in the Moche Valley and those in Nepeña, a fact that might be interpreted as resulting from a single established tradition (see Bonavia, 1959b, p. 24; Kroeber, 1930, p. 71; 1949, p. 430; Schaedel, 1970, pp. 318–19). On the prepared, still-damp plaster a coat of dense white color was applied to serve as ground. Once the ground color was dry, the figures were outlined with incision and then filled with paint.[1] There may have been a variant in which the motifs were incised while the plaster was still fresh, as Morales Gamarra thinks was done at Moche (ms.a). These incisions were firm, continuous, and not very deep. In some cases they were filled with black paint so that the figures would be more conspicuous. The brush strokes also demonstrated skill, almost never exceeding the limits circumscribed by the incisions. The only major variation seems to have been at La Mayanga in Lambayeque, where the colors were applied while the ground color was still damp. We know nothing yet about the techniques used in Middle Horizon paintings outside of the Moche tradition.

Although there are various examples of paintings from the Late Intermediate Period, our only evidence regarding the techniques used comes from the Túcume mural. The treatment of the motif on this mural is Chimú, but there are two aspects of special interest. While the technique of execution is evidently Moche, the checkerboard may have Middle Horizon antecedents. Thus the mural may be an indication of cultural continuity in Lambayeque, which, in its conception and technology, would find its direct antecedents in the artistic canons used at La Mayanga, only varying in the basic motif.

Regarding paintings from Inca times, while it was Wiener who first attempted to describe application technique in a footnote referring to the painted walls of Pachacámac (1880, p. 495), the major contribution to this subject is clearly that of Muelle and Wells (1939), who found considerable evidence *in situ* of great importance for the interpretation and reconstruction of technology. Like the French traveler, they made their observations at Pachacámac.

> . . . initially, the wall, of adobes made in a wooden mold, . . . was covered with an uneven [coat of] plaster. Over this "finish" the paint was applied with large wads of cotton. We separated from the walls the remains of cotton fibers that had remained stuck to the paint, and also, at the foot of the terracing, recovered sample 39.1–

42 consisting of fibers impregnated with ochre-pink, the same shade as that used on the walls. Probably in this operation the ancient Peruvians used rags soaked in paint with which they repeatedly moistened the wall, or hides with wool as is done today to make the so-called "broqueles," [2] but we have found nothing in this case that would prove it. Once the base was painted, the motifs were put on top, drawn without previous planning, with brushes made of hanks of human hair, which have also been found near the terracing. It is not difficult even now to find some strands of hair caught between the layers of paintings. The decorative figures had a black outline which was not the first sketch, but rather was added *a posteriori*, doubtless to emphasize the delimitation. (Muelle and Wells, 1939, pp. 274, 277; see also their fig., p. 267)

They also found evidence for the renewal of the paintings, including sixteen superimposed layers of paint at the entrance to the top platform of the Temple of Pachacámac (see above, p. 144). Of the ten brushes reportedly of human hair, later examination suggested that one was of alpaca fiber (Muelle, personal communication, 1972). I shall refer later to the remains of paint that were found and analyzed. In addition to these items, however, Muelle and Wells also found some of the vessels used to mix the colors. Of these they wrote:

> They reduced the colors to powder on grinding stones[3] and [in] small stone mortars, some of which still preserve vestiges. The paste was prepared and deposited in vessels of various sizes and classes, depending on the amount to be used. For small quantities, especially the fine colors destined to cover wood, there are multicellular recipients carefully carved of stone or wood, and everything from shells to small cane tubes and little skin packets was used to store the colored powders. But at Pachacámac, as might be expected given the quality of the colors and extent of the painted surfaces, the paste was stored in terracotta pots and the powders also in pots, [as well as] small cloth bags and even gourds. . . . (Muelle and Wells, 1939, p. 277)

The Huadca paintings were produced by a process similar to that used on the other murals, that is, the work was painted on a prepared, painted plaster ground. The only difference is that the Huadca figures were first outlined with a thick black line and then filled in with color. In summary, technological variations are very small and limited to the method of delineating the figures.

Another important problem in studying these paintings is that of color. Properly speaking, use of the word "color" is incorrect when applied to pigments and colorants. The proper term would be "colored substance," since we are dealing with materials that adhere to others or penetrate them (either with or without a chemical reaction taking place), thus providing coloration.[4] All that pigments can do is reflect, absorb, or cause the selective transmission of light (Chambers, 1964; Trucco, 1934; Mueller and Mae, 1969). It should also be kept in mind that "in many cases . . . the color does not depend so much on the molecular constituents of the pigment or the dominant color of the light as on the structure of the surface of the object" (Mueller and Mae, 1969, p. 98). Thus, although I shall continue to use the word color, for the sake of convenience, it is important to keep in mind that it refers basically to the identification of the hues and the descriptive terminology used for that purpose. It should be unnecessary to allude to the importance of individual judgment in assigning values to a given color, or to how great individual variation may be, up to and including pathological conditions. Infinite sensations are caused by the union of colors, which the human eye perceives as a function of the laws of optics and chromatics, so that fixed rules cannot be established in this regard. It is a function of instinct, of culture, and of the expression of the artistic spirit of each individual or group (Wagner, 1972). In the words of Mueller and Mae:

> . . . human vision has its own laws, often disconcerting, that can vary from one person to another. Frequently logical deductions based on the characteristic traits of the physical colors may not apply to color vision. Naturally the laws of physics have something to do with human color perception and are the basis upon which the analysis of color vision is based, but they serve only as a starting point in a process influenced by the physiology of the eye and the brain as well as by human psychology. (1969, p. 113)

The only way to deal with these problems is by the use of standardized color charts for classification purposes, since, aside from the total difference between the means of achieving the colors with light and with pigments, the names given to the different shades of a color are utterly inadequate from a scientific standpoint; rarely can any two people agree on the exact tone described by a name. Obviously a precise nomenclature is needed (Mueller and Mae, 1969, pp. 95, 108). In other words, a standard must be used that will minimize error. While any color chart or color dictionary may be used, in the case of these ancient murals experience has shown that, since all the pigments are derived from minerals, it is preferable to work with the terms used for classifying soils, which generally order the colors according to three attributes: hue, brilliance, and saturation.[5]

It is unfortunate that such dictionaries have been used

extensively only at Pañamarca and the Huaca de la Luna (Bonavia, 1959b; Morales Gamarra, ms.a), and to a lesser extent by Muelle at Pachacámac (Muelle and Wells, 1939). Thus, any comparative study is impeded by the great diversity of terms that have been used, terms that make the true chromatic significance impossible to determine.

Establishment of the type of pigments used in antiquity to paint murals is another basic problem. A review of the literature on this topic reveals that, while information is not abundant, numerous authors express opinions on the matter. In most cases, however, these are no more than opinions, and often unsupported. Thus Florián speculates that the colors used to paint the walls at the Huaca del Oro were of mineral and vegetable origin (1951, p. 12), while Stumer, describing the paintings of Cerro Culebra, states categorically that "the paints were vegetable" (1954, p. 227). Tello, referring to the paints used in Chavín structures, mentions colored earths but adds "cochineal, certain molluscs and plants" (1956, p. 66), while Wiener, commenting on paints in general, wrote that they were ochres (1880, p. 495). Oscar Lostaunau, describing the Túcume mural, conjectured that copper oxides and coal had been used to achieve some of the colors (personal communication, 1958), and Ravines suggests, in the case of the paints of Cerro Trinidad, that manganese was used for black and chalk or calcium carbonate for white (ms.). I myself remarked in field notes made during the study of the Huadca painting that the black was probably based on manganese, yellow on limonite, and red on iron oxide. Of the paint used at the Huaca de la Luna, Morales Gamarra wrote that the white was based on kaolin (with a high content of aluminum oxide), the black on iron silicate, the cadmium yellow on limonite (ferric oxide), and the red on hematite (iron oxide) (ms.a, p. 5). And Schaedel suggested, on the basis of my earlier analyses from other sites (Bonavia, 1974, Appendix), that at the Huaca Pintada the red could be from cinnabar, the yellow from hydrated iron oxides, and the black a pyrolusite or black iron oxide (Schaedel, 1978, p. 33). But I repeat that these are simply opinions, of no scientific value until confirmed.

It may be possible to find interesting references in the chronicles, since early observers might have seen a wall being painted, witnessed the preparation of colors, or simply gathered information on the subject. The following quote about Peru from Oviedo is suggestive of what might be expected: "[There are] veins of earth of all colors, and especially yellow, green, red and a very fine blue: the green is [from a] plant and the others, as noted, are earths." (Oviedo y Valdés, lib. XLVI, cap. XVII; 1855, p. 231).

To my knowledge the first scientific analyses of mural paints in Peru were done by Wells at Muelle's request on samples collected at Pachacámac. Wells concluded that they were basically iron combinations, principally the natural ochres. Sample 1, obtained from a blue-green rock, was a ferrous oxide. The red of samples 2, 4, 5, 6, and 8 resulted from a content of anhydrous ferric oxide (Fe_2O_3, or hematite). The yellow color of samples 3 and 7 was from hydrous ferric oxide ($2Fe_2O_3 \cdot 3H_2O$, or limonite). Moreover, Wells noted that the permeable substances were impregnated with soluble salts, sulfates, and chlorides. One sample of a yellow color was an arsenic sulfide, pentasulfide As_2S_5, while in two of the green samples, he detected copper salts, oxichloride, atacamite ($CuCl_2 \cdot 2CuO \cdot 4H_2O$), and ferrous iron silicates. The black sample was an impure hematite in the form of specular iron or shining hematite, which produces a red-colored pigment when reduced to a powder. Finally, another yellow sample came from sulfates of ferric iron, which, when ground, give a rather weak yellow color that may have been used as an intermediate substance in the preparation of red pigment by burning. Wells comments, as speculation, that since iron sulfates are found mainly in the desert regions of Chile (coquimbite, copiapite), their being found in such a distant region might indicate trade (Muelle and Wells, 1939, pp. 279–82).

The analysis of twelve samples of Moche paint from Pañamarca that I requested indicated that what had been used was basically calcium carbonate, the different colors being obtained from varieties of iron oxides. Thus the cream-white tones (for color dictionary definitions, see Bonavia, 1959b) and dark sepia derived from limonite; a gray-white, a dark black, and two shades of dark sky-blue from a greater or lesser proportion of magnetite; dark orange, dark brick-red, red-brown, and ochre-red from different proportions of hematite; while to achieve a light orange, a mixture of limonite and hematite was used (Bonavia, 1959b, pp. 48–49).

The La Mayanga paints were analyzed by David Weide at the request of Christopher Donnan. For the red pigment he found two diagnostic X-ray lines indicating that the material could have been cinnabar (HgS). This identification could be made only tentatively, since the other line characteristic of cinnabar was masked by a very strong line from quartz found in the adobe material on which the paint was laid. No hematite spectra were present. In the case of the yellow pigment a very definite

X-ray pattern indicates that the material was goethite/limonite $Fe_2O_3 \cdot H_2O$. This material commonly appears as a bright yellow crust on highly oxidized soils. For the black pigment three partially diagnostic lines indicate that the material could be pyrolusite (MnO_2). A definite X-ray pattern shows that the material for the white pigment was calcined lime, which might have been obtained from burning limestone or shells (Donnan, 1972, p. 88).

Hermann Trimborn informed me that analyses that he had ordered on paint samples from the Huaca Chotuna in Lambayeque had also revealed the presence of iron oxide (Fe_2O_3).

Most recently, excellent results were obtained by Charles R. Ross II on pigments from the Chornancap mural submitted to him by Donnan. The analysis, using X-ray diffraction, provided the following results: the red pigments are partly hematite, Fe_2O_3, and partly goethite, $FeO(OH)$; yellow is hematite, Fe_2O_3, goethite, $FeO(OH)$, and alunite, $(K,Na)Al_3(SO_4)_2(OH)_6$; both the dark and light green pigments are malachite, $Cu_2CO_3(OH)_2$, and paratacamite, $Cu_2(OH)_3Cl$; white is calcite, $CaCO_3$, and plagioclase, $NaAlSi_3O_8 - CaAl_2Si_2O_8$; the black is graphite, C, and chalcosiderite, $CuFe_6(PO_4)_4(OH)_8 4H_2O$. On the basis of these results, Ross suggested that the red and yellow pigments could have been obtained from the same mineral source. In fact, goethite and hematite are generally found together in mineral deposits and could have been selected by eye by the ancient artisans, the coloration thus resulting from the use of different proportions of the two minerals. Ross also mentioned that the differences in coloration could be the result of the degree to which the minerals were pulverized. The smaller the grain size, the greater the tendency to shift from red to yellow. The grains of hematite can be seen to be smaller in the yellow pigment than in the red. The two shades of green also seem to have originated from a single source. Geologically malachite and paratacamite appear together. The first tends to be a lighter green than the second, so that when chunks of these minerals were removed, a lighter or darker tone would simply represent a variation in the proportions of these two minerals (Donnan, ms.).

A series of samples I was able to obtain that had been gathered from Illimo (Huaca Pintada?), the ruins of Pachacámac, Tambo Colorado, Huaca Licapa, Túcume, and the walls of a looted tomb in the cemetery of Los Alamos in the Huarmey Valley turned out to be iron oxides, and in one case clay with lime. The data on these analyses are presented in detail in the Appendix.

Finally, although it is not directly related to the matter

at hand, Mejía Xesspe mentions (1968, p. 24) that in the rock paintings at Udima (Monte Calvario, Cataче), the ochre-red is an iron oxide or hematite (Fe_2O_3); ochre-yellow, an iron hydroxide or limonite ($HFeO_2 \cdot H_2O$); the dark brown or black, manganese dioxide (MnO_2); the blue from lapis lazuli has an animal fat content; the green is copper carbonate or malachite ($Cu_2(OH)_2CO_3$) and the white, a calcium carbonate ($CaCO_3$) or perhaps volcanic ash. He attributes these data to Asbjorn Pedersen but does not state whether the material was analyzed or whether these results are simply conjecture.

Thus, while it has been said that the various colors achieved in the paintings were perhaps the result of colored substances obtained from several origins, animal (shells, cochineal or some mollusc), vegetable, or mineral, the analyses allow us to state firmly that only mineral pigments were employed in the preparation of mural paints in ancient Peru.

Much more complicated than determining the sources of pigments is the problem of ascertaining whether some material was used to fix the colors and, if so, what this material might have been. Not only has this question not been investigated but, according to specialists, its investigation involves serious technical problems. Ravines noted that fixing colors, especially some of them, must have been one of the problems faced by the prehispanic painters (ms.). But Florián's statement about the Huaca del Oro mural, that "at the last moment of its execution it might have received a wash or vegetable varnish, brightening it" (1951, p. 12), is simply speculation. The same is true of Villar Córdova's statement that the color was mixed with the clay and the surface carefully burnished so the paintings could resist weathering (1942, pp. 252–53). In fact, we owe the only serious comment on the subject, even though still hypothetical, to Jorge C. Muelle:

> Although the vehicle employed in fixing the pigments cannot be determined, it is easy to guess that it was a vegetable substance of the same sort as that used throughout the highlands today by Indians who use the following procedure: They cut slices of *gigantones* (*Cereus*) and leave them overnight in clear water to release the viscous sap; in this way a sort of gum water is procured in which they dissolve the earths, thus preparing the paint. The analysis of sample 39.1–41 (5) indicates the presence of an organic vehicle and we also have the testimony of chroniclers like Betanzos: "So that the mixture that was to be brought for finishing the houses, both inside and out, would adhere and not crack, [Inca Yupanqui] ordered that they bring for that time a great quantity of some cacti that they call *agua*

colla quisca with the juice of which these walls were bathed. . . ." (Muelle and Wells, 1939, p. 277)

Muelle's reference to sample 39.1-41 is based on the analysis by Wells, who wrote in one of the appendixes to the Pachacámac study: "under the blowpipe the powder first acquires a black color, returning, as the burning continues, to its original color, suggesting that some organic substance was used as mordant or vehicle for the application of the color . . ." (Muelle and Wells, 1939, p. 280).

The fragment from Betanzos quoted by Muelle is of sufficient interest to warrant reproduction of the entire passage from the original sixteenth-century source:

> Thus, [Inca Yupanqui] ordered that when the buildings were made and complete and placed in the proportion and appearance that they were to have, and so that the mixture that was to be brought for finishing the houses, both inside and out, would adhere and not crack, he ordered that they bring for that time a great quantity of some cacti that they call *aguacolla quizca* with the juice of which these walls were to be bathed; and the mixture being very well kneaded and mixed with a great quantity of wool, it was to be put on the walls over the wetting that you have already heard, of the aforesaid cacti, and that into this mixture, if they did not want to add wool, they might add dry grass, which was to be very finely ground, and thus provide luster to those walls and buildings. (Betanzos, cap. XVI; 1880, pp. 109–10)

Cobo also comments on the matter in describing the cacti: "From some kinds of them is made a glue for whitening the walls; which is made by cooking some tender slices and the water in which they are cooked becomes glutinous and appropriate for the purpose" (Cobo, *Historia*, lib. 5, cap. IV; 1956, tomo 91, pp. 203–204). Ravines also thinks that this was the procedure that, he says, is still used in the Peruvian highlands (1980, p. 345).

Furthermore, the same procedure was employed in the Colonial Period, although beaten egg was added to the mixture, an obvious European influence.

> We know practically nothing of how these civil or religious murals were painted between the sixteenth and nineteenth centuries. The majority were not frescos as shown by the slight penetration of the colorant into the surface. Most generalized, at least in the second half of the eighteenth century, was a technique consisting of the application to the walls of Ccontay (white earth) fixed with the juice of the Aguaccollay or Gigantón (Cactus). Upon this dry whitened surface the painting was done with so-called "earth colors," of local origin dissolved in glue, gum and beaten egg with water. The same procedure was used when murals were repainted

as can be seen on the principal arch in Checacupe. (Macera, 1975, p. 66)

It is hard to tell exactly which species of cactus was used, since the common name *gigantón* applies in general to *Trichocereus* Riccob., of which a dozen species are known from the Peruvian coast and highlands (Soukup, 1970).

Arturo Jiménez Borja experimented with a fixative based on the sap of *Cereus* in repainting the Cerro Sechín motifs, apparently with good results (personal communication, April 1974).

Discussing Pachacámac, Petersen repeats Muelle and Wells's statements but also mentions zapote gum (*Capparis angulata*) as a fixative agent (1970, p. 18), an interesting datum in view of the large quantity of zapote growing on the north coast of Peru. Petersen told me in 1973 that this information was of ethnographic origin. I have ascertained personally that *zapote* gum is still used in the area of Motupe, department of Lambayeque, as a fixative in the preparation of paint for walls. The gum is dissolved in water and the paint mixed with this solution. Apparently the process is empirical and no exact proportions are given for the preparation.

In the Old World the acacia, a member of the Leguminosae, was used for fixing colors (Branzani, 1935, p. 39). A member of the plant family commonly found in Peru is the *huarango* (*Acacia macracantha*) (Towle, 1961, p. 42), which may well have served the same purpose.

Schaedel believes that no fixative was used at the Huaca del Dragón and that the colors on the walls were constantly retouched while the edifice was in use (1967a, pp. 445–46). He does not, however, offer any evidence to support this conjecture.

Closely related to these other technical procedures are those of repainting and of remodeling, a frequent occurrence on these monuments, which were often occupied or used for many centuries. Generally, when a wall was to be repainted, the previous painting was simply covered with a more or less dense layer of color, but in several places there is evidence that the artisans preferred to cover the walls with a thin layer of plaster, without erasing or destroying the underlying painting, and then repeat the entire painting process. This procedure was first noted by Max Uhle at Pachacámac (1903, p. 80) and Tambo Colorado, where he describes it very clearly: ". . . the uppermost covering of color [was] not the only one applied. Many covers of colors, sometimes separated by thin layers of uncolored clay, had been applied in most of the cases . . ." (ms., f. 62). Later Muelle

encountered the same phenomenon at Pachacámac (Muelle and Wells, 1939, p. 277), as did I at Huadca.

In some cases, however, rather than simply overpainting, another wall was raised in front of the painting to be replaced, taking special care to prevent damage to the covered paintings. This is a practice that merits a separate study in and of itself. In the absence of such a work, however, I have gathered information on several cases, and shall simply present it.

José Eulogio Garrido had observed this practice and tried to analyze it in his anonymous discussion of decorated walls both painted and with reliefs: "All the decorated walls . . . were covered . . . or rather walled in . . . purposefully at certain times. . . ." He then presented some unanswered questions, revealing that he had checked the facts in each case, adding:

> The fact is that all the decorated walls were covered by parallel walls very close to them, so close that from the exterior nothing suggested the ornamentation, but always assuring that the covering walls would cause no damage, almost not even scratches on the decoration. Startling but true. And the same occurred with the walls discovered in the last century, as with those recently brought to light. And the same also in edifices of the Chavín Culture. . . . The good preservation of the decorations that have recently been uncovered shows that the ancient folk took singular pains to care for them and cover them very carefully. (Garrido, 1956b, p. 7)

Garrido's information seems to me to be of great value since throughout his life he knew the coastal monuments intimately. Time is proving his observations to be correct.

Mejía Xesspe recalled that the Temple of Puncurí, with Chavín relationships, was covered with clay in some sectors, but in such a way that it had clearly been applied with special care not to damage the decorations (personal communication, 1973). The discoverer of the monument, John B. Harrison, recalls that the well-known clay idol was covered by a layer of fine river sand that had probably been purposely placed there and held in by a wall as protection for the painting. At the Huaca Lucía, of the same time period, as I noted earlier, Shimada reports "its architectural features [were] carefully 'entombed' in thick layers of pure white sand," which he tentatively interprets, given the excellent state of preservation, the quantity of sand, and the form in which it was found, as possibly a sort of "ritual burial" of the architecture (1981, pp. 39–40).

I observed a similar phenomenon at the Huaca Licapa, where the flat reliefs were also covered by a layer of very clean, fine clay, applied directly over the decoration, thus avoiding the slightest harm to it. When I was at the site in 1955, part of the decoration was still covered with this coating, and we proved that it could be removed with great ease, since the colored pigments had not allowed it to adhere tightly to the decoration. Moreover, the room upon whose walls this decoration was placed had been filled at some time with sand, and still the decorative elements remained intact. Florián, who saw the monument before I did, wrote that "the principal panel, the upper secondary panels, are covered by a layer of silty clay and soil," and when the site was abandoned, "to hide the famous reliefs . . . they filled the entire chamber with clean sand" (Florián, 1954, p. 2). I disagree with Schaedel, who states that this sand resulted from flooding (1957, p. 94 caption to fig. 2). Evidence to support my position is clearly visible in the photograph illustrating one of my articles (Bonavia, 1965b) and in fig. 27. The reader will recall that the Huaca Licapa is related to the Gallinazo style of the north coast.

Stumer encountered similar evidence when he uncovered the polychrome painting of Cerro Culebra, which is in the Lima style. The original edifice upon which the paintings were executed was at some time covered by another later structure. Nevertheless, not only were the paintings covered in some parts with a fine plaster, but the builders had clearly endeavored not to hurt them, since they were found in a good state of preservation (Stumer, 1954, p. 227).

We have more evidence from the Moche culture. Bennett, referring to Pañamarca (although he calls it Pañamarquilla), notes that many of the painted walls "have been completely covered in later building periods" (1939, p. 17). Indeed, when Schaedel worked at the site he observed a very similar phenomenon in the main plaza (1951, 1967b, 1970). He interpreted this as a reoccupation of the Moche monument by "Tiahuanacoids," who covered the existing paintings. The question of who covered the paintings is debatable and not important here. What is important is the fact that the murals were covered at some time, and on this point Schaedel's observations are important:

> The Tiahuanacoids must have been responsible for some of the partitioning between the main and corner buildings, but we could not determine how much. The corner building itself appears to have been filled in and covered up externally by the Tiahuanacoids, as we could determine by the courses of adobe covering the paintings. They apparently followed a similar procedure with the sunken plaza. In the area where we cleared away

the material immediately in front of the friezes, we found that the friezes themselves had been covered up by two courses of adobes and that further toward the center the plaza seemed to be filled with miscellaneous refuse. This suggests that the Tiahuanacoids utilized the sunken plaza as a dumping ground. Although it is not clear as to their reasons, it would appear that they levelled the top of the wall lining the plaza so that the heads of all of the figures were destroyed [fig. 30]. While it is conceivable that the Mochicas themselves may have placed the adobe covering against the friezes, it is difficult to explain away the architectural decapitation. (Schaedel, 1951, pp. 150–51; 1967b, pp. 110–11)

I know only two other documented examples of paintings being damaged or destroyed during prehispanic architectural changes. I noted earlier that a door was opened through part of one of the Huaca de la Luna murals, and Shimada reported that an entire painted wall was removed in the course of ancient remodeling at the Huaca Corte (1981, p. 43). In all other cases, I repeat, the pictorial decoration has been respected. In 1972 I was able to confirm Schaedel's statements, since, as I explained in discussing the Pañamarca murals, following his work new figures were found that he had not seen. Not only was there a parallel adobe wall closely placed some 20 cm in front of the painted wall, but the space between the two walls had been filled in with very fine, clean sand to protect the paintings. I also reached the conclusion that the mural painting that I studied at the same site had been purposely covered in the Moche epoch, since it can be seen that the walls, painted in a single epoch, are superimposed one on another, always respecting the pictorial motifs. When I discussed this matter with Horkheimer, he told me that he had observed a similar phenomenon many times on Moche and Chimú coastal ruins. In fact, there is yet another example of it at Pañamarca. It is very clear that the wall painted with the mural Schaedel labeled B (pl. 7) and I called the "feline snail" cut another wall, also painted, which appeared to be of the same epoch (Schaedel, 1970, illustration on p. 315; Bonavia, 1959b, pp. 26–27).

Yet another example is to be found in the Middle Horizon mural brought to light at the Huaca de la Luna in 1955, which was on a

> wall that had been uncovered by *huaqueros* accidentally in perforating the earth in search of tombs, when the unpainted wall that totally covered the decorated one collapsed. It should be noted that this is not a unique occurrence, since we have confirmed that all the decorated walls—painted or in relief—that have been discovered in other prehispanic monuments of the same

culture as the Huaca de la Luna, in various places of the Trujillo and Ancash coast, were purposely and mathematically covered by others built perhaps only for this reason, the same having been observed in edifices of later periods at Chan Chan. (Garrido, 1956a, p. 28)

Garrido's statement was confirmed by the investigations of the Chan Chan–Moche Valley Project (Mackey and Hastings, 1982).

As already noted, Donnan found that the paintings at Chornancap were carefully covered before other structures were erected over them (personal communication, April 1982). The Túcume mural had also been covered by a wall that concealed it without harm when the doorway it adorned was walled up (Lostaunau, personal communication, 1958). And finally, the mural found by Charles Wiener at Paramonga was "covered by adobes" and "very well preserved" when discovered (Wiener, 1880, p. 495).

There are also historical references to such usage. A quote from Squier is suggestive, although I must confess that I have not been able to locate his original source. Moreover, his translation of a fragment from Calancha, which I did locate, is so bad as to be almost unintelligible as well as inaccurate, which casts some doubt on the accuracy of this passage. Nevertheless, because of its interest, I present the statement of a "native author" who, in turn, cites Pinelo (it is not clear to whom the following words regarding the temple of the oracle of Rímac are due): "They painted in this temple, as hieroglyphics, the answers most favoring their ideas. And, to make mysterious these paintings, which are to be seen on the walls of this structure, they covered them with other walls, without allowing the junction of those that served as curtain to obliterate the figures they concealed" (Squier, 1877, pp. 84–85). The quotation continues: "The Padre Calancha adverts to the same things with myself . . . ," but here I revert to Calancha for the words. Of the buildings at the place called "Lima Tanbo" by the Spaniards and "Rimac Tanpu" by the Indians, he says:

> I marveled seeing in one of those Palaces, or houses, two walls right together, which with the earthquakes have been separated at the top part, and they are painted with figures of Indians and animals. Some [people], discussing how it was possible to plaster and paint one wall that they put right against the other, think (seeing that these are large walls) that they painted one tapia [section] and attached it, and then another, and thus they went, placing and getting higher; but they do not notice, that were it thus, the joins between tapia [sec-

tion] and tapia [section] would be marked, and the paintings with lines and breaks showing the division. Surely what must be thought is, that the multitude of Indians had a means of placing the entire wall after plastering and painting, joining it to another, and with obedience and thousands of Indians still more difficult things are made possible. (Calancha, lib. I, cap. XXXVII; 1638, p. 236)

Later, discussing the painting of the Huaca del Sol, Calancha amplifies these comments: ". . . how did they put one wall so close to another on whose surfaces figures of men and animals were painted? This has been discussed speaking of other huacas, and it was that the thousands of Indians and the machines joined wall to wall, so that the paintings might be preserved and the memorials not be lost" (Calancha, lib. II, cap. XXXV; 1638, p. 486). But Calancha does not provide any basis for this last observation, and it may well be no more than conjecture. Any attempt to explain this pattern on the basis of the existing evidence must be speculative. But we can surmise that it might have been related to magico-religious practices and, if we follow Squier, might in some cases have had something to do with the oracular phenomenon.

There is one final technical aspect to be considered, relating to the technical category in which the ancient Peruvian mural paintings really belong. With rare exceptions they are always called "al fresco paintings" or simply "frescos." Even authors expert in the subject matter have fallen into this error, among them Uhle (1903, p. 20), Kroeber (1930, p. 71), Bennett (1946, p. 100), Tello (1942, pp. 24, 89) and Mesa and Gisbert (1973, p. 300). Only a few have classified these paintings as belonging to the "distemper" technique or, to be more exact, "matte distemper": Larrabure y Unanue referring to Paramonga (1935, p. 216), Muelle and Wells on Pachacámac (1939, p. 266), Bonavia on Pañamarca (1959b, p. 24), and Ravines on the Cerro Trinidad murals (ms.).

I believe that the proliferation of these erroneous classifications results from a very common phenomenon in Peruvian archaeology, that is, repetition of earlier statements that are considered to be true *a priori* with no effort made to check their validity. I am not entirely sure, but it seems to me that the first author to call these mural paintings "frescos" was Wiener in 1880 (p. 494), referring to Paramonga. Perhaps he is to blame for this error which has been perpetuated to the present day.

It is well known that al fresco mural painting is a

watercolor technique resulting from a long process of development.

> ... it is basically a mixture of lime and sand or another component applied fresh to the wall and painted with mineral colors either pure or mixed with lime. From this emulsion (fresh plaster—mineral color) will be produced, once dry, a chemical fixing process which differentiates it substantially from any other known technique [and should not be confused with other techniques] executed dry, with pigments emulsified with an adhesive (resins, gums, etc.) which, technically speaking, have nothing to do with the "buon fresco." (Aschero, 1968, p. 37)[6]

Al fresco painting is, thus, a very elaborate technique that requires a profound knowledge of the problems—knowledge not present in the prehispanic societies of what is now Peru. This fact is best demonstrated by the Moche paintings, in which a coat of ground color was allowed to dry before the figures to be painted were outlined and later filled in with the desired color. Since the mark left on fresh clay by the pointed outlining tool is very different from that left on a dry surface, there is no room for doubt in this regard.

The Peruvian paintings were executed in matte distemper, that is, watercolors in which the colors were mixed with some glutinous substance to fix them. The colors of these paintings were, in general, matte and impermanent (especially when exposed to weathering); they covered small areas that were almost always protected; and they were applied to clay surfaces exclusively, on walls that were not very smooth. Mineral pigments found in the natural state in the country were used.

As far as I know, in the entire Western Hemisphere, only the ancient Mexicans and the Mayas knew and used the true fresco (Littman, 1973), which reached its apogee during the Classic Period. Ponce Sanginés mentions "pieces of al fresco mural painting" found at Tiahuanaco but offers no evidence for the statement (1972, p. 74). I consulted Teresa Gisbert on the matter, and she wrote: "At present nothing is to be seen, but I remember that when they opened those chambers, a sort of chullpa, that were inside the Kalasasaya, there was talk of frescos. What I saw personally was a very loose layer of a sort of white lime on the floor" (personal communication, 1974).

In Ponce Sanginés's report on the work carried out at Tiahuanaco, in the section dealing with the Kalasasaya, he says: "The walls are painted in colors, largely tones of white and gray" (1961, p. 19). In that paragraph, however, he is referring to the "Classic" or "Epoch IV" in general, and it is unclear whether the statement applies specifically to the Kalasasaya or to some other unspecified place. Nevertheless, he definitely does not refer to frescos, not even to murals. Lumbreras, referring to Ponce's report, speaks of "mural painting," which is ambiguous and could lead to errors (Lumbreras, 1974, p. 143).[7]

Furthermore, referring to the "Semisubterranean Temple" excavated by Ponce Sanginés, Lumbreras states that there were "traces of painted coating on its walls" (1974, p. 140). This statement is incorrect or, at best, misleading. It may have resulted from a careless reading of Ponce's report (1964; 1969), or misinterpretation of a statement by Bennett that "Around [the] Calasasaya, are other smaller units, all made with carefully cut and dressed stone. Many of the stones, when first excavated, showed traces of painted designs" (Bennett, 1949, p. 40). Bennett's statement is probably based on the report of the French scientific mission of 1903, which, under the direction of Georges Courty, excavated at Tiahuanaco. The summary (and only) report of this work contains several references to the use of colors. In the Semisubterranean Temple, while no color was reported on the actual wall faces, an ochrous-red was preserved on the tenon heads in the lines of the eyes, nose, ears, and mouth (Créqui-Montfort, 1906, p. 536). Moreover, some walls both of earth and of stone, near a small structure just off the northwest corner of the Kalasasaya, were "covered with white and red colors" and the stones of the entrance to a small enclosure just west of the Kalasasaya revealed traces of a blue-green color "with which they had been intentionally covered" (Créqui-Montfort, 1906, pp. 540–41). Even these comments, however, do not tell us whether the colors were applied directly to the walls or onto a plaster coating, nor do they indicate whether the colors formed any sort of patterned decoration or merely areas of solid color. Therefore, although we have firm reports of painting on some walls of Tiahuanaco, the existence of "al fresco mural painting" at the site remains in doubt.

It is worth commenting that similar terminological errors have been, and are still being, committed with respect to other aspects of Peruvian art. For example, the word "arabesque" has been used to refer to the clay flat reliefs especially common in the final epochs of Andean architecture. In fact, according to the dictionary of the Spanish language of the Royal Academy, an arabesque is any "design or ornament composed of traceries, foliage, bands and volutes most commonly used in friezes, socles, and borders." Sometimes, rather than arabesque, the term used is "stuccoes," which is also incorrect, since, according to the same source, a stucco is a "mass of white plaster and gum water with which many objects are made and prepared for later gilding or painting," clearly not the case in our material. The terms "high relief" and "low relief" are also used to refer to these clay decorations, the vast majority of which are really flat reliefs, probably in imitation of stone carvings.

It is to be hoped that such incorrect terminology will be abandoned, since it leads to confusion and errors, especially among those scholars who do not have the opportunity to know the materials at firsthand and must work exclusively from published descriptions.

—9—
Final Considerations

On the basis of the foregoing material, some general conclusions can be drawn. The most evident one is negative: we have only minimal information regarding prehispanic mural painting in Peru. There may be some additional data on this topic in the scientific literature that I have not seen, but I doubt that they are extensive. Sources where more information may yet be found are the monographic regional histories and descriptions, local publications of limited distribution, newspaper ar-

ticles, and, of course, the Spanish chronicles, which have not been thoroughly sifted.

While there is no doubt that painting, in the broadest sense, played an important role in prehispanic Peruvian architecture, we shall never fully comprehend the phenomenon, in part because serious studies were not carried out when it was possible, and in part because of the present deteriorated state of the ancient remains. The reader will have been struck by the extent to which our data come from the coast, with only vague information for most of the vast highland region. I have commented that it is unbelievable that mural art was an exclusively coastal phenomenon, and I am inclined to believe that climatic factors are largely responsible for the differential preservation we find today. Nevertheless, it should not be forgotten that highland architecture, being of stone, was not always plastered, and, since cut stone walls were relatively rare, the possibility of decorating the walls was more limited than on the coast. But here we enter the realm of speculation; the matter requires further investigation, keeping in mind the fact that there are indications of painting applied directly to stone walls in some cases.

Another factor affecting the sample that has reached us is the generalized custom in prehistoric times of reusing the same buildings in different epochs, remodeling them in various ways. For all these reasons, only a minute fraction of what must have been a much greater reality has reached us, the rest to remain forever unknown. Even with respect to the known fraction, we are greatly handicapped in trying to interpret the phenomena because of the few concrete data we possess. This factor is greatly accentuated in the case of pictorial art in which animals, men, and objects interact, and in scenes that, besides being partial, represent a world foreign to our mentality and ultimately almost impenetrable.

After praising Moche sculptural work, Kroeber commented that the Moche "were scarcely less successful as painters, both in monochrome red or brown on the cream slip of their pottery, and in larger flat-color frescoes . . ." (1949, p. 429). I would not say, however, that mural painting should be considered one of the high points of aboriginal art, either aesthetically or technically. In this context, it is worth recalling Muelle's words:

> In Peru the plastic arts did not achieve emancipation from their technical resources and we see them in servile subjugation to a decorative will, even in cases which we might consider representational art. . . . Even in works of larger scope, like the paintings at the temple of the Huaca de la Luna at Moche, the wall frieze is not abandoned. Thus there is an intimate interdependence between the expression and the means of expressing it: *métier* and *matériel*. (Muelle, 1951, p. 11)

I think that this opinion may be extended to all prehispanic Andean paintings.

It is useless, of course, to compare these paintings to the murals of the Old World, as some have done. While there is a vast technical difference, comparison from other angles is entirely out of the question. Art is one of the most important expressions of the spirit of a people and is intimately linked to their culture. This fact is more noticeable the farther back in time we go. If Andean mural painting is to be understood, it must be placed within its proper context and related to it by a series of conditioning factors from which it is indivisible, among which religion is one of the most important. But such considerations lead to a disquisition on the artistic phenomenon in general, which is inappropriate here.

In spite of its limitations, however, native Andean mural painting reached a level that makes it worthy of a place among mural paintings from other parts of the world. It should not be despised or totally ignored, as has been the case so far in studies of art history. This neglect has been from lack of knowledge or information. To say that American painting "is an infantile art, happy with bright and clashing colors" (Naval Ayerve, 1950, pp. 300–301), is to demonstrate the grossest possible ignorance. Obviously part of the responsibility for this informational gap lies with the archaeologists themselves. In general they have shown little interest in the theme, and even when they have pursued it, they have done so only superficially. Thus, they have contributed to a distorted visualization, a misuse of technical terms, and the classification of these paintings into categories to which they do not belong, as noted earlier.

But mural painting is not the only aspect of architectural adornment that has been neglected. While I have purposely limited the scope of this study, a holistic treatment of architectural decoration must consider other closely related arts and techniques. The native Peruvians had recourse to other devices to achieve the greatest beauty and enhance the quality of their houses, temples, and palaces. We do not know all the other materials that were combined with painting to achieve such effects. There is evidence that gold, at least, was an important element and also that metal objects were often painted for unknown reasons. The same is true of painting on wood. References to the painted boards of Puquín Cancha ("pictorial museum," according to Porras Barrenechea, 1955, p. 112) in Cuzco, mentioned by Cristóbal de Molina and Bernabé Cobo, are of special interest, as are the many fragments of wood bearing the remains of painting that are frequently found in prehispanic ruins on the coast, but whose use and function are unknown in many cases. Textiles are also closely related to this theme, since decoration was probably one of the functions of cloth that has been least mentioned and studied, as Lathrap suggested (1973, p. 98). It is probable that painted textiles and tapestries were intended basically as wall decoration, and that in the last periods, flat reliefs in adobe, perhaps easier to make, may have replaced them, while still providing a similar sensation, as Mesa and Gisbert have so aptly noted (1973, p. 300). Andean tapestries may have fulfilled fundamentally the same function as the much-vaunted tapestries of the European Medieval period.

We can only begin to comprehend the importance of the use of color on architecture, whether as simple wall painting or in murals, although it was very widespread in ancient Peru from the earliest times. While the destruction of the urban complexes prevents our achieving complete understanding of this aspect of Andean culture, we can imagine the monotony of the coast broken by the colors of the dwellings and sacred edifices, which, in the highlands, would have stood out against the green or gold of the mountains. Evidence for this visualization may be seen in the pottery representations of painted structures from different times on exhibit in museums and illustrated in many publications. A few examples will serve to illustrate the point.

Schmidt published a Recuay-style house model, from Recuay, that apparently had a flat roof with two rear skylights. It has a square window with something like a grate composed of crossed elements above it. The side door, apparently higher than the base of the house, was reached by means of a stairway. There is even a modeled person looking out through the window and another standing at the doorway. The house is entirely painted with typical Recuay-style motifs, that is, feline stylizations and various geometric elements. The decoration is distributed in horizontal bands on the top of each wall and vertical bands at the corners. The doorway has a special decoration, as does the stairway (Schmidt, 1929, p. 237, fig. 2). Similar configurations are common in this style from the Callejón de Huaylas.

Another example from Chuquitanta in the Lima Valley, dating to the Middle Horizon, is illustrated in the same book (Schmidt, 1929, p. 262, fig. 2). It represents a house with a flat roof with "merlons" on the sides, a roofed courtyard at the front, and a window that is decorated with broad lines in two alternating colors. Similar pieces exist in several museums and private collections in Lima.

In the Museo Amano in Lima is another Recuay-style vessel, on top of which is the representation of what seems to be a courtyard, since it has no roof, that is totally enclosed by high walls (Anonymous, n.d., specimen no. 0014). In the front wall is a doorway with decorative molding, and the side and central walls are topped by a decorative stepped element. All the walls are adorned with typical Recuay-style motifs. The façade has a horizontal band of step frets on the top.

The most interesting example of this ceramic form that I have seen is in the collections of the Detroit Institute of Arts (Anonymous, 1956, p. 68, cat. no. 55-334). In the published catalog it is called a Moche-style piece from Chavín, and it is interpreted as a "prison." The piece is not Moche, however, but a Middle Horizon style from the central coast, and it is important since it shows a complex structure. The artist's intention was clearly to show that the structure was elevated above ground level, since it is reached by a stairway. The most interesting aspect of this vessel is that the façade of the edifice bears a mural painting in the form of a broad band, bordered by two heavy lines, containing two parallel series of repeated inverted stepped elements. The side wall of the back courtyard is entirely covered with a two-color checkerboard, in which light-colored squares alternate with dark ones that contain a lighter, dotted circular element. Moreover, on the side wall of the parallelepiped section, one of the sides is bordered by a broad, vertical dark-colored band extending from roof to ground. This specimen is evidently a good example of the established custom of painting structures.

Keeping in mind the difficulties in discussing colors mentioned in the preceding chapter, I still think it worth the effort to attempt to synthesize our knowledge on this point. There is, of course, a wide margin of error, and the concepts I shall use are those of artists rather than of physicists.

In general, the most frequently used colors in ancient Peruvian mural paintings are five: red, blue, yellow, white, and black. These are followed in frequency by violet, orange, brown, and green. I shall, naturally, not mention all the variations in tones that have been obtained on the basis of these colors. If we exclude from the most frequently used colors black, which is really an absence of color, and white, as an all-inclusive one, we are left only red, blue, and yellow, precisely the colors considered to be "primary." Of the next most common ones, three are "secondary" (green, violet, and orange), and only one, brown, is "tertiary," as are all the shades that were used less frequently. From this count it is clear that the indigenous artist preferred those colors called *warm* to those called *cold*.

On a more speculative note, when the need was to define an incision or simply outline a figure, the preferred color was black, which makes the motifs stand out. It is well known that the effect of depth can be achieved through the interplay of warm and cold colors, and that cold colors are those used to give an impression of greater depth. I do not know if this effect resulted randomly or from empirical knowledge, but the effect itself is evident.

In painting walls there seems to have been a certain preference for the color red, a fact noted by Raimondi, who commented on "the walls painted red, a characteristic of all the structures of the Indians of the coast . . ." (1942, p. 167). The observation of Rostworowski de Diez Canseco is also of interest in this regard. "Red should be considered a sacred color, and it should be noted that the Temple of the Sun, built under the Cuzco domination of Pachacamac, was painted vermillion" (1972, p. 39).

As far as the murals are concerned, there is no evidence for a preference for certain colors at certain times or the predomination of any color over any others. But it is clear that the Moche palette was the richest and most varied. During the Early Horizon red, blue, and white are most common, with a limited use of yellow and black. The greatest number of colors was used at Puncurí, where nine were recorded. In the Early Intermediate Period reds, blacks, whites, and yellows predominate, with occasional brown and orange, and very little light blue. At Pañamarca, however, as many as twelve distinct tones have been recorded. During the Middle Horizon the same colors were always used: yellow, red, white, blue, and occasionally black. A similar range, five tones, is found at both the Huaca de la Luna and La Mayanga. During the Late Intermediate Period two colors, red and white, stand out with occasional black and blue. Finally, in the Late Horizon preference is shown for red, black, and yellow and, to a lesser extent, green and white, while orange and light blue are very rare. With five tones each, Pachacámac and Huadca are the sites of this period where the greatest number of colors were employed.

Practically all the colored substances used are readily found in nature. While this fact does not exclude the possibility that new colors may have been sought through mixture, neither does it explain the poverty of coloring when, with the three primary colors plus black and white, there was a potential to achieve any color. I believe that the limiting factor was the lack of technical knowledge, perhaps combined with cultural phenomena of which we know nothing.

One possible approach to understanding colors as a cultural phenomenon is through language, but in our case this is a practical impossibility. Even for the Yunga language, which has been attributed to the Moche, the small amount of linguistic evidence available is confined to limited aspects of life; but what little we have suggests that color terms were few. Fernando de la Carrera's *Arte de la lengua yunga* of 1644 (Carrera, 1939) contains no words referring to colors. More recent vocabularies, including those published by Bastian, Middendorf, Villarreal, and Larco Hoyle, were collated by Zevallos Quiñones (1946), together with some of his own data, resulting in the color terms in Table 2.

TABLE 2

YUNGA COLOR TERMS

English	Spanish	Yunga
black	negro	chafca, fag, fak
white	blanco	ziku, zikuyu, tsekku, aja
red	rojo	kuj *or* kul
yellow	amarillo	tsam
green	verde	iss
brown (gray?)	pardo	cham

Other words he includes pertaining to color are *tsuk* = light, and *cucho* = colored or red (*colorado*). Kosok published two brief word lists collected by Antonio Rodríguez Suy Suy, including terms for black (*colpan*), red (*cuyupe*), and white (*secúye*). (Kosok, 1965, pp. 248–49).

If we compare the Moche palette to these terms, we find that it contains the more important colors mentioned, but not green, which, to my knowledge, was not used by that culture. On the other hand, there is no mention of certain other colors that were widely used, for example, orange and blue. Clearly we are limited by our lack of knowledge of the native languages, although it should be recalled that in other parts of the world, in literary works of fundamental importance to their cultures, one may not find words for some colors that were doubtless considered important in the cultural context. Evidence of such cases may be found in the writings of Aristotle, the Homeric poems, the Veda, the Zend-Avesta, the Koran, etc. Empedocles and Pythagoras mention only four colors (Trucco, 1934, pp. 412–13). This limitation is also evident in the writings of the Spanish chroniclers, who "are seen to be noticeably restricted by the lack of vocabulary. It is curious, for example, that the range of colors that the sixteenth-century Europeans were able to identify was strictly limited" (Elliot, 1972, p. 35).

Although I cannot explain it, it seems both evident and important that all the painted murals that have been found on the coastal plain come from the north and central parts. Possible exceptions are the murals reported by Engel and Mejía Xesspe from the south coast, probably dating to the Early Horizon, and two or three examples from Inca times found at the border between the south and central coasts.

In spite of these exceptions, the general distribution in time and space could lead us to think that the *idea* of mural paintings belongs to the Chavín style, *sensu lato*, and that it acquired its own definite characteristics on the north coast in the Moche tradition, which is clearly derived from Chavín. Evidence to support this suggestion is found in the artistic expressions like Caballo Muerto, Puncurí, Moxeque, Cerro Blanco, Cerro Sechín, or Garagay, as well as the temple of Chavín de Huántar itself. Preventing a more definite statement on this point is the fact that we do not know the precise associations of the painted structures with the different phases of the Chavín style. Be that as it may, I believe that the hypothesis, although speculative, is logical and should stimulate us to seek the reasons that this aspect of art did not develop in the south.

Not only is this artistic mode a very ancient tradition in the Andean area, developing throughout all prehispanic time, but it continued into the Colonial Period. For example, we find at Huaytará a church built on Inca walls during the Colonial Period. Framing the trapezoidal windows of purest Inca style are white bands, and above them, but inside the niche, are motifs based on volutes painted in red, probably to give more color to the walls (fig. 124). Moreover, at the Palace of Sayri Thupa, or Incahuasi, in Yucay in the Urubamba Valley near Cuzco, there are paintings in pure Inca style but probably executed during the Colonial Period. I believe that these examples provide a good basis for arguing the continuity of an old native tradition.

With regard to the stylistic treatment of the murals, I am forced to repeat yet again that there is not enough evidence to draw firm conclusions. What little we can deduce is, therefore, subject to revision when more data are available.

It would seem that in the Early Horizon there were at least two modes of expression, one realistic, the other conventional. The realistic would include the feline and fish at Cerro Sechín, and the conventional, the painted column at Casa Grande illustrated by Kosok and perhaps the one from the Huaca Lucía discovered by Shimada. In the realistic renderings the motifs are represented in profile; the artist has simply outlined the figures without adding much detail. The conventional mode appears to be copied from the compositions that appear on stone, with combined fullface and profile representations, some seminatural elements, and others that are completely conventionalized and stylized, all perfectly integrated and in total accord.

In the Early Intermediate Period the murals of the Lima and Moche styles are different. We have two examples in the Lima style, and both appear to include the same motifs with slight variations in treatment. The motifs are interlocking designs, probably copying themes already appearing on pottery in this style as well as other Peruvian styles of several epochs. The problem is more complex in the Moche-style murals, since they show true scenes. In all known examples the treatment is the same. The figures are in profile and turned right or left, depending on the requirements of the composition or perhaps simply the whim of the artist. Although the compositions are relatively complex, true perspective was unknown. But there was a good sense of volume, and the figures represented by the Moche artist, whatever their nature, are shown in different sizes, a device apparently solving two basic problems. On the one hand, it provides a sense of depth, replacing the lacking perspective, and on the other, it underlines the rank of certain personages. The Moche, moreover, clearly abhorred empty spaces, so that their representations display a certain rhythm in the distribution of the elements within a scene (Muelle, 1936, p. 68; Bonavia, 1959b, p. 25). Kroeber correctly remarked that the Moche gave freer rein to their fancy in murals than was usual in pottery decoration (1930, p. 71).

These comments on the Moche style also apply in general terms to the treatment of the figures of the Middle Horizon murals, which, in fact, fall within the same tradition. It is the composition that varies, since it now represents not scenes but either isolated personages or figures repeated in such a way as to give the impression of being isolated in spite of being physically proximate.

It is difficult to make even a superficial judgment on the Late Intermediate Period paintings, specifically those in the Chimú style. The Túcume mural has very simple and stylized bird shapes, and there are problems regarding the only complete illustration of the painting of the Huaca del Oro. The Huaca Corte paintings seem to have been similar to the Huaca del Oro one.

In the Late Horizon there are again two well-defined tendencies in mural paintings. One is decoration based on geometric elements, probably copied from Inca ceramic themes, although with a still more limited motif

Fig. 124.
Huaytará, Huancavelica, painted decoration in trapezoidal window in the church of San Juan Bautista, which was raised on the Inca palace, demonstrating continuity of the indigenous tradition into the Colonial Period.

vocabulary; the other represents scenes. In the scenes the motifs are still stylized and represented in profile, and the same principles regarding size and distribution used in Moche murals may be applied. However, while some care was taken in the treatment of the nonhuman images, even including a certain amount of detail, in anthropomorphic figures exactly the opposite is true, that is, they were outlined without detail and even with a certain intentional carelessness. I do not know if this treatment is simply coincidental or reflects norms imposed on the artists; further study of the question would be interesting.

Here I must repeat as generally applicable a point I have previously made with specific regard to the Moche style (Bonavia, 1959b, p. 47). This point is that the execution of paintings does not necessarily carry over all the canons of style shown in the pottery motifs. There are variations, sometimes important ones. Consequently, it is difficult to apply the chronological criteria established on ceramics to murals without encountering certain limitations. We do not know the reasons for these differences, but it is reasonable to suggest that they result basically from the material upon which the artist was working. Even though pottery offers the artist a smooth surface upon which to exhibit his or her skill in details (as in the case, for example, of Moche decoration, especially its final manifestations), the large wall surfaces permit greater freedom to the development of expressive impulses, allowing creation without the natural limitations imposed by a vessel, be it ever so large. Moreover, it is possible that the master artisans (mastercraftsmen, to use Bennett's term) who painted the walls were not the same ones who decorated the pottery.

No one has so far endeavored to study the changes within the various forms of art in ancient Peru; we do not even know if there is enough evidence to do so. A few authors have, however, sketched some ideas in this area that might possibly assist future investigators. For example, in his notes on Cerro Blanco in Nepeña, Tello expresses his belief that the clay relief figures were later replaced by others simply outlined by incision on the wall plaster and that this incision finally disappears, giving way to painting alone: "The high-relief figures of the bottom level are monochrome at Chavin; on the coast they are painted in various colors which diminish in number in the top levels" (Tello, 1942, pp. 115–16). Later, dealing with the problem of the spread of the Chavín culture and the changes that some coastal monuments underwent because of the medium, he repeats

something very similar: "Thus the structures of the principal buildings are of stone and adobe (Moxeque, Sechin Alto and Cerro Sechin; the decorations carved in stone are replaced by mural paintings or by relief figures in clay stucco (Punkuri and Cerro Blanco in Nepeña, Ipuna in Santa); the stone statues are replaced by other similar ones made of stone and clay (Punkuri and Moxeque)" (Tello, 1960, pp. 36–37). Accordingly, the sequence of the development of art would be: (1) figures carved and sculpted in stone followed by figures modeled in clay and painted; (2) incised and painted figures; and finally (3) exclusively painted figures.

Kroeber suggested that in Chimú, "relief friezes or arabesques [replaced] the Mochica frescoes" (1949, p. 432), while Schaedel thinks that "The sequel to the stucco relief in the Lambayeque area for wall decoration appears to be a return to polychrome painting . . ." (1967a, p. 456). All these ideas are clearly isolated and based on little data; indeed, I would say they are mere impressions, but all are worthy of consideration.

We also lack the information necessary to permit any decision regarding which period in ancient Peru produced the best murals. To do so we should have a broad and complete repertoire, and even then the decision would be subjective. On the basis of the little we do know, however, I believe that the best results were achieved in the Early Intermediate Period Moche murals.

It is clear that the application of solid-color paint to walls was much more common at all times than were any of the varieties of mural painting. And while it is also clear that buildings with some special function, religious or not, were the most elegant, I venture to state that painted walls were not at all confined to such edifices. Anyone who has explored the prehispanic ruins of the Peruvian coast knows how frequently the remains of painting are found on fallen houses and, in general, on structures that were simple dwellings, storage structures, etc. The discovery of tombs with painted walls relates this mode to funerary architecture as well. The painting of edifices was a much more widespread custom than we have thought, but what we do not know is whether it obeyed cultural patterns directed and determined by established norms or was simply the result of the personal, innate, aesthetic impulses of the Andean peoples.

The case of mural paintings is very different. There is, to my knowledge, no example from any time period in which artistic manifestations of this nature have been found on structures not related to religion. Mural paintings are always found on the ruins of temples or palaces, courtyards or other structures that are somehow connected with ceremonial or sacred architecture. The scenes represented are intimately linked to religious patterns and in only a few cases show images of animals whose relationship to ideas of the epoch we do not know. In Moche art this relationship is clear, since the elements created in murals are also found represented on ceremonial pottery, where they practically always form part of much more complex and conventional scenes. In this context the contribution of Donnan (1976; 1977) is especially important. These paintings, then, represented a very important, if not vital, part of magico-religious ritual in ancient Peru. The only doubtful cases that might arise would be the few examples of painting of a geometric character that the peoples of Inca times have left us, to be discussed below.

There are two aspects of the treatment of mural paintings in antiquity that reflect their special status. The first is found in the evidence that roofs or shelters were often built especially to protect the paintings from the effects of weathering. These coverings were probably of perishable materials, so that evidence of their existence is extremely hard to find without the most careful excavation. Nevertheless, Squier, referring to the decorations at Chanquillo or Calaveras in the Casma Valley, remarked that the places where there were traces of figures in relief and paintings were "protected" (1877, p. 212). Later Tello observed at Cerro Blanco in Nepeña that the paintings showed no signs of having been exposed to weathering. He also found traces of holes so arranged that they suggested to him the existence of a protecting roof supported by wooden columns (1942, p. 115). He made a similar observation when working at Cerro Sechín. Referring to the central building of the temple, he wrote in his field notes: "It is noteworthy that the top faces of these walls appear to be plastered. This would indicate that the rafters did not rest directly on them. It is possible that there may have been wooden or clay columns to support the roof" (Tello, 1956, pp. 251–52). He is referring here to the same sector in which the feline painting discussed earlier was found. Furthermore, the photograph published by Kosok of a Chavín structure on the lands of the former Hacienda Casa Grande shows two cylindrical columns decorated with paintings located in front of a structure that was probably a temple. Those columns may have served to support some type of roof.

More solid evidence has been presented by Schaedel (1967a) and Stumer (1954). At the Huaca del Dragón

Schaedel concluded, on the basis of evidence found *in situ*, that the flat reliefs on the terrace of the monument had been protected by a roof with a cornice that was also decorated (1967a, p. 422). A similar conclusion was reached by Stumer, also on the basis of indirect evidence, when he excavated the temple of Cerro Culebra (1954, p. 227). And proof of the same sort was found in the city of Chanchan during the work carried out in 1972 by the Harvard University project (Kent Day, personal communication, 1973).

The second indication of the importance of these paintings is the fact that even when walls bearing a mural had to be remodeled or repainted for some reason, the existing painting was usually not destroyed, but simply covered with either a coat of fresh plaster or another wall, always taking care not to mar the covered paintings. The many cases of this treatment reported in the preceding chapter show clearly, as I said in 1959, that covering paintings, whether of earlier epochs or contemporary ones, with walls or fill was not accidental but rather a very widespread and deeply rooted cultural pattern, insufficiently examined by archaeologists, and found from the Early Horizon to the Late Horizon (Bonavia, 1959b, p. 47). Thus the conclusion that murals represented a respectable element within the ritual life of the Andean world is supported not only by the fact that they occupied privileged locations, but also because they were protected both when they were exposed to view and when they had to be covered.

As I noted in the case of each mural, although general comments can be made, interpretation of the scenes represented is difficult. In the Early Horizon the animals, or symbolism based on zoomorphic elements, are always of the sort that form part of the religious repertoire of the Chavín culture.

The murals related to the Lima style provide a complex problem. Basically they represent the interlocking motif based on a stylized fish element. We do not know what value this symbol had in the Lima culture, but it was probably more than merely decorative. In fact, with slight modifications, we see it on the ceremonial pottery of several other styles, especially Nasca and Recuay.

Moche not only is a different problem but has another aspect, especially because of the figurative realism of its expression. In Moche art there are true scenes including religious ceremonies, as at Pañamarca, or perhaps symbolizing ancient rites, as in the case of the Huaca de la Luna murals studied by Seler and Kroeber, and perhaps the one at Pampa Grande. We can say nothing, however, about the later murals at the Huaca de la Luna, La Mayanga, Huaca Pintada, and Chornancap, which, although following the same tradition, have been modified by new ideas, since in this case, as with the Lima style, the cultural value is unknown to us. And the same is true of the Late Intermediate Period murals, but the situation there is more complex since, with rare exceptions, we do not even have good descriptions and illustrations.

Regarding the mural paintings of Inca times, it is worth asking ourselves whether all of them had the same significance. I have noted that there are two clearly separable design categories: geometric decorations, like those at the Huaca de la Centinela and most of the elements of the "fortress" of Paramonga, and scenes based on anthropomorphic and/or zoomorphic elements, as in the Pachacámac and Huadca paintings. Do we have here pure decoration in one case and religious motifs in the other? While such an explanation is possible, in view of the mind and spirit of native culture, I tend to doubt it. Interpretation is surely one of the most slippery fields that can be trod by the investigator of ancient Peruvian culture, but it is also undeniably almost virgin soil awaiting cultivation, and the possibilities for its study are limitless.

In spite of all the preceding material, I am convinced that I have presented only a minimal sample of what prehispanic mural painting in the central Andean area really was. Although much was destroyed in the Spanish conquest and during the Colonial Period, it is undeniable that much, too much, has also been destroyed since Peru enacted laws to protect its cultural patrimony. A grave responsibility rests on the institutions and authorities charged with enforcing those laws. Many paintings still exist, both discovered and yet to be discovered, and it is to be hoped that in the future their importance will be recognized.

I have endeavored to salvage this evidence that has been so long overlooked by historians of prehispanic American art. It is worthy of attention. It cannot and must not be forgotten again.

Appendix
Pigment Analysis

TABLE A-1

QUALITATIVE SPECTROGRAPHIC ANALYSIS OF PIGMENTS

S	M	m	St	W	V	Color
1	Fe Si	Al Mg	Mn	Ca Na+	Ag B Ba Cr Cu Ga Pb Ti V Zn	Red (D-26) and black (H-10)
2	Fe Si	Al+ Mg	Ca	Na+	Ag B Ba Cr Cu Ga Ge Pb Ti V Zn	Gray-blue (B-10)
3	Fe Si	Al	Ca K− Mn Na+	Mg+	B Ba Co Cr Cu Ga Ni Pb Ti V Zn	Red (C-23)
4	Al Ca Si	Fe+ Mg+	K Na	Cr Mn P+	B Ba Co Ni Pb Ti V Zn	White (A-81)
5	Fe Si	Al+ Ca	K+ Mg Na P	Cr Cu Mn	B Ba Co Mo Ni Pb Ti V Zn	Yellow (C-63)
6	Fe Si	Al+	Ca Mn	Mg Na	B Cr Cu Mo Pb Ti V Zn	Red (F-28)
7	Ca Mg	Al− Fe+	Mn− Na Si+		B Ba Co Cr Cu Ga Ni Pb Ti Zn	White (A-81)
8	Fe Si	Al+	Ca Mn−	Mg+ Na+	B Ba Cr Cu Ga Ge Ni Pb Ti V Zn	Red (E-16)
9	Si	Al Fe+	Ca+ Mn−	Mg+ Na+	B Ba Cr Cu Ga Ni Pb Ti Zn	Pale red (E-16)
10	Al Fe− Mg− Si	Ca	Mn−	Na	B Ba Cr Cu Ga Ni Pb Ti	Pale yellow (A-82)
11	Fe Si	Al Mg	Ca Ti	Mn	Ag B Ba Cr Cu K Ni Pb V Zn	Red (C-14)
12	Ca	Fe Mg+ Si	Al	Mn Na	Ba Cr Cu Pb Ti Zn	White (A-81)

KEY

S = Sample
M = Major component (probably more than 10%)
m = Minor component (probably 1–10%)
St = Strong traces (probably 0.1–1%)
W = Weak traces (probably 0.01–0.1%)
V = Very weak traces (less than 0.01%)

The symbols between parentheses in the Color column refer to the Cailleux and Taylor terminology.

1 = Illimo (Lambayeque)
2 = Illimo (Lambayeque)
3 = Pachacamac (Lima)
4 = Tambo Colorado (Ica)
5 = Tambo Colorado (Ica)
6 = Tambo Colorado (Ica)
7 = Huaca Licapa (La Libertad)
8 = Huaca Licapa (La Libertad)
9 = Los Alamos (Ancash)
10 = Los Alamos (Ancash)
11 = Túcume (Lambayeque)
12 = Túcume (Lambayeque)

Note: the signs + and − do not refer to ionic charge, but to the relative proportion in which the elements are found.

TABLE A-2

QUALITATIVE SPECTROGRAPHIC ANALYSIS OF PIGMENTS

S	M	m	St	W	V	Color	S	M	m	St	W	V	Color	S	M	m	St	W	V	Color
1 B	Fe Si+	Al− Ca− Na−	K+ Mg Mn	Cr	Ag B Ba Co Cu Ga Ni Pb Ti V	(Red and black)	2 B	Fe Si+	Al+ Ca− Na−	K+ Mg Mn−	Cr	Ag B Co Cu Ga Ni Pb Ti V	(Gray-blue)	3 B	Fe Si	Al+ Ca K Na	Mg+	Cr+ Mn	B Co Cu Ga Ni Pb Ti V Zn	(Red)
4 B	Fe− Si	Al Ca K Na	Cr− Mg+	Mn	B Co Cu Ga Ni Pb Ti V Zn	(White)	5 B	Fe Si	Al Ca K Na+	Cr− Mg+	Mn	B Co Cu Ga Mo Ni Pb Ti V Zn	(Yellow)	6 B	Fe Si	Al Ca K− Na	Mg Mn−	Cr	Co Cu Ga Ni Pb Ti V Zn	(Red)
7 B	Fe Si	Al Ca K− Na	Mg	Cr Mn	Co Cu Ga Mo Ni Pb Ti V Zn	(White)	8 B	Fe− Si	Al Ca K− Na	Mg	Cr+ Mn	Co Cu Ga Mo Ni Pb Ti V Zn	(Red)	9 10 B	Fe− Si	Al+ K− Na+	Ca+ Mg−	Cr+ Mn	Co Cu Ga Ni Pb Ti V Zn	(Pale red and pale yellow)
11 B	Fe Si	Al Mg	Ca Mg Mn Na+ Ti	Cr K Ni	B Ba Cu Pb V Zn	(Red)	12 B	Fe Si		Al Na+ Ti	Ca Cr Mg Mn	B Ba Cu K Ni Pb V Zn	(White)							

Note: This additional qualitative analysis was carried out on the base of the colored substances whose analysis results are shown in Table A-1. The key is the same, except a *B* has been added to the number of each sample to indicate that it is a "base."

TABLE A-3

QUALITATIVE ANALYSIS (WET)

Sample number	Color	Fe^{+++}	Fe^{++}	Ca^{++}	$CO_3^=$	$SO_4^=$
1	Red and black (D-26) (H-10)	+	+	+	−	−
3	Red (C-23)	+	+	+	−	−
4	White (A-81)	+	+	+	−	−
5	Yellow (C-63)	+	+	+	+	−
6	Red (F-28)	+	+	+	+	−
8	Red (E-16)	+	+	+	+	−
11	Red (C-14)	+	+	+	+	−
12	White (A-81)	+	−	+	+	−

Note: The sample numbers refer to the key used for Tables A-1 and A-2.

COMMENTARY ON THE ANALYSIS OF THE PIGMENTS OF SOME OF THE PAINTINGS STUDIED

Carlos Núñez Villavicencio

[The qualitative analyses by spectrography that are presented in this appendix were carried out in the laboratories of the Research Department of the Cerro de Pasco Corporation in La Oroya; the qualitative wet analyses were performed in the Chemistry Laboratory of the Universidad Peruana Cayetano Heredia. Samples 1 and 2 were collected by the personnel of the Museo Nacional de Antropología y Arqueología, Lima, and were given to me by Toribio Mejía Xesspe; samples 11 and 12 were collected by Oscar Lostaunau; the remainder were collected by Duccio Bonavia. (DB)]

Samples 1, 3, 5, 6, and 8 probably owe their coloration to the presence of mixtures of iron oxides; the red color would be explained by the use of a higher proportion of hematite or red ochre than of limonite, and the yellow of sample 5 would indicate that yellow ochre, or limonite, was used as colorant in a higher proportion than hematite. The results obtained in the analysis by spectroscopic emission on the five samples indicate the presence of iron as the predominant element, along with silicon. The wet qualitative analyses show the presence of iron in its two states of oxidation, Fe(II) and Fe(III); this would be explained by considering the presence of some variety of ferric-ferrous oxide in which the stability of the ferrous form resulted from the presence of small quantities of manganese, an element that appears in the spectrographic analysis of all the samples, and confirms our suggestion regarding the use of yellow ochre, since, as is known, the yellow ochres are mixtures of limonite and clay, and the red ochres are earthy varieties of the hematites.

Sample 4 is white. This coloration probably results from a mixture of clay and lime ($Ca(OH)_2$), and, in fact, the spectrographic analyses show the predominant elements to be calcium, silicon, and aluminum, with iron as a minor component, in contrast to observations on the other samples. In the wet analyses the presence of appreciable quantities of sulfates and carbonates was disregarded, permitting us to state that the white coloration did not derive from the use of calcium carbonate (lime), limestone, or dolomites.

Wet analyses of samples 5, 6, and 8 showed the presence of appreciable quantities of carbonates. The presence of this anion would be explained if we assumed that some calcareous material was used as base for these samples, perhaps limestones and dolomites, and we even suspect the presence of ferrous carbonate or siderite.

The results of the analyses of sample 11 are similar to those of sample 8. The red color results from the use of red ochre, which is some earthy variety of the hematites. In the analysis of anions the presence of carbonates was detected, which makes us think of the possibility that the red ochre used was mixed with calcareous materials and very probably contained siderite (ferrous carbonate), since the presence of ferrous iron was also confirmed. In scratching the sample to obtain the painted portion, it was observed that there is a zone of yellow color, which would probably be composed of limonite (yellow ochre).

In sample 12 calcium and carbonates are found in abundance, from which the fact is deduced that the white color resulted basically from the use of limestone mixed, perhaps, with lime.

It must be emphasized that the earthy material has a high carbonate content, which suggests that the mud used is rich in limestone and perhaps in ferrous carbonate.

It is not possible to specify exactly what minerals were used in the preparation of pigments, since it is possible that they reacted with the material used as a base and even with the clay from which the walls were made, in addition to having suffered changes from the action of water and atmospheric carbon dioxide.

NOTES

Chapter 2: The Early Andean Images

1. I expressed my opinion of this restoration in an article written jointly with Rogger Ravines (Bonavia and Ravines, 1973).

2. In all descriptions of murals, unless otherwise indicated, the terms "right" and "left" are used as though the observer is facing the wall.

3. Information supplied by Mejía Xesspe is of special value, since he was Tello's chief assistant, working constantly at his side. Moreover, after Tello's death, Mejía continued to edit and see through publication the excavation reports resulting from their work, until his own death in 1983.

4. Although Samaniego says in his note 2 (1980, p. 332) that he is simply summarizing material published "up to 1974," he cites works as recent as 1977, so had he wished to correct the points I criticized in the first edition of this book (Bonavia, 1974), he could have done so.

5. For additional information on the site, see Proulx, 1968 and 1973.

6. On this point Mejía Xesspe seems to have erred, since he recalled that, had the figure been completed, it would have been on the lower part, while Antúnez de Mayolo's data make it clear that such a hypothetical completion would have had to be on the top.

Chapter 3: Further Developments

1. *Tapia* is tamped earth construction using forms. (PJL)

2. All color identifications using the Cailleux and Taylor (n.d.) key were made personally by the author.

3. In 1982 a note on this mural was published, in which the author inaccurately claims to have discovered the paintings (Silva Pérez, 1982). He is, in fact, the student I mentioned, who learned of the discovery and informed the Instituto Nacional de Cultura so that it could take appropriate action. His note is superficial and lacks scientific value; the drawing he presents is a distortion of the original painting.

Chapter 4: The Moche Tradition

1. Since Anders's article (1979) was translated into Spanish from an original English text, this material regarding her work was sent to Anders to verify its accuracy. She was kind enough to insert her original color terminology as well as to correct some errors that appeared in the published text. The most important such error was the translation of "waist" by *muñeca* ("wrist") in the description of the small warrior figure. Other errors that we have corrected refer to the colors of the plumage of the large fullface figure, the color of the circles on the pink bands flanking that figure, and the colors of the elements above the head of the small warrior. Anders also indicated that the entire wall bearing the mural was painted white, not just its north end as implied by the wording of her published article.

Chapter 5: Late Expressions on the North Coast

1. Schaedel appears to have misread this comment, since he says that Horkheimer found friezes "painted in red and yellow" (Schaedel, 1967a, p. 386); the phrase used by Horkheimer is "eran pintados en un amarillo rojizo" (1944, p. 70 caption to fig. 60). This misinterpretation led Schaedel to search for traces of red paint, which, naturally, he did not encounter in this part of the structure.

2. *Adobón* translates literally as "large adobe." The term is used in Peru, however, to refer to very large unbaked clay blocks, often about a meter in length, which are used, like adobes, to build walls. Construction based on these blocks is often called "tapia" in the Andean area. Duccio Bonavia provided the following information to me. The term "tapia" is not native, being introduced by the Spaniards together with an Old World technology that has mingled with the indigenous one. European technology introduced the use of planks to make the large forms used to shape the adobe blocks. While it has been said that the same was done in the prehispanic period, but with reed molds, there is no concrete evidence for such usage, and it appears that the large clay blocks were simply formed by hand on the spot and allowed to dry before making another on top. For further details, see Muelle, 1963. (PJL)

Chapter 6: Late Manifestations on the Central Coast

1. Although Cobo entitled this chapter of his work "Of the famous temple of Pachacama," his description is clearly of the Temple of the Sun. Probably the term "Pachacama" was applied, as it is today, to the entire great complex, and the chron-

icler simply failed to specify the name of the structure bearing the paintings.

2. See Muelle and Wells (1939, figs. 5 and 6) for color-coded scale drawings of the painted terrace faces.

3. The code referred to here is *A Dictionary of Color*, by Maerz and Paul (Muelle and Wells, 1939, p. 267).

4. The color coding used in this drawing is as follows: vertical hachure, ochre-rose; horizontal hachure, light blue; dotted, Naples yellow (Muelle and Wells, 1939, p. 278, note to fig. 5). While Muelle here indicated the color code used only for figure 5, as noted, it can be inferred that it applies equally to all the drawings published in the article (Muelle and Wells, 1939).

Chapter 7: Murals in the Inca Empire

1. *Cancha* is a Quechua word meaning "enclosure." The term is often applied, as here, to a particular kind of compound: "a walled rectangular block enclosing groups of one-room buildings destined for dwelling and other uses" (Gasparini and Margolies, 1977, p. 186; 1980, p. 181). (PJL)

2. The work here cited as "Noticia del Perú" has been published several times, attributed to Miguel de Estete (e.g., Noticia del Perú, 1938). In fact, as Rowe indicated to Gasparini and Margolies, the author of this work could not possibly have been Estete, though we do not know his name (Gasparini and Margolies, 1980, p. 333, n. 24).

3. There is a fine model of the monument in the Museo Nacional de Antropología y Arqueología, Lima. A photograph of this model was published by Hardoy (1973, fig. 72), and most of the kinds of ornamental brickwork mentioned by Uhle can be seen in it.

4. Rather than translate the Uhle passages back into English from Haase's article, I have taken them directly from the original letter (Uhle, ms.). All material within quotation marks in the material quoted from Haase comes from the original letter, and the folio numbers in square brackets refer to the letter, not to Haase's article. (PJL)

5. Uhle's use of "confining" in this passage results from the admixture of Spanish in his already imperfect English. The Spanish verb *confinar* means to border, abut, or adjoin. Thus, the "confining triangles" to which he refers are simply the adjacent or adjoining triangles. (PJL)

6. This site of Huaycán is not to be confused with the complex of Huaycán de Pariachi in the Rímac Valley.

7. For an exact location and description of the architectural complex, I refer the reader to Bonavia, Matos, and Caycho (1963, p. 131). To orient the painted wall, the Maranga Ha-

cienda house was to the south, Huaca Concha to the north-west, and the Naval Hospital to the north-northeast.

8. See note 2, chap. 5.

9. See note 2, this chapter.

Chapter 8: Materials and Techniques

1. Coincidentally, the same technique was used in the ancient Mediterranean.

2. In Peru today *broquel* refers to an implement used to apply whitewash or calcimine paints to buildings and walls. It consists of a sheepskin or one or more rags attached to a handle, which varies in length depending on the location to be painted. The applicator material is soaked in paint and repeatedly slapped against the surface being treated. (PJL)

3. The term used in the original is *batanes*. In this context, in Peru, *batán* refers to the grinding implement sometimes called "Andean rocker mill" in English. It consists of a large, flat horizontal stationary stone upon which the element to be ground is placed. The upper element is a good-sized stone, usually more or less semicircular, which is rocked by hand back and forth over the material to be ground. In the eastern lowlands, both elements are often of wood. Mills of this kind were used to grind everything from metal ores and clay to all kinds of foodstuffs. (PJL)

4. The difference in acceptation here between "pigment" and "colorant" is the same used in chemistry, in which the essential characteristic of pigments is their insolubility in water and oil, while colorants are soluble.

5. To identify colors, I suggest the use of charts like Munsell or Cailleux and Taylor, although the dictionaries of Maerz and Paul (1950 and other editions), Séguy (1936), or Ostwald (1930–39), which are the best known and relatively easy to acquire, are also useful.

6. For more detail, see any vocabulary of technical terms or handbook of painting, e.g., Adeline (1887), Branzani (1935), Reau (1930), or Mayer (1959).

7. While the phrase "mural painting" is not at all ambiguous in English, its equivalent in Spanish, *pintura mural*, can mean either "mural painting" or "wall painting." Since the work of Lumbreras referred to here is a translation to English from Spanish, which was not corrected by the author before publication (Lumbreras, personal communication to Lyon, 1982), it is probable that the original Spanish was *pintura mural*, which is indeed ambiguous, as Bonavia notes, but not incorrect; it was then translated into a factual error. (PJL)

REFERENCES

Adeline, J.
1887   *Vocabulario de términos de arte.* Traducido y aumentado por José Ramón Mélida. Madrid: La Ilustración Española y Americana.

Alva Maúrtua, Abelardo V.
n.d.   *Tradiciones chinchanas y versos inéditos.*

Alvarez M., Carlos E.
ms.   El monumento de Sacachique; un aporte a la prehistoria peruana. Tesis para optar el título de Bachiller en Educación. Universidad Nacional de Trujillo, Facultad de Educación, 1956. Trujillo, Peru.

Amano, Yoshitaro
1961   *Huacos precolombinos del Perú.* Tokyo: Bijutsu Shuppan-Sha.

Anders, Martha B.
1979   Sistema de depósitos en Pampa Grande, Lambayeque. *Revista del Museo Nacional,* tomo XLIII, 1977, pp. 243–79. Lima.

Anonymous
n.d.   *Huacos y tejidos precolombinos del Perú; Museo Amano.* Lima: Edición de "La Sociedad Latino-Americana."
1933   Nuevas excavaciones arqueológicas serán practicadas en la próxima quincena en el palacio de "Cerro Blanco" en Nepeña. (El Dr. Tello explica a un representante de Cadelp los recientes hallazgos.) *El Comercio,* no. 47255, martes 3 de Octubre, p. 13. Lima.
1952   Importante hallazgo arqueológico a dieciseis kilómetros de Lima. *El Comercio,* 12 de Diciembre, pp. 3–4. Lima.
1956   Arts of ancient Peru. *Bulletin of the Detroit Institute of Arts,* vol. XXXV, 1955–56, no. 3, pp. 62–75. Detroit.
1967   Exploraciones arqueológicas en Huancavelica. *Boletín del Museo Nacional de Antropología y Arqueología* 6. Pueblo Libre, Peru.
1972   El mundo preincaico. *Gran historia de Latinoamérica.* La aventura del continente, pueblos y países, 5. Tomo I, pp. 41–48. Buenos Aires.
1973   Telas precolombinas. *Dominical,* 10-6, p. 27. Lima: El Comercio.

Antúnez de Mayolo, Santiago.
1933   Los trabajos arqueológicos en el valle de Nepeña. *El Comercio,* no. 47277, domingo 15 de Octubre, pp. 16–17. Lima.

Aschero, Carlos A.
1968   *La pintura al fresco.* Buenos Aires: Centro Editor de América Latina.

Banco Popular
1979   *El arte y la vida vicús: colección del Banco Popular del Perú.* Text: Luis Guillermo Lumbreras. Lima: Banco Popular del Perú.

Bennett, Wendell Clark
1937   Chimu archeology; the archeology of the north coast of Peru. *The Scientific Monthly,* vol. XLV, no. 1, July, pp. 35–48. Lancaster, Pennsylvania.
1939   Archaeology of the north coast of Peru. An account of exploration and excavation in Viru and Lambayeque valleys. *Anthropological Papers of the American Museum of Natural History,* vol. XXXVII, pt. 1. New York.
1946   The archeology of the Central Andes. *Handbook of South American Indians.* Bureau of American Ethnology, Bulletin 143, vol. 2, pp. 61–147. Washington.
1949   Religious structures. *Handbook of South American Indians.* Bureau of American Ethnology, Bulletin 143, vol. 5, pp. 29–51. Washington.
1950   The Gallinazo Group; Viru Valley, Peru. *Yale University Publications in Anthropology,* no. 43. New Haven, Connecticut.

Benson, Elizabeth P.
1972   *The Mochica, a culture of Peru.* New York, Washington: Praeger Publishers.

Berezkin, Yuri E.
1972   Mifologiya Mochika (Peru). *Sovetskaya Arkheologiya,* 1972, 4, pp. 171–92. Moscow. [Abstract: La mythologie des Mochicas (le Pérou)]

Betanzos, Juan de
1880   *Suma y narración de los Incas . . .* [1551]; publícala Marcos Jiménez de la Espada. Biblioteca Hispano-Ultramarina, vol. V, second paging. Madrid: Imprenta de Manuel G. Hernández.

Beuchat, Henri
1912   *Manuel d'archéologie américaine*. Paris: Librairie Alphonse Picard et Fils.

Bonavia, Duccio
1959a   Una nueva pintura mural en Pañamarca. *El Comercio, Suplemento dominical*, no. 309, domingo 5 de Abril, pp. 6–7. Lima
1959b   Una pintura mural de Pañamarca, valle de Nepeña. *Arqueológicas 5*, pp. 21–54. Lima
1961   A Mochica painting at Pañamarca, Perú. *American Antiquity*, vol. 26, no. 4, April, pp. 540–43. Salt Lake City.
1962   Decoraciones murales de la vieja Lima. *El Comercio, Suplemento dominical*, domingo 2 de Diciembre, pp. 6–7. Lima.
1965a   Arqueología de Lurín; seis sitios de ocupación en la parte inferior del valle. *Publicaciones del Museo Nacional de la Cultura Peruana*. Serie: Tesis Antropológicas, no. 4. Lima.
1965b   Pinturas murales precolombinas. *El Comercio, Dominical*, 15 de Agosto, p. 6. Lima.
1966   [Compiler and editor] Sitios arqueológicos del Perú (primera parte). *Arqueológicas 9*. Lima.
1974   *Ricchata quellccani; pinturas murales prehispánicas*. Lima: Fondo del Libro del Banco Industrial del Perú.
1981   Pañamarca nuevamente: Una aclaración. *Revista del Museo Nacional*, tomo LXIV, 1978–80, pp. 239–48. Lima.

Bonavia, Duccio; Matos, Ramiro; and Caycho, Félix
1963   Informe sobre los monumentos arqueológicos de Lima. *Junta Deliberante Metropolitana de Monumentos Históricos, Artísticos y Lugares Arqueológicos de Lima (Equipos Técnicos)*, no. 2, 1962–63. Lima.

Bonavia, Duccio, and Ravines, Rogger
1973   Arqueología científica o farsa turística. *Oiga*, año XII, no. 507, 12 de Enero, pp. 34–36. Lima.

Branzani, Luigi
1935   *Le tecniche, la conservazione, il restauro delle pitture murali*. Città di Castello: Società An. Tipogràfica "Leonardo Da Vinci."

Brüning, Enrique
1916   Provincia de Lambayeque (contribución arquelógica [*sic*]). *Boletín de la Sociedad Geográfica de Lima*, tomo XXXII, trim. II y III, Septiembre 30 de 1916, pp. 197–201. Lima. [Author's name misspelled Brünning]

Bueno Mendoza, Alberto
1971   Arqueología peruana. Sechín: Síntesis y evaluación crítica del problema. *Boletín Bibliográfico de Antropología Americana*, vol. XXXIII–XXXIV, 1970–71, pp. 201–21. México.
1975   Sechín: síntesis y evaluación crítica del problema. *Anales Científicos de la Universidad del Centro del Perú 4*, pp. 135–65. Huancayo, Peru.

Bueno Mendoza, Alberto, and Grieder, Terence
1979   Arquitectura precerámica de la sierra norte. *Espacio*, año I, no. 5. Lima.

Bueno Mendoza, Alberto, and Samaniego Román, Lorenzo

1969   Sechín: una nueva perspectiva. *Amaru*, no. 11, Diciembre, pp. 31–38. Lima.

Cailleux, A., and Taylor, B.
n.d.   *Code expolaire (notice sur le code expolaire)*. Paris: Editions en français N. Boubée & Cie.

Calancha, Antonio de la
1638   *Coronica moralizada del Orden de San Avgvstín en el Perv, con svcesos egenplares en esta monarqvia*. [Tomo primero]. Barcelona: Pedro Lacavalleria.

Campana, Cristóbal.
ms.   Información sobre descubrimiento frisos Chimú–Huaca Cotón. Informe presentado al Instituto Nacional de Cultura de Lima. 1981.

Carrera, Fernando de la
1939   *Arte de la lengua yunga* (1644). Reedición, con introducción y notas por Radamés A. Altieri. Universidad Nacional de Tucumán, Publicación no. 256. Departamento de Investigaciones Regionales, Publicaciones Especiales del Instituto de Antropología. Tucumán.

Carrión Cachot, Rebeca
1942   La luna y su personificación ornitomorfa en el arte chimú. *Actas y Trabajos Científicos del XXVIIº Congreso Internacional de Americanistas (Lima, 1939)*, tomo I, 1940, pp. 571–87. Lima: Librería e Imprenta Gil, S.A.
1948   La cultura Chavín. Dos nuevas colonias: Kuntur Wasi y Ancón. *Revista del Museo Nacional de Antropología y Arqueología*, vol. II, no. 1, primer semestre, pp. 99–172. Lima.

Chambers
1964   *Diccionario tecnológico español, inglés, francés, alemán*. Barcelona: Ediciones Omega, S.A.

Cieza de León, Pedro de
1922   *La crónica del Perú* [1550]. Los Grandes Viajes Clásicos, no. 24. Madrid: Espasa-Calpe, S.A.
1967   *El señorío de los Incas (2ª parte de la Crónica del Perú)* [1553]. Lima: Instituto de Estudios Peruanos.

Cisneros G., Carmen (Director)
1981   *Perú*. Cuadernos de viaje, travel notebook, cahiers de voyage, no. 4. Lima: Embajada del Viajero S.A.

Cobo, Bernabé
1956   *Obras del P. Bernabé Cobo de la Compañía de Jesús*. Biblioteca de Autores Españoles (continuación), tomos 91–92. Madrid: Ediciones Atlas.

Collier, Donald
1962   Archaeological investigations in the Casma Valley, Peru. *Akten des 34. Internationalen Amerikanistenkongresses, Wien, 18. bis 25. Juli 1960*, pp. 411–17. Horn-Vienna: Verlag Ferdinand Berger.

Créqui-Montfort, Guy de
1906   Fouilles de la mission scientifique française a Tiahuanaco. Ses recherches archéologiques et ethnographiques en Bolivie, au Chili et dans la République Argentine. *Internationaler Amerikanisten-Kongress, vierzehnte Tagung, Stuttgart 1904*, zweite Hälfte, pp. 531–50. Berlin, Stuttgart, Leipzig: Verlag von W. Kohlhammer.

Díaz D., Máximo R.
1940   Frescos murales en el arte del antiguo Perú. Algo sobre el fragmento de un fresco de los muchos que han existido en los paramentos del templo de la Luna en Moche. *Revista de la Universidad de La Libertad*, año XVI, no. 13, Diciembre, pp. 61–65. Trujillo, Peru.

Donnan, Christopher Bruce
1972   Moche-Huari murals from northern Peru. *Archaeology*, vol. 25, no. 2, April, pp. 85–95. New York.
1973   Moche occupation of the Santa Valley, Peru. *University of California Publications in Anthropology*, vol. 8. Berkeley, Los Angeles, London.
1975   The thematic approach to Moche iconography. *Journal of Latin American Lore*, vol. 1, no. 2, Winter, pp. 147–62. Los Angeles.
1976   Moche art and iconography. *UCLA Latin American Studies*, vol. 33. Los Angeles.
1977   The thematic approach to Moche iconography. *Pre-Columbian art history; selected readings*, Alana Cordy-Collins and Jean Stern, editors, pp. 407–20. Palo Alto, California: Peek Publications.
1978   *Moche art of Peru, pre-Columbian symbolic communication.* Los Angeles: Museum of Cultural History, University of California, Los Angeles.
1983   Dance in Moche art. *Ñawpa Pacha* 20, 1982, pp. 97–120. Berkeley.
1984   Ancient murals from Chornancap, Peru. *Archaeology*, vol. 37, no. 3, May/June, pp. 32–37. New York.
ms.   An ancient mural from Chornancap, Peru.

Donnan, Christopher Bruce, and Mackey, Carol Joy
1978   *Ancient burial patterns of the Moche Valley, Peru.* Austin & London: University of Texas Press.

Duviols, Pierre
1968   Un inédit de Cristóbal de Albornoz: la Instrucción para descubrir todas las guacas del Pirú y sus camayos y haziendas [c. 1582]. *Journal de la Société des Américanistes*, tome LVI-1, 1967, pp. 7–39. Paris.

Elliott, J. H.
1972   *El viejo mundo y el nuevo (1492–1650).* Madrid: Alianza Editorial.

Engel, Frédéric André
1967   El complejo El Paraíso en el valle del Chillón, habitado hace 3,500 años; nuevos aspectos de la civilización de los agricultores del pallar. *Anales Científicos de la Universidad Agraria*, vol. V, Julio–Diciembre, nos. 3–4, pp. 241–80. Lima.
1972   *Le monde précolombien des Andes.* Paris: Librairie Hachette.
1976   *An ancient world preserved; relics and records of prehistory in the Andes.* Translated by Rachel Kendall Gordon. New York: Crown Publishers, Inc.

Enríquez de Guzmán, Alonso
1960   *Libro de la vida y costumbres de don Alonso Enríquez de Guzmán* [1547]. Publicado por Hayward Keniston. Biblioteca de Autores Españoles (continuación), tomo 126. Madrid: Ediciones Atlas.

Feldman, Robert A.
1978   Informe preliminar sobre excavaciones en Aspero, Perú, y sus implicancias teóricas. *Investigación Arqueológica*, 2, pp. 20–27. Trujillo, Peru.

Florián, Mario
1951   *Un icono mural en Batán Grande.* Lima: Imprenta "Amauta."
1954   Descubrimiento de un friso Mochica en Paiján. *El Comercio, Suplemento dominical*, no. 89, domingo, 7 de Noviembre, pp. 2, 10, 11. Lima.

Fung Pineda, Rosa
1969   Observaciones arqueológicas sobre la obra: Perú antes de los Incas. *Tecnia* 3, Setiembre, pp. 142–52. Lima.
1971   [Editor] *Apuntes Arqueológicos* 1. Lima.

Fung Pineda, Rosa, and Pimentel Gurmendi, Víctor
1974   Chankillo. *Revista del Museo Nacional*, tomo XXXIX, 1973, pp. 71–80. Lima.

Fung Pineda, Rosa, and Williams León, Carlos
1979   Exploraciones y excavaciones en el valle de Sechín, Casma. *Revista del Museo Nacional*, tomo XLIII, 1977, pp. 111–55. Lima.

García Rosell, César
1968   *Diccionario arqueológico del Perú.* Lima: [the author].

Garcilaso de la Vega, "El Inca"
1945   *Comentarios reales de los Incas* [1609]. Edición al cuidado de Angel Rosenblat (segunda edición). Buenos Aires: Emecé Editores. 2 vols.

Garrido, José Eulogio
1956a   Descubrimiento de un muro decorado en la "Huaca de la Luna" (Moche). *Chimor, Boletín del Museo de Arqueología de la Universidad de Trujillo*, año IV, no. 1, Noviembre, pp. 25–31. Trujillo, Peru. [Signed J.E.G.]
1956b   El problema de la conservación de las decoraciones murales prehistóricas. *Chimor, Boletín del Museo de Arqueología de la Universidad de Trujillo*, año IV, no. 1, Noviembre, pp. 1–8. Trujillo, Peru. [Published anonymously]

Gasparini, Graziano, and Margolies, Luise
1977   *Arquitectura inka.* Caracas: Centro de Investigaciones Históricas y Estéticas, Facultad de Arquitectura y Urbanismo, Universidad de Venezuela.
1980   *Inca architecture.* Translated by Patricia J. Lyon. Bloomington and London: Indiana University Press.

Giesecke, Alberto
1939   Las ruinas de Paramonga. *Boletín de la Sociedad Geográfica de Lima*, tomo LVI, trimestre 2°, pp. 75–123. Lima.

Haase, Ynez
1958   Notas preliminares de la visita de Max Uhle a Tambo Colorado. Paper presented to the Mesa Redonda de Ciencias Antropológicas, Universidad Nacional Mayor de San Marcos, Lima. Mimeographed.

Hagen, Victor Wolfgang von
1976   *The royal road of the Inca.* London: Gordon & Cremonesi Ltd.

Hardoy, Jorge E.
1973   *Pre-Columbian cities.* Translated by Judith Thorne. New York: Walker and Company.

Hastings, Charles Mansfield, and Moseley, Michael Edward
1975   The adobes of Huaca del Sol and Huaca de la Luna. *American Antiquity,* vol. 40, no. 2, April, pp. 196–203. Washington.

Hocquenghem, Anne Marie, and Lyon, Patricia Jean
1981   A class of anthropomorphic supernatural females in Moche iconography. *Ñawpa Pacha* 18, 1980, pp. 27–48. Berkeley.

Horkheimer, Hans
1944   *Vistas arqueológicas del noroeste del Perú.* Trujillo, Peru: Librería e Imprenta Moreno.
1965   Identificación y bibliografía de importantes sitios prehispánicos del Perú. *Arqueológicas* 8. Lima.

Imbelloni, José
1943   La "Weltanschauung" de los amautas reconstruida: Formas peruanas del pensamiento templario. *Actas y Trabajos Científicos del XXVII° Congreso Internacional de Americanistas (Lima, 1939),* tomo II, 1942, pp. 245–71. Lima: Librería e Imprenta Gil, S.A.
1960   *Civiltà andine; creazioni plastiche e stili degli antichi popoli delle Ande.* Le Piccole Storie Illustrate, 36. Florence: Sansoni.

Ishida, Eiichiro, and others
1960   *Tōkyō Daigaku Andesu chitai gakajutsu chōsa dan 1958 nendo hōkokusho. Andes; the report of the University of Tokyo Scientific Expedition to the Andes in 1958.* Report 1. Tokyo: Bijitsu Shuppan Sha.

Izumi, Seiichi, and Terada, Kazuo
1972   *Andes 4. Excavations at Kotosh, Peru, 1963 and 1966.* Tokyo: University of Tokyo Press.

Jérez, Francisco de
1938   Verdadera relación de la conquista del Perú y provincia del Cuzco, llamada la Nueva Castilla . . . [1534]. In *Los cronistas de la conquista.* Biblioteca de Cultura Peruana, 1st ser., no. 2, pp. 15–115. Paris: Desclée, De Brower.

Jiménez Borja, Arturo, and Samaniego Román, Lorenzo
1973   *Guía de Sechín.* Casma, Peru.

Kauffmann Doig, Federico
1964   *La Cultura Chimú.* Las Grandes Civilizaciones del Antiguo Perú, tomo IV. Lima: Peruano Suiza S.A.
1970   *Arqueología peruana; visión integral.* Lima: Ediciones Peisa. [Revised editions entitled *Manual de arqueología peruana* were published in 1973, 1978, and 1981.]

Kosok, Paul
1965   *Life, land and water in ancient Peru.* New York: Long Island University Press.

Krickeberg, Walter
1928   Mexikanish-Peruanische Parallelen. Ein Ueberblick und eine Ergänzung. *Festschrift/Publication d'hommage offerte au/ P.W. Schmidt,* pp. 378–93. Vienna: Mechitharisten-Congregations-Buchdruckerei.

Kroeber, Alfred Louis
1926   The Uhle pottery collections from Chancay by . . . with Appendix by Max Uhle. *University of California Publications in American Archaeology and Ethnology,* vol. 21, no. 7, pp. 265–304, pls. 80–90. Berkeley and London.
1930   Archaeological explorations in Peru. Part II. The northern coast. *Field Museum of Natural History, Anthropology Memoirs,* vol. II, no. 2, pp. 45–116. Chicago.
1944   *Peruvian archeology in 1942.* New York: Viking Fund Publications in Anthropology, no. 4.
1949   Art. *Handbook of South American Indians.* Bureau of American Ethnology, Bulletin 143, vol. 5, pp. 411–92. Washington.

Kutscher, Gerdt
1950   *Chimu; eine altindianische Hochkultur.* Berlin: Verlag Gebr. Mann.
1954   *Nordperuanische Keramik; figürlich verzierte Gefässe der Früh-Chimu. Cerámica del Perú septentrional; figuras ornamentales en vasijas de los chimúes antiguos.* Monumenta Americana I. Berlin: Verlag Gebr. Mann.

Langlois, Louis
1938   Paramonga. Translated from the unpublished French by José Eugenio Garro. Biblioteca del Museo Nacional de Lima [Perú], Servicio de Traducciones, Publicación no. 2. *Revista del Museo Nacional,* tomo VII, no. 1, I semestre, pp. 21–52; no. 2, II semestre, pp. 281–307. Lima.

Lanning, Edward Putnam
1963   An early ceramic style from Ancon, central coast of Peru. *Ñawpa Pacha* 1, pp. 47–59. Berkeley.
1967   *Peru before the Incas.* Englewood Cliffs, New Jersey: Prentice-Hall, Inc.

Larco Hoyle, Rafael
1938   *Los Mochicas.* Tomo I. Lima: Casa Editora "La Crónica" y "Variedades."
1939   *Los Mochicas.* Tomo II. Lima: Empresa Editorial "Rimac" S.A.
1946   A culture sequence for the north coast of Perú. *Handbook of South American Indians.* Bureau of American Ethnology, Bulletin 143, vol. 2, pp. 149–75. Washington.
1948   *Cronología arqueológica del norte del Perú.* Hacienda Chiclín-Trujillo (Peru): Biblioteca del Museo de Arqueología "Rafael Larco Herrera." Buenos Aires: Sociedad Geográfica Americana.

Larrabure y Unanue, Eugenio
1935   *Manuscritos y publicaciones.* Historia y arqueología, tomo II. Lima: Imprenta Americana.

Lathrap, Donald Ward
1970   La floresta tropical y el contexto cultural de Chavín. In *100 años de arqueología en el Perú,* ed. Rogger Ravines, pp. 235–61. Fuentes e Investigaciones para la Historia del Perú 3. Lima: Instituto de Estudios Peruanos, Edición de Petróleos del Perú.
1971   The tropical forest and the cultural context of Chavín. *Dumbarton Oaks Conference on Chavín, October 26th and 27th, 1968,* Elizabeth P. Benson,

editor, pp. 73–100. Washington: Dumbarton Oaks Research Library and Collection.
1973   Gifts of the cayman: Some thoughts on the subsistence basis of Chavín. In *Variation in anthropology: Essays in honor of John C. McGregor*, edited by Donald W. Lathrap and Jody Douglas, pp. 91–105. Urbana, Illinois: Illinois Archaeological Survey.

Lavallée, Danièle
1970   *Les représentations animales dans la céramique mochica*. Mémoires de l'Institut d'Ethnologie, IV. Paris.

León Barandiarán, Augusto
1938   *Mitos, leyendas y tradiciones lambayecanas. Contribución al folklore peruano*. Lima: Club de Autores y Lectores de Lima.

Leroi-Gourhan, André
1965   *Préhistoire de l'art occidental*. Paris: Éditions d'Art Lucien Mazenod.

Littmann, Edwin R.
1973   The physical aspects of some Teotihuacán murals. Appendix to *The mural paintings of Teotihuacán*, by Arthur G. Miller, pp. 175–86. Washington: Center for Pre-Columbian Studies, Dumbarton Oaks.

Lumbreras, Luis Guillermo
1970   *Los templos de Chavín*. Guía de monumentos y exposiciones del Museo de Arqueología y Etnología de la Universidad Nacional Mayor de San Marcos, vol. 1. Lima: Proyecto Chavín.
1973   Los estudios sobre Chavín. *Revista del Museo Nacional*, tomo XXXVIII, 1972, pp. 73–92. Lima.
1974   *The peoples and cultures of ancient Peru*. Translated by Betty J. Meggers. Washington: Smithsonian Institution Press.
1977   *Los orígenes de la civilización en el Perú*. Lima: Editorial Milla Batres.

Lyon, Patricia Jean
1981   Arqueología y mitología: La escena de "los objetos animados" y el tema de "el alzamiento de los objetos." *Scripta Ethnologica*, vol. VI, pp. 105–108. Buenos Aires.

Macera, Pablo
1975   El arte mural cuzqueño siglos XVI–XX. *Apuntes*, año II, no. 4, pp. 59–113. Lima.

Mackey, Carol Joy
ms.   Murals from the Pyramid of the Moon. Paper presented at the Annual Meeting of the Society for American Archaeology, San Francisco, California, 1973.

Mackey, Carol Joy, and Hastings, Charles Mansfield
1982   Moche murals from the Huaca de la Luna. In *Pre-Columbian art history; selected readings* [second edition], edited by Alana Cordy-Collins, pp. 293–312. Palo Alto, California: Peek Publications.

Maerz, Aloys, and Paul, Rea M.
1950   *A dictionary of color*. New York: McGraw-Hill Book Company, Inc.

Massey, Sarah Ann
ms.   A Paracas temple in the lower Ica Valley. Paper presented at the 23rd Annual Meeting of The Institute of Andean Studies, January 8–9, 1983, Berkeley, California.

Mayer, Ralph
1959   *The artist's handbook of materials and techniques*. New York: The Viking Press.

Mejía Xesspe, Toribio
1956   Historia de la Expedición Arqueológica al Marañón de 1937. Appendix to *Arqueología del Valle de Casma*, by Julio C. Tello, pp. 319–37. Publicación Antropológica del Archivo "Julio C. Tello" de la Universidad Nacional Mayor de San Marcos, vol. I. Lima: Editorial San Marcos.
1968   Pintura chavinoide en los lindes del arte rupestre. *San Marcos* no. 9, segunda época, Junio–Julio, Agosto, pp. 15–32. Lima.

Mendizábal Losack, Emilio
1961   Don Phelipe Guaman Poma de Ayala, señor y príncipe último quellqacamayoc. *Revista del Museo Nacional*, tomo XXX, pp. 228–330. Lima.

Menzel, Dorothy
1964   Style and time in the Middle Horizon. *Ñawpa Pacha* 2, pp. 1–105. Berkeley.
1968   *La Cultura Huari*. Las Grandes Civilizaciones del Antiguo Perú, tomo VI. Lima: Compañia de Seguros y Reaseguros Peruano-Suiza S.A.
1969   New data on the Huari empire in Middle Horizon Epoch 2A. *Ñawpa Pacha* 6, 1968, pp. 47–114. Berkeley.
1977   *The archaeology of ancient Peru and the work of Max Uhle*. Berkeley: R. H. Lowie Museum of Anthropology, University of California, Berkeley.

Mesa, José de, and Gisbert, Teresa
1973   Culturas de los Andes. *Historia del Arte Salvat*, vol. I, fascicle 124–25, Marzo, pp. 281–319. Barcelona: Salvat Editores.

Middendorf, Ernst Wilhelm
1973   *Perú. Observaciones y estudios del país y sus habitantes durante una permanencia de 25 años* [1894]. Translated by Ernesto More. Tomo II, *La costa*. Lima: Universidad Nacional Mayor de San Marcos.

Moorehead, Elisabeth L.
1979   Highland Inca architecture in adobe. *Ñawpa Pacha* 16, 1978, pp. 65–94. Berkeley.

Morales Gamarra, Ricardo
ms.a   Conservación de pinturas murales de la Huaca de la Luna. Informe final presentado al Instituto Nacional de Cultura (Filial de Trujillo), 1980. Trujillo, Peru.
ms.b   Pinturas murales de la Huaca Cotón (Trabajos de emergencia para su conservación). 1981. Trujillo, Peru.

Moseley, Michael Edward
1978   An essay on five ancient styles. In *Peru's golden treasures*, pp. 4–67. Chicago: Field Museum of Natural History.

Muelle, Jorge C.
1936   Chalchalcha (Un análisis de los dibujos muchik). *Revista del Museo Nacional*, tomo V, no. 1, pp. 65–88. Lima.

1937   Filogenia de la estela Raimondi. *Revista del Museo Nacional*, tomo VI, no. 1, I semestre, pp. 135–50. Lima.

1951   El arte y los estilos. *Perú ayer y hoy*, pp. 11–34. Buenos Aires: Herbert Kirchoff.

1959   Función i forma en arqueología. *Cuadernos*, Centro de Estudiantes de Antropología Universidad Nacional Mayor de San Marcos, vol. I, nos. 2–3, 22 de Diciembre 1958/22 de Enero de 1959, pp. 45–51. Lima.

1963   Tecnología del barro en el Perú precolombino. In *A Pedro Bosch-Gimpera en el septuagésimo aniversario de su nacimiento*, pp. 327–30. México.

Muelle, Jorge C., and Wells, J. Robert
1939   Las pinturas del Templo de Pachacámac. *Revista del Museo Nacional*, tomo VIII, no. 2, II semestre, pp. 265–82. Lima.

Mueller, Conrad G., and Mae, Rudolph
1969   *Luz y visión.* Amsterdam: Time-Life International.

Munsell
1954   *Munsell soil color charts.* Baltimore: Munsell Color Company.

Museo Nacional
1948   Revista del Museo Nacional de Antropología y Arqueología, vol. II, no. 1, primer semestre. Lima.

Nakamura H., Félix
1973   Reynaldo Luza: Telas chancay 1973. *7 Días del Perú y del Mundo*, año XXIII, no. 780, Junio 15, pp. 16–17. Lima.

Naval Ayerve, Francisco
1950   *Curso breve de arqueología y bellas artes.* Madrid: Editorial Coculsa.

Netherly, Patricia Joan
1978   Local level lords on the north coast of Peru. Ph.D. Diss. in Anthropology, Cornell University, 1977. University Microfilm International, 78-7792. Ann Arbor, Michigan.

Noticia del Perú
1938   Noticia del Perú. In *Los cronistas de la conquista.* Biblioteca de Cultura Peruana, 1st. ser., no. 2, pp. 195–251. Paris: Desclée, De Brouwer.

Oberem, Udo
1953   La obra del obispo Don Baltazar Jaime Martínez Compañón como fuente para la arqueología del Perú septentrional. *Revista de Indias*, Año XIII, nos. 52–53, pp. 233–75. Madrid.

Orrego V., Lorenzo S.
1927   La Huaca Pintada; su antigüedad y origen probable, su importancia como fuente histórica. *Monografía general del departamento de Lambayeque*, Ricardo A. Miranda, pp. CCXXV–CCXXXVI. Chiclayo, Peru: Talleres Tipográficos "El Tiempo."

Ostwald
1930–39   *Die kleine Farbmesstafel.* Göttingen: Munster Schmidt.

Oviedo y Valdés, Gonzalo Fernández de
1855   *Historia general y natural de las Indias, islas y tierra-firme del mar océano.* Tercera parte, tomo IV. Madrid: Real Academia de la Historia.

Patterson, Thomas Carl
1966   Pattern and process in the Early Intermediate Period pottery of the central coast of Peru. *University of California Publications in Anthropology*, vol. 3. Berkeley and Los Angeles.

PESCA Perú
1981   *La pesca en el Perú prehispánico.* Lima: Empresa Pública de Producción de Harina y Aceite de Pescado (PESCA Perú).

Petersen G., Georg
1970   Minería y metalurgía en el antiguo Perú. *Arqueológicas* 12. Lima.

Pizarro, Pedro
1944   Relación del descubrimiento y conquista de los reinos del Perú y del gobierno y orden que los naturales tenían, y tesoros que en ella se hallaron, y de las demás cosas que en él han subcedido hasta el día de la fecha hecha por . . . conquistador, [etc.] [1571]. Editorial Futuro, Buenos Aires.

Ponce Sanginés, Carlos
1961   Informe de labores; Octubre 1957–Febrero 1961. *Centro de Investigaciones Arqueológicas en Tiwanaku*, Publicación no. 1. Tiwanaku.

1964   Descripción sumaria del Templete Semisubterráneo de Tiwanaku. *Centro de Investigaciones Arqueológicas en Tiwanaku*, Publicación no. 2. Tiwanaku.

1969   Descripción sumaria del Templete Semisubterráneo de Tiwanaku. Tercera edición revisada. *Academia Nacional de Ciencias de Bolivia*, Publicación no. 20. La Paz, Bolivia.

1972   Tiwanaku: Espacio, tiempo y cultura. Ensayo de síntesis arqueológica. *Academia Nacional de Ciencias de Bolivia*, Publicación no. 30. La Paz, Bolivia.

Porras Barrenechea, Raúl
1954   La raíz índia de Lima. *Miraflores*, año III, no. 28, Junio, pp. 9–16, 22. Organo del Concejo Distrital de Miraflores.

1955   *Fuentes históricas peruanas.* Lima: Juan Mejía Baca y P.L. Villanueva Editores.

Pozorski, Thomas
1976   El complejo Caballo Muerto: Los frisos de barro de la Huaca de los Reyes. *Revista del Museo Nacional*, tomo XLI, 1975, pp. 211–51. Lima.

Prescott, William H.
1942   *History of the conquest of Peru* [1847]. Introduction by Thomas Seccombe. Everyman's Library, no. 301. London: J. M. Dent & Sons Limited. New York: E. P. Dutton & Company.

Proulx, Donald Allen
1968   An archaeological survey of the Nepeña Valley, Peru. *Department of Anthropology, University of Massachusetts, Research Reports*, no. 2. Amherst, Massachusetts.

1971   Headhunting in ancient Peru. *Archaeology*, vol. 24, no. 1, January, pp. 16–21. New York.

1973   Archaeological investigations in the Nepeña Valley, Peru. *Department of Anthropology, University of*

Massachusetts, Research Reports, no. 13. Amherst, Massachusetts.

1983   Territoriality in the Early Intermediate Period: The case of Moche and Recuay. *Ñawpa Pacha* 20, 1982, pp. 83–96. Berkeley.

Raimondi, Antonio
1942   *Notas de viajes para su obra "El Perú"* 1855–1860. 1$^{er.}$ Volumen. Lima: Imprenta Torres Aguirre.

Ravines, Rogger
1980   [Editor] *Chanchan, metrópoli chimú.* Fuentes e Investigaciones para la Historia del Perú 5. Lima: Instituto de Estudios Peruanos, Instituto de Investigación Tecnológica Industrial y de Normas Técnicas.
ms.   Sobre una pintura mural en el valle de Chancay. 1963.

Ravines, Rogger, and Isbell, William H.
1976   Garagay: Sitio ceremonial temprano en el valle de Lima. *Revista del Museo Nacional*, tomo XLI, 1975, pp. 253–75. Lima.

Reau, Louis
1930   *Dictionnaire illustré d'art et d'archéologie.* Paris: Librairie Larousse.

Rivero, Mariano Eduardo de, and Tschudi, Juan Diego de
1851   *Antigüedades peruanas.* Vienna: Imprenta Imperial de la Corte y del Estado.

Roe, Peter Guy
1974   A further exploration of the Rowe Chavín seriation and its implications for North Central Coast chronology. *Studies in Pre-Columbian Art and Archaeology*, no. 13. Dumbarton Oaks. Washington.

Rostworowski de Diez Canseco, María
1972   Breve ensayo sobre el señorío de Ychma o Ychima. *Arqueología PUC*, no. 13, Enero–Diciembre, pp. 37–51. Publicación no. 86 del Instituto Riva-Agüero. Lima.
1978   *Señoríos indígenas de Lima y Canta.* Historia Andina 7. Lima: Instituto de Estudios Peruanos.

Rowe, John Howland
1946   Inca culture at the time of the Spanish conquest. *Handbook of South American Indians.* Bureau of American Ethnology, Bulletin 143, vol. 2, pp. 183–330. Washington.
1962   *Chavín art; an inquiry into its form and meaning.* New York: The Museum of Primitive Art.
1967   Form and meaning in Chavin art. In *Peruvian archaeology; selected readings*, edited by John Howland Rowe and Dorothy Menzel, pp. 72–103. Palo Alto, California: Peek Publications.
1974   Kunst in Peru und Bolivien. In *Das alte Amerika* von Gordon R. Willey. Propyläen Kunst Geschichte, Bd. 18, pp. 285–350. Berlin: Propyläen Verlag.

Ruiz de Arce, Juan
1933   Relacion de los servicios en Indias de don Juan Ruiz de Arce, conquistador del Peru [1543]. Edited by Antonio del Solar y Taboada and José de Rújula y de Ochotorena. *Boletín de la Academia de la Historia*, tomo CII, cuaderno II, Abril–Junio, pp. 327–84. Madrid.

Samaniego Román, Lorenzo
1972a   Sechín: Pasado, presente y futuro. *Revista de Chimbote*, no. 12, Diciembre, pp. 37–44. Chimbote, Peru.
1972b   Sechín testimonio de una epopeya. *Acero*, año II, no. 4, Mayo, pp. 28–35. Chimbote, Peru.
1973   *Los nuevos trabajos arqueológicos en Sechín, Casma, Perú.* Trujillo, Peru: Larsen Ediciones.
1980   Informe sobre los hallazgos en Sechín; monumento arqueológico en la costa norte del Perú. *Indiana 6*, Gedenkschrift Walter Lehmann, Teil 1, pp. 307–48. Berlin.

Sancho de la Hoz, Pedro
1550   Relatione per sua maestà di quel che nel conquisto & pacificatione di queste provincie della nuova Castiglia è successo & della qualità del paese dopo che il capitano Fernando Pizarro si partì & ritorno a sua Maestà. Il rapporto del conquistamento di Caxamalca & la prigione del cacique Atabalipa [1534]. *Terzo Volume Delle Navigationi et Viaggi*, ff. 398v–414v. Venice: Di Hiunti.

Sawyer, Alan Reed
1954   *The Nathan Cummings Collection of ancient Peruvian art (formerly Wassermann-San Blas Collection).* Handbook. Chicago: Art Institute of Chicago.

Schaedel, Richard P.
1951   Mochica murals at Pañamarca. *Archaeology*, vol. 4, no. 3, September, pp. 145–54. Cambridge, Massachusetts.
1957   Highlights of Andean archaeology, 1954–1956. *Archaeology*, vol. 10, no. 2, June, pp. 93–99. Cincinnati, Ohio.
1967a   The Huaca El Dragón. *Journal de la Société des Américanistes*, tome LV-2, 1966, pp. 383–496. Paris.
1967b   Mochica murals at Pañamarca. In *Peruvian archaeology; selected readings*, edited by John Howland Rowe and Dorothy Menzel, pp. 104–14. Palo Alto, California: Peek Publications.
1970   Murales mochicas en Pañamarca. Translated by M. Cárdenas M. In *100 años de arqueología en el Perú*, edited by Rogger Ravines, pp. 309–20. Fuentes e Investigaciones para la Historia del Perú 3. Lima: Instituto de Estudios Peruanos, Edición de Petróleos del Perú.
1978   The Huaca Pintada of Illimo. *Archaeology*, vol. 31, no. 1, January/February, pp. 27–37. New York.
1980   La Huaca Pintada de Illimo. *Humboldt*, año 21, no. 71, pp. 61–69. Munich.

Schmidt, Max
1929   *Kunst und Kultur von Peru.* Berlin: Propyläen-Verlag.

Séguy, E.
1936   *Code universel des couleurs.* Paris: Le Chevalier.

Seler, Eduard
1893   *Peruanische Alterthümer, insbesondere altperuanische Gefässe, und Gefässe der Chibcha und der Tolima- und Cauca-Stamme, Goldschmuck etc.* Königliche Museen zu Berlin. Berlin: Dr. E. Mertens & Cie.

1912   Archäologische Reise in Sud- und Mittel-Amerika. *Zeitschrift für Ethnologie*, 44. Jahrgang, Heft I, pp. 201–42. Berlin.

1923   Viaje arqueológico en Perú y Bolivia. *Inca*, vol. I, no. 2, Abril–Junio, pp. 355–74. Lima.

Shimada, Izumi
1981   Temples of time: the ancient burial and religious center of Batan Grande, Peru. *Archaeology*, vol. 34, no. 5, September/October, pp. 37–45. New York.

Silva Pérez, Hernán I.
1982   Hallazgo de pinturas murales en la Huaca de "Cotón." *Investigación Arqueológica* 4, pp. 48–49. Trujillo, Peru.

Soukup, Jaroslav
1970   *Vocabulario de los nombres vulgares de la flora peruana*. Lima: Colegio Salesiano.

Squier, Ephraim George
1877   *Peru; incidents of travel and exploration in the land of the Incas*. New York: Harper & Brothers, Publishers.

Stumer, Louis M.
1954   The Chillon Valley of Peru, excavation and reconnaissance 1952–1953. Part 2. *Archaeology*, vol. 7, no. 4, Winter, pp. 220–28. New York.

1955   History of a dig. *Scientific American*, vol. 192, no. 3, March, pp. 98–104. New York.

Tabío, Ernesto
1977   *Prehistoria de la costa del Perú*. Havana: Academia de Ciencias de Cuba.

Tello, Julio César
1923   Observaciones del Editor al discurso del Profesor Seler. *Inca*, vol. I, no. 2, Abril–Junio, pp. 375–82. Lima.

1933a   Las ruinas del valle de Nepeña. *El Comercio*, no. 47261, viernes 6 de Octubre, p. 4. Lima.

1933b   Las ruinas del valle de Nepeña. II. Los testimonios de la más vieja y más adelantada civilización del Perú, recientemente descubierta. *El Comercio*, no. 47266, lunes 9 de Octubre, p. 7. Lima.

1933c   Las ruinas del valle de Nepeña. III. De la necesidad de preservar y estudiar los tesoros arqueológicos descubiertos en el valle de Nepeña. *El Comercio*, no. 47275, sábado 14 de Octubre, p. 7. Lima.

1936   Los monumentos arqueológicos de Magdalena Vieja y la necesidad de conservarlos. *Gaceta Municipal, Magdalena Vieja*, Enero. [Lima].

1937   Los trabajos arqueológicos en el departamento de Lambayeque. *El Comercio*, no. 49460, 29 de Enero, p. 5; no. 49462, 30 de Enero, p. 10; no. 49464, 31 de enero, p. 7. Lima.

1939a   Algunos monumentos arqueológicos existentes entre Lima y Paramonga. *El Comercio*, no. 51213, 26 de Setiembre, p. 3. Lima.

1939b   Sobre el descubrimiento de la cultura Chavín del Perú. *Actas de la primera sesión celebrada en la C. de México en 1939, del vigesimoséptimo Congreso Internacional de Americanistas*, tomo 1, pp. 231–52. México: Instituto Nacional de Antropología e Historia, Secretaría de Educación Pública.

1942   *Origen y desarrollo de las civilizaciones prehistóricas andinas*. Reimpreso de las Actas del XXVII Congreso de Americanistas de 1939. [Greatly expanded]. Lima: Librería e Imprenta Gil, S.A.

1943a   Discovery of the Chavín culture in Peru. *American Antiquity*, vol. IX, no. 1, July, pp. 135–60. Menasha, Wisconsin.

1943b   Sobre el descubrimiento de la cultura Chavín en el Perú. *Letras*, no. 26, tercer cuatrimestre, pp. 226–373. Lima.

1956   *Arqueología del Valle de Casma. Culturas: Chavín, Santa o Huaylas Yunga y Sub-Chimú. (Informe de los trabajos de la Expedición Arqueológica al Marañón de 1937)*. Publicación Antropológica del Archivo "Julio C. Tello" de la Universidad Nacional Mayor de San Marcos, vol. I. Lima: Editorial San Marcos.

1960   *Chavín. Cultura matriz de la civilización andina*. Primera parte. Con revisión de Toribio Mejía Xesspe. Publicación Antropológica del Archivo "Julio C. Tello" de la Universidad Nacional Mayor de San Marcos, vol. II. Lima: Imprenta de la Universidad de San Marcos.

1970   Sobre el descubrimiento de la cultura Chavín en el Perú. In *100 años de arqueología en el Perú*, edited by Rogger Ravines, pp. 69–110. Fuentes e Investigaciones para la Historia del Perú 3. Lima: Instituto de Estudios Peruanos, Edición de Petróleos del Perú.

Thompson, Donald Enrique
1962   Additional stone carving from the north highlands of Peru. *American Antiquity*, vol. 28, no. 2, October, pp. 245–46. Salt Lake City.

1964   Formative period architecture in the Casma Valley, Peru. *XXXV Congreso Internacional de Americanistas, México, 1962, Actas y Memorias*, pp. 205–12.

Toledo, Francisco de
1924   Libro de la visita general del Virrey Don Francisco de Toledo 1570–1575. *Revista Histórica*, tomo VII, entrega II, pp. 113–216. Lima.

Towle, Margaret A.
1961   *The ethnobotany of pre-Columbian Peru*. Viking Fund Publications in Anthropology, no. 30. New York: Aldine Publishing Company.

Trucco, Giovanni (a cura di)
1934   *Grande dizionario enciclopedico*. Vol. III. Turin: Unione Tipogràfica–Editrice Torinese.

Tschudi, Johann Jacob von
1847   Travels in Peru during the years 1838–1842. Translated from the German by Thomasina Ross. Part I. New York: Wiley & Putnam.

Ubbelohde-Doering, Heinrich
1936   *Old Peruvian art*. New York: E. Weyhe.
1967   *On the royal highways of the Incas; archaeological treasures of ancient Peru*. Translated from the German by Margaret Brown. New York, Washington: Frederick A. Praeger, Publishers.

Uhle, Max
1903   *Pachacamac. Report of the William Pepper M.D., LL.D., Peruvian Expedition of 1896*. Translated by

C. Grosse. Philadelphia: Department of Archaeology of the University of Pennsylvania.

1910a   Las civilizaciones primitivas en los alrededores de Lima. Traducción del alemán al francés por el R.P. Ph. Kieffer . . . y del francés al español por . . . María Wiesse. *Revista Universitaria*, año V, vol. 1, [no. 4], Abril, pp. 333–47. Lima.

1910b   Über die Frühkulturen in der Umgebung von Lima. *Verhandlungen des XVI. Internationalen Amerikanisten-Kongresses, Wien, 9. bis 14. September 1908*, zweite Hälfte, pp. 348–70. Vienna and Leipzig: A. Hartleben's Verlag.

1924   Explorations at Chincha. Edited by A. L. Kroeber. *University of California Publications in American Archaeology and Ethnology*, vol. 21, no. 2, pp. 55–94. Berkeley.

1935   *Die alten Kulturen Perús im Hinblick auf die Archäologie und Geschichte des amerikanischen Kontinents*. Berlin: Wilhelm Süsserott Verlag.

ms.   Letter to Phoebe Apperson Hearst, September 24, 1901. Field Catalogue, vol. IV, ff. 37–74. R. H. Lowie Museum of Anthropology, Berkeley.

Urteaga, Horacio H.

1917   Perú descriptivo; las antiguas tradiciones del valle de Lambayeque. . . . *Variedades*, año XIII, no. 477, 21 de Abril, pp. 449–51. Lima.

Vega, Juan José

n.d.   *La guerra de los Viracochas*. Lima: Populibros Peruanos.

Villar Córdova, Pedro Eduardo

1935   *Las culturas pre-hispánicas del departamento de Lima*. Lima: Auspiciado por la H. Municipalidad de Lima.

1942   Las ruinas de Ascona. *Revista Histórica*, tomo XV, entrega III, pp. 248–55. Lima.

Wagner, Günther S.p.A.

1972   *Dipingere, colorare, costruire*. Milan: Pelikan.

Wallace, Dwight Tousch

1971   Valles de Chincha y Pisco. *Arqueológicas* 13. Sitios arqueológicos del Perú (Segunda entrega). Lima.

Wiener, Charles

1880   *Pérou et Bolivie. Recit de voyage suivi d'études archéologiques et ethnographiques et des notes sur l'écriture et les langues des populations indiennes*. Paris: Librairie Hachette et Cie.

Willey, Gordon Randolph

1951   The Chavín problem: A review and critique. *Southwestern Journal of Anthropology*, vol. 7, no. 2, Summer, pp. 103–44. Albuquerque, New Mexico.

1970   El problema de Chavín: Revisión y crítica. In *100 años de arqueología en el Perú*, edited by Rogger Ravines, pp. 161–214. Fuentes e Investigaciones para la Historia del Perú 3. Lima: Instituto de Estudios Peruanos, Edición de Petróleos del Perú.

1971   *An introduction to American archaeology*. Volume Two, *South America*. Englewood Cliffs, New Jersey: Prentice-Hall, Inc.

Yakovleff, Eugenio

1932   Las falcónidas en el arte y en las creencias de los antiguos peruanos. *Revista del Museo Nacional*, [tomo I], no. 2, pp. 33–111. Lima.

Zevallos Quiñones, Jorge

1946   Un diccionario yunga. *Revista del Museo Nacional*, tomo XV, pp. 163–88. Lima.

1971   *Cerámica de la cultura "Lambayeque" (Lambayeque I)*. Trujillo, Peru: Imprenta de la Universidad Nacional de Trujillo.

CREDITS FOR ILLUSTRATIONS

Map. Drawing by Félix Caycho Quispe.
Fig. 1. After Izumi and Terada, 1972, fig. 82, p. 140.
Fig. 2. After Izumi and Terada, 1972, fig. 94, p. 160.
Fig. 3. Photo Wilfredo Loayza.
Fig. 4. Redrawn by Margaret MacLean from Tello, 1956, fig. 108, p. 250, with minor modifications.
Fig. 5. Photo Duccio Bonavia.
Fig. 6. After Tello, 1956, fig. 109, p. 252.
Fig. 7. Photo Donald Collier.
Fig. 8. Photo Donald Collier.
Fig. 9. Photo Duccio Bonavia.
Fig. 10. Photo Abraham Guillén.
Fig. 11. After *Acero*, año 2, no. 4, Mayo de 1972, cover. Chimbote, Peru.
Fig. 12. Redrawn by Margaret MacLean from Larco Hoyle, 1938, fig. 18, p. 32, somewhat simplified.
Fig. 13. Redrawn by Margaret MacLean from Larco Hoyle, 1938, fig. 19, p. 33; format and labeling by Patricia Lyon.
Fig. 14. Photo John Harrison.
Fig. 15. Photo John Harrison.
Fig. 16. After Carrión Cachot, 1948, lám. XIX-4, p. 143.
Fig. 17. Photo John Harrison.
Fig. 18. After Kosok, 1965, fig. 32. Reproduced by permission of Long Island University.
Fig. 19. Drawing by Carlos Elera and Izumi Shimada.
Fig. 20. Photo Abraham Guillén.
Fig. 21. Photo Abraham Guillén.
Fig. 22. Photo Abraham Guillén.
Fig. 23. Photo Abraham Guillén.
Fig. 24. Photo Abraham Guillén.
Fig. 25. After Uhle, 1935, fig. 13, p. 27.
Fig. 26. Drawing by Rogger Ravines.
Fig. 27. Photo Hans Horkheimer.
Fig. 28. Redrawn by Margaret MacLean from Bonavia, 1959b, lám. I (which was adapted from Schaedel, 1951, fig. 3, p. 147), with some simplification and change in lettering.
Fig. 29. Redrawn by Margaret MacLean from Bonavia, 1959b, lám. II, with changes in lettering.
Fig. 30. Photo Abraham Guillén.
Fig. 31. Photo Abraham Guillén.
Fig. 32. Drawing by Pedro Azabache from Kosok, 1965, p. 203. Reproduced by permission of Long Island University.
Fig. 33. Photo Hans Horkheimer.
Fig. 34. Drawing by Pedro Azabache from Kosok, 1965, fig. 10b, p. 207. Reproduced by permission of Long Island University.
Fig. 35. Drawing by Pedro Azabache from Kosok, 1965, fig. 10a, p. 206. Reproduced by permission of Long Island University.
Fig. 36. Reconstruction drawing by Pedro Azabache from Kosok, 1965, fig. 10, pp. 206–207. Reproduced by permission of Long Island University.
Fig. 37. Photo Abraham Guillén.
Fig. 38. Photo Abraham Guillén.
Fig. 39. Abraham Guillén photo of replica painted by Félix Caycho.
Fig. 40. Photo Hans Horkheimer.
Fig. 41. Photo Hans Horkheimer.
Fig. 42. Photo by Billing.
Fig. 43. Abraham Guillén photo of replica painted by Félix Caycho.
Fig. 44. Photo Hans Horkheimer.
Fig. 45. Abraham Guillén photo of replica painted by Félix Caycho.
Fig. 46. Photo by Billing.
Fig. 47. Photo Hans Horkheimer.
Fig. 48. Abraham Guillén photo of replica painted by Félix Caycho.
Fig. 49. Photo Hans Horkheimer.
Fig. 50. Abraham Guillén photo of replica painted by Félix Caycho.
Fig. 51. Abraham Guillén photo of replica painted by Félix Caycho.
Fig. 52. Drawing by Rogger Ravines based on his own tracing.
Fig. 53. Redrawn by Margaret MacLean from plan by Chan Chan–Moche Valley Project on file in Instituto Nacional de Cultura, Trujillo, Peru, with slight modifications and added letters.
Fig. 54. After Seler, 1912, Abb. 13, p. 220.
Fig. 55. Photo Abraham Guillén.
Fig. 56. Photo Alfred L. Kroeber, courtesy Field Museum of Natural History, Chicago.
Fig. 57. Photo Alfred L. Kroeber, courtesy Field Museum of Natural History, Chicago.
Fig. 58. Reoriented and redrawn by Margaret MacLean after Kroeber, 1930, pl. XXVIIa.

Fig. 59a–d. Drawings based on tracings by Alfred L. Kroeber, courtesy Field Museum of Natural History, Chicago.

Fig. 60. Wilfredo Loayza photo of anonymous drawing, courtesy Museo Nacional de Antropología y Arqueología, Lima.

Fig. 61. After Díaz, 1940.

Fig. 62. Photo Ricardo Morales Gamarra.

Fig. 63. Drawn by Francisco Carré from original by staff of Chan Chan–Moche Valley Project, courtesy Chan Chan–Moche Valley Project.

Fig. 64. Photo Ricardo Morales Gamarra.

Fig. 65. Photo Ricardo Morales Gamarra.

Fig. 66. Drawn by Francisco Carré from original by staff of Chan Chan–Moche Valley Project, courtesy Chan Chan–Moche Valley Project.

Fig. 67. Photo Ricardo Morales Gamarra.

Fig. 68. Hans Horkheimer photo of painting by Pedro Azabache.

Fig. 69. Photo Antonio Rodríguez Suy Suy.

Fig. 70. Photo Antonio Rodríguez Suy Suy.

Fig. 71. Photo Martha B. Anders.

Fig. 72. After Anders, 1979, fig. 20, p. 267.

Fig. 73. After Archaeology, vol. 25, no. 2, April 1972, cover. New York.

Fig. 74. After Donnan, 1972, p. 89.

Fig. 75. After Schaedel, 1978, p. 30. Reproduced by permission of Archaeology.

Fig. 76. Photo Heinrich Brüning, courtesy Hamburgisches Museum für Völkerkunde.

Fig. 77. Photo Heinrich Brüning, courtesy Hamburgisches Museum für Völkerkunde.

Fig. 78. Photo Oscar Lostaunau.

Fig. 79. Photo Hans Horkheimer.

Fig. 80. Duccio Bonavia photo of drawing provided by Oscar Fernández de Córdoba, based on documentation in the files of the Museo Arqueológico Brüning, Lambayeque.

Fig. 81. After Carrión Cachot, 1942, fig. 17, p. 585.

Fig. 82. Photo Richard P. Schaedel.

Fig. 83. After Florián, 1951, p. 9.

Fig. 84. Drawing by Izumi Shimada.

Fig. 85. Drawing by Izumi Shimada.

Fig. 86. Drawing by Izumi Shimada.

Fig. 87. Drawing courtesy Christopher B. Donnan.

Fig. 88. Drawing courtesy Christopher B. Donnan.

Fig. 89. Drawing courtesy Christopher B. Donnan.

Fig. 90. Drawing courtesy Christopher B. Donnan.

Fig. 91. Drawing courtesy Christopher B. Donnan.

Fig. 92. Photo courtesy Christopher B. Donnan.

Fig. 93. Photo courtesy Christopher B. Donnan.

Fig. 94. Photo courtesy Christopher B. Donnan.

Fig. 95. Photo courtesy Christopher B. Donnan.

Fig. 96. Photo courtesy Christopher B. Donnan.

Fig. 97. Detail, with inserted north arrow and scale, from complete site plan drawn by Uhle (1903).

Fig. 98. Photo Hans Horkheimer.

Fig. 99. After Uhle, 1903, fig. 6, p. 20.

Fig. 100. After Uhle, 1903, fig. 7, p. 21.

Fig. 101. After Uhle, 1903, fig. 8, p. 21.

Fig. 102. After Uhle, 1903, fig. 9, p. 21.

Fig. 103. Photo Abraham Guillén.

Fig. 104. Photo Abraham Guillén.

Fig. 105. Photo Abraham Guillén.

Fig. 106. After Muelle and Wells, 1939, fig. 7, p. 275.

Fig. 107. After Muelle and Wells, 1939, fig. 8, p. 275.

Fig. 108. After Muelle and Wells, 1939, fig. 9, p. 275.

Fig. 109. Photo Abraham Guillén.

Fig. 110. Photo Rogger Ravines.

Fig. 111. Anonymous photo courtesy Hans Horkheimer.

Fig. 112. Photo Duccio Bonavia.

Fig. 113. Photo Duccio Bonavia.

Fig. 114. Drawn by Jane Becker from sketches, notes, and measurements taken by John H. Rowe in 1958.

Fig. 115. Redrawn by Jane Becker from original by Félix Caycho Q. based on aerial photographs with ground control.

Fig. 116. Photo Duccio Bonavia.

Fig. 117. Redrawn by Jane Becker from original by Duccio Bonavia.

Fig. 118. Photo Abraham Guillén.

Fig. 119. Air photo by Servicio Aerofotográfico Nacional of Peru.

Fig. 120. Redrawn by Margaret MacLean from Langlois, 1938, unnumbered plan preceding p. 281; letters added by Patricia Lyon.

Fig. 121. After Wiener, 1880, p. 494.

Fig. 122. Photo Duccio Bonavia.

Fig. 123. After Squier, 1877, p. 243.

Fig. 124. Photo Duccio Bonavia.

COLOR PLATES

Plate 1. Photo Duccio Bonavia.

Plate 2. Photo Juan Ossio.

Plate 3. Photo Juan Ossio.

Plate 4. Photo Juan Ossio.

Plate 5. Photo Ricardo Morales Gamarra.

Plate 6. Photo Duccio Bonavia.

Plate 7. Photo Duccio Bonavia.

Plate 8. Photo Hans Horkheimer.

Plate 9. Photo Hans Horkheimer.

Plate 10. Photo Hans Horkheimer.

Plate 11. Photo Duccio Bonavia.

Plate 12. Photo Duccio Bonavia.

Plate 13. Photo Duccio Bonavia.

Plate 14. Photo Ricardo Morales Gamarra.

Plate 15. Photo Gustavo Alvarez Sánchez.

Plate 16. Photo Gustavo Alvarez Sánchez.

Plate 17. Photo Gustavo Alvarez Sánchez.

Plate 18. Photo Ricardo Morales Gamarra.

Plate 19. Photo Martha B. Anders.

Plate 20. Photo of painting by N. Moreno, courtesy of Hamburgisches Museum für Völkerkunde.

Plate 21. Photo Abraham Guillén.

Plate 22. Photo Izumi Shimada.

Plate 23. Photo Christopher B. Donnan.

Plate 24. Photo Christopher B. Donnan.

Plate 25. Photo Christopher B. Donnan.

Plate 26. Photo Christopher B. Donnan.

Plate 27. Photo Christopher B. Donnan.

Plate 28. Photo Christopher B. Donnan.

Plate 29. Photo Abraham Guillén.

Plate 30. Photo Abraham Guillén.

Plate 31. Photo John H. Rowe, 1958.

Plate 32. Photo Duccio Bonavia.

Plate 33. Photo Duccio Bonavia.

Plate 34. Photo Duccio Bonavia.

INDEX OF
PERSONS AND
AUTHORS CITED

Adeline, J., 206
Albornoz, Cristóbal de, 159
Alva Maúrtua, Abelardo V., 155
Alvarez M., Carlos E., 31
Alvarez Sánchez, Gustavo, 97
Amano, Yoshitaro, 133
Anders, Martha B., 97, 99, 205
Antúnez de Mayolo, Santiago, 24, 27, 28, 205
Antze, Gustavo, 116
Apperson Hearst, Phoebe, 153
Aschero, Carlos A., 185
Atabalipa. *See* Atahualpa
Atahualpa, 175
Aurich, Osvaldo, 100
Avila, Francisco de, 82
Azabache, Pedro, 58, 89–91, 93

Bances, Augusto, 100
Bandelier, Adolphe F., 153
Bennett, Wendell Clark, 24, 27, 28, 30, 43, 45, 49, 71, 73, 80, 104, 112, 116, 152, 155, 171, 183–85, 193
Benson, Elizabeth P., 43, 48, 84
Berezkin, Yuri E., 84
Betanzos, Juan de, 181
Beuchat, Henri, 169
Bonavia, Duccio, 38, 40, 43, 46, 49, 58, 59, 64, 71, 85, 89, 94, 97, 99, 148, 158, 160, 178–80, 183, 184, 191, 193, 194, 205, 206
Branzani, Luigi, 182, 206
Brüning, Enrique, 104–106, 108
Bueno Mendoza, Alberto, 9, 21, 23

Cailleux, A., 43, 46, 49, 70, 103, 115, 116, 153, 199, 205, 206
Calancha, Antonio de la, 72, 159, 184
Campana, Cristóbal, 31, 43, 45
Cárdenas, Mercedes, 31
Carrera, Fernando de la, 190
Carrión Cachot, Rebeca, 104, 109, 116, 117, 121, 125
Castro Talledo, Víctor, 45
Caycho, Félix, 59, 61, 64, 66, 68, 70, 148, 160, 206
Ccosi Salas, Luis, 27, 28
Chambers, 179
Chauchat, Claude, 31, 97
Chávez Ballón, Manuel, 40, 174

Cieza de León, Pedro de, 137, 157, 168–71, 174, 175
Cisneros G., Carmen, 85
Cobo, Bernabé, 137, 152, 166, 175, 181, 188, 205
Collier, Donald, 16, 19–21, 24
Conrad, Geoffrey W., 95
Courty, Georges, 185
Créqui-Montfort, Guy de, 185
Cuismancu, 147

Dávila. *See* Avila, Francisco de
Day, Kent C., 72, 194
Díaz D., Máximo R., 80, 83
Disselhoff, Hans Dietrich, 112
Donnan, Christopher Bruce, 43, 47, 48, 58, 59, 64, 71, 72, 84, 94, 97, 99–101, 103, 104, 117, 125–27, 130–32, 134, 180, 184, 194
Duviols, Pierre, 159

Eguiguren, Luis Antonio, 159
Elliot, J. H., 190
Engel, Frédéric André, 9, 11, 191
Enríquez de Guzmán, Alonso, 173
Estete, Miguel de, 137, 168, 171, 206

Feldman, Robert A., 9, 112
Fernández de Córdova, Oscar, 112
Florián, Mario, 43, 109, 118, 120–22, 179, 181, 183
Ford, James A., 100, 101, 103
Fung, Pineda Rosa, 23

García Rosell, César, 105
Garcilaso de la Vega, "El Inca," 147, 157–59, 169, 171, 172, 174
Garrido, José Eulogio, 43, 73–75, 80, 84, 85, 88, 89, 91, 93, 96, 104, 112, 182, 184
Gasparini, Graziano, 152, 171, 174, 206
Giesecke, Alberto, 140, 171
Gisbert, Teresa, 184, 185, 189
Gonzáles, Nicolasa, 118
Grieder, Terence, 9
Grossman, Joel, 100
Guainacaba. *See* Guaynacapac
Guaynacapac (Huayna Capac), 173, 174
Guillén, Abraham, 112, 164
Guillén G., Edmundo, 174

Haase, Inez, 153, 206
Haberland, Wolfgang, 105
Hagen, Victor Wolfgang von, 43
Hardoy, Jorge E., 206
Harrison, John B., 25, 28, 182
Hastings, Charles Mansfield, 43, 75, 85, 90, 93, 94, 96, 104, 184
Hocquenghem, Anne Marie, 59, 117
Horkheimer, Hans, 43, 74, 104, 112, 149, 183, 205
Huapaya, Cirilo, 46

Imbelloni, José, 80, 84
Isbell, William H., 11
Ishida, Eiichiro, 155
Izumi, Seiichi, 10

Jahnsen, Eduardo, 172
Jérez, Francisco de, 168, 175
Jiménez Borja, Arturo, 11, 13, 19, 23, 182

Kauffmann Doig, Federico, 25–27, 30, 33, 55, 96, 104, 122, 171
Kaulicke, Peter, 46
Kosok, Paul, 30, 33, 40, 118, 120, 121, 190, 191, 194
Krickeberg, Walter, 82, 84
Kroeber, Alfred Louis, 7, 33, 40, 73–75, 79–85, 155, 171, 178, 188, 191, 193, 194
Kutscher, Gerdt, 84, 95, 99

Langlois, Louis, 170–72
Lanning, Edward Putnam, 21, 23, 42, 171
Larco Hoyle, Rafael, 24, 25, 27, 28, 47, 64, 70, 74, 95, 125, 133. 134, 190
Larrabure y Unanue, Eugenio, 157, 158, 169, 184
Lathrap, Donald Ward, 23, 188
Lavallée, Danièle, 95
León Barandiarán, Augusto, 108, 118
Leroi-Gourhan, André, 6
Littmann, Edwin R., 185
Lostaunau, Oscar P., 43, 112, 115, 179, 184, 203
Lumbreras, Luis Guillermo, 21, 32, 64, 185, 206
Luza, Reynaldo, 30
Lyon, Patricia Jean, 59, 84, 117, 134, 206

Macedo, José Mariano, 149
Macedo Mas, Armando, 149
Macera, Pablo, 6, 181
Mackey, Carol Joy, 75, 85, 90, 93, 94, 96, 104, 131, 134, 184
Mae, Rudolph, 179
Maerz, Aloys, 206
Margolies, Luise, 152, 171, 174, 206
Martin, Phyllis, 97
Martínez Compañón, Baltazar Jaime, 112
Massey, Sarah Ann, 11
Matos, Ramiro, 148, 160, 206
Mayer, Ralph, 206
Mejía Xesspe, Toribio, 6, 11, 16, 19, 27, 80, 149, 159, 181, 182, 191, 203, 205
Mendizábal Losack, Emilio, 174
Menzel, Dorothy, 94–96, 109, 133, 155
Mesa, José de, 184, 189
Middendorf, Ernst Wilhelm, 137, 155, 159, 169, 171, 172, 190
Molina, Cristóbal de (El Cuzqueño), 188
Montalvo, 72
Moorehead, Elizabeth L., 174
Morales Chocano, Daniel, 174
Morales Gamarra, Ricardo, 45, 85, 93, 96, 97, 178, 179
Moreno, N., 106
Moseley, Michael Edward, 43, 85, 93–96, 104
Muelle, Jorge Clemente, 32, 33, 58, 94, 137, 139–41, 143–47, 178–82, 184, 188, 191, 205, 206
Mueller, Conrad G., 179
Munsell, 85, 93, 206

Nakamura H., Félix, 31
Naval Ayerve, Francisco, 188
Netherly, Patricia Joan, 72

Oberem, Udo, 72
Odriozola, Manuel, 159
Orrego H., Augusto, 104, 106, 108
Orrego V., Lorenzo S., 116, 117
Ossio, Juan, 158
Ostwald, 206
Oviedo y Valdés, Gonzalo Fernández de, 179, 180

Pachacútec (Pachacuti), Inca, 118
Patterson, Thomas Carl, 38
Paul, Rea M., 206
Pedersen, Asbjorn, 181
Peralta, Eduardo de, 116
Perkovich, N., 149
Petersen G., Georg, 182
Pimentel Gurmendi, Victor, 23
Pinelo (León Pinelo, Antonio Rodríguez de?), 158, 184
Pizarro, Francisco, 174
Pizarro, Hernando, 137, 146, 166, 171
Pizarro, Pedro, 174, 175
Ponce Sanginés, Carlos, 185
Porras Barrenechea, Raúl, 166, 188
Pozorski, Thomas, 31
Prescott, William H., 174
Proctor, 169
Proulx, Donald Allen, 20, 23, 28, 30, 70, 71, 132, 205

Raimondi, Antonio, 169, 190
Ravines, Rogger, 11, 40, 42, 149, 158, 174, 177, 179, 181, 184, 205
Reau, Louis, 206
Respaldiza, José Ricardo, 140
Rivero, Mariano Eduardo de, 112, 152, 172
Rodríguez Suy Suy, Antonio, 190
Roe, Peter Guy, 23, 28
Rojas Ponce, Pedro, 15, 16, 19, 74, 171, 174
Rondon, Jorge, 100, 109, 112, 121, 125
Ross, Charles R., 181
Rostworowski de Diez Canseco, María, 159, 190
Rowe, John Howland, 11, 22, 23, 28, 30–32, 43, 71, 93, 95, 96, 152, 155, 157, 171, 174, 206
Ruiz de Arce, Juan, 173

Samaniego Román, Lorenzo, 11, 13, 15, 19, 21–23, 205
San Román, Miguel, 149
Sánchez Vera, Manuel, 89, 91, 96
Sancho de la Hoz, Pedro, 174
Sawyer, Alan Reed, 59
Schaedel, Richard P., 43, 49, 53, 54–56, 58, 70, 74, 100, 104–106, 108, 109, 112, 116, 118, 119, 121, 125, 178, 179, 182, 183, 193, 194, 205
Schmidt, Max, 43, 84, 99, 132, 133, 189
Séguy, E., 206
Seler, Eduard, 73–75, 82, 125, 194
Semper, Gottfried, 94, 132
Shimada, Izumi, 31, 109, 122, 123, 125, 182, 183, 191
Silva, Gerónimo de, 159
Silva Pérez, Hernán I., 205
Soukup, Jaroslav, 181
Squier, Ephraim George, 23, 49, 71, 72, 112, 137, 158, 159, 169, 171, 173, 174, 184, 194
Stumer, Louis M., 36–38, 40, 177, 179, 183, 194

Tabío, Ernesto, 59, 172
Taylor, B., 43, 46, 49, 70, 103, 115, 116, 153, 199, 205, 206
Tello, Julio César, 11, 13, 15, 16, 18, 19, 22–26, 28, 30, 32, 71, 74, 75, 80, 97, 148, 149, 171, 177, 179, 184, 193, 194, 205
Terada, Kazuo, 10

Thompson, Donald Enrique, 16, 20
Toledo, Francisco de, 152
Towle, Margaret A., 182
Trimborn, Hermann, 180
Trucco, Giovanni, 179, 190
Tschudi, Johann Jacob von, 112, 152, 171, 172
Tunga, Anto, 118

Ubbelohde-Doering, Heinrich, 72, 74, 84, 95
Uceda, Santiago, 72
Uhle, Max, 38, 40–42, 75, 94, 96, 137, 139, 140, 143, 144, 146, 153, 155, 156, 182, 184, 206
Unanue Pavón, José Hipólito, 172
Urteaga, Horacio H., 105

Vargas Ugarte, Rubén, 159
Vega, Juan José, 173

Velásquez, José, 59–68
Villar Córdova, Pedro Eduardo, 137, 148, 160, 181
Villarreal, Federico, 190

Wagner-Günter, 179
Wallace, Dwight Tousch, 155
Weide, David, 180
Wells, Robert, 137, 139, 140, 143, 144, 178–82, 184, 206
Wiener, Charles, 137, 169–71, 178, 179, 184
Willey, Gordon Randolph, 21, 23, 80
Williams León, Carlos, 23

Yacovleff, Eugenio, 120
Yupanqui, Inca (Pachacuti Inca Yupanqui), 181
Yupanqui, Inca (Topa Inca Yupanqui), 169

Zevallos Quiñones, Jorge, 125, 134, 190

INDEX OF MONUMENTS

Ancón, 132
Armatambo, 3, 166
Aspero, 9

Batán Grande, 31, 100, 122, 123

Caballo Muerto, 31, 191
Cajamarca, 175
Calaveras. *See* Chanquillo
Callango, 11
Campo de las Flores, 3, 158
Canta, 46
Cañahuaca. *See* Huaca Sacachique
Casa Grande, 3, 30, 191, 194
Castillo, 72
Castillo de las Calaveras. *See* Chanquillo
Cerro Blanco, 3, 11, 13, 20, 22, 24, 25, 28, 32, 191, 193, 194
Cerro Culebra, 3, 35–38, 40, 179, 183, 194
Cerro de la Horca, 172
Cerro Sechín, 3, 11, 13–23, 182, 191, 193, 194
Cerro Trinidad, 3, 38, 40–42, 179, 184
Chancaillo. *See* Chanquillo
Chanchan, 3, 96, 112, 169, 184, 194
Chanquillo, 3, 23, 194
Chavín. *See* Chavín de Huántar
Chavín de Huántar, 3, 11, 31–33, 189, 191
Checacupe, 182
Chiripa, 31
Chornancap, 3, 125–34, 180, 184, 195
Chuquitanta, 189
Cuzco, 3, 174, 188

El Alamo, 46, 180, 199
El Castillo, 46
El Paraíso, 9
El Purgatorio. *See* Túcume
El Templo del Sol. *See* Huaca del Sol

Fortaleza de Paramonga. *See* Paramonga

Galindo, 74, 95
Gallito Ciego, 3, 97
Garagay, 3, 10, 13, 191
Guarco, 3, 157

Hacienda Casa Grande. *See* Casa Grande
Herederos, 31
Huaca Chotuna, 125, 180
Huaca Cientopiés. *See* Huaca del Dragón
Huaca Concha, 3, 148, 206
Huaca Corte, 3, 122–25, 131, 183, 191
Huaca Cotón, 3, 45, 125
Huaca de la Centinela, 3, 155–57, 195
Huaca de la Luna, 3, 43, 48, 72–75, 79, 80, 82–97, 99, 103, 104, 125, 133, 179, 183, 184, 188, 190, 194, 195
Huaca de las Llamas, 149
Huaca de los Chinos, 31
Huaca de los Idolos, 9
Huaca de los Reyes, 31
Huaca del Dragón, 3, 96, 112, 182, 194
Huaca del Estanque. *See* Maranga
Huaca del Horno, 122
Huaca del Oro, 3, 109, 118–22, 125, 131, 179, 181, 191
Huaca del Sol, 3, 43, 48, 72, 94, 96, 184
Huaca Facho. *See* La Mayanga
Huaca Grande (Túcume), 116
Huaca La Palma, 115, 159
Huaca La Ventana, 97
Huaca Licapa, 3, 43–45, 97, 180, 182, 183, 199
Huaca Lucía, 3, 31–33, 182, 191
Huaca Mocan. *See* Huaca Licapa
Huaca Pintada, 3, 94, 100, 104–106, 108, 109, 116–18, 121, 122, 125, 179, 180, 195
Huaca Sacachique, 31
Huaca Tacaynamo, 112
Huaca Tres Palos. *See* Maranga
Huaca Ureña, 31
Huacas de Ascona. *See* Huacas de Mateo Salado
Huacas de Mateo Salado, 3, 148
Huadca, 3, 147, 159–62, 164, 178, 179, 182, 190, 195
Huari, 46
Huatica. *See* Huadca
Huatica Marca. *See* Huadca
Huaycán, 158, 206
Huaycán de Pariachi, 206
Huaytará, 191, 192

Illimo, 180, 199
Incahuasi (Lunahuaná, Cañete Valley), 3, 158

Incahuasi (Yucay, Urubamba Valley). *See* Palace of Sayri Thupa
Ipuna, 193

Jusape, 43

Kotosh, 3, 10

La Mayanga, 3, 94, 99, 101, 103, 104, 109, 178, 180, 190, 195
Las Aldas, 21, 22
Licape. *See* Huaca Licapa
Lima, 3, 7, 10
Lima Tambo. *See* Rimac-tampu
Limatambo. *See* Rimac-tampu
Loma Quemada, 43
Los Alamos. *See* El Alamo

Macusani, 3, 174
Machu Picchu, 174
Manache, 46
Maranga, 115, 148, 159, 160
Mojeque, 3, 20, 21, 23, 32, 149, 191, 193
Moxeque. *See* Mojeque

Ñaña, 3

Oracle of Apurímac, 174

Pacatnamú, 130, 132
Pachacámac, 3, 72, 117, 125, 132, 133, 135–41, 143–47, 158, 164,
    166, 178–82, 184, 190, 195, 199
Palace of Sayri Thupa (Yucay), 191
Palace of the Inca (Island of Titicaca), 173
Palace of the Virgins of the Sun (Island of Coati; Lake Titicaca),
    173
Palca, 173
Pampa Grande, 3, 97–99, 194

Pañamarca, 3, 48, 49, 52–57, 59, 61, 62, 64, 66, 67, 70, 71, 73, 93,
    99, 104, 125, 132, 179, 180, 183, 184, 190, 194
Pañamarquilla. *See* Pañamarca
Paramonga, 3, 23, 166, 168–70, 172, 184, 195
Potrero de Santa Lucía, 158
Puncurí, 3, 13, 20, 22, 24–28, 32, 177, 182, 190, 191, 193
Punguri. *See* Puncurí
Punkuri. *See* Puncurí

Raqchi. *See* Temple of Viracocha
Rimac-Tam-pu. *See* Rimac-tampu
Rimac-tampu, 158, 159, 184
Rimac Tanpu. *See* Rimac-tampu
Rúpac, 46

Sacsahuaman, 3
San Juan, 3, 148
Sechín Alto, 23, 193
Tambo Colorado, 3, 153, 154, 174, 180, 182, 199
Tambo Inga, 158
Temple of the Columns. *See* Huaca Lucía
Temple of the Crossed Hands. *See* Kotosh
Temple of Viracocha (Raqchi, San Pedro de Cacha), 3, 174
Tiahuanaco, 104, 185
Tres Palos. *See* Huaca Tres Palos
Túcume, 3, 104, 105, 112–16, 125, 131, 147, 178–80, 184, 191,
    199
Tumbes, 3, 173
Tumebamba, 175

Udima, 6, 181

Vilcabamba, 174

Waka de las Llamas. *See* Huaca de las Llamas
White Temple. *See* Kotosh

DUCCIO BONAVIA is University Professor in the
Department of Biology (Laboratory of Prehistory)
at the Universidad Peruana Cayetano Heredia,
Lima, and Research Associate of the Department of
New World Archaeology of the Royal Ontario
Museum of Canada.

editor: Risë Williamson
book designer: Sharon Sklar
jacket designer: Sharon Sklar
production coordinator: Harriet Curry
typeface: Sabon
typesetter: G&S Typesetters, Inc.
printer: Malloy Lithographing, Inc.
paper: (70) Glatco matte
binder: John H. Dekker and Sons, Inc.
cover material: Kingston natural